TAYLOR'S VERSION

TAYLOR'S VERSION

THE POETIC AND MUSICAL GENIUS OF TAYLOR SWIFT

STEPHANIE BURT

BASIC BOOKS
NEW YORK

Copyright © 2025 by Stephanie Burt
Cover design by Chin-Yee Lai
Cover image © Alexandre Paes Leme Durão/Dreamstime.com
Cover copyright © 2025 by Hachette Book Group, Inc.

Hachette Book Group supports the right to free expression and the value of copyright. The purpose of copyright is to encourage writers and artists to produce the creative works that enrich our culture.

The scanning, uploading, and distribution of this book without permission is a theft of the author's intellectual property. If you would like permission to use material from the book (other than for review purposes), please contact permissions@hbgusa.com. Thank you for your support of the author's rights.

Basic Books
Hachette Book Group
1290 Avenue of the Americas, New York, NY 10104
www.basicbooks.com

Printed in the United States of America

First Edition: October 2025

Published by Basic Books, an imprint of Hachette Book Group, Inc.
The Basic Books name and logo is a registered trademark of the Hachette Book Group.
The Hachette Speakers Bureau provides a wide range of authors for speaking events. To find out more, go to www.hachettespeakersbureau.com or email HachetteSpeakers@hbgusa.com.

Basic books may be purchased in bulk for business, educational, or promotional use. For more information, please contact your local bookseller or the Hachette Book Group Special Markets Department at special.markets@hbgusa.com.
All lyrics © copyright of their respective owners.

The publisher is not responsible for websites (or their content) that are not owned by the publisher.

Library of Congress Cataloging-in-Publication Data

Names: Burt, Stephanie, 1971– author.
Title: Taylor's version : the poetic and musical genius of Taylor Swift / Stephanie Burt.
Description: First edition. | New York : Basic Books, 2025. | Includes bibliographical references and index.
Identifiers: LCCN 2025010825 | ISBN 9781541606234 (hardcover) | ISBN 9781541606258 (ebook)
Subjects: LCSH: Swift, Taylor, 1989– —Criticism and interpretation. | Popular music—History and criticism. | Country music—History and criticism.
Classification: LCC ML420.S968 B87 2025 | DDC 782.421642092—dc23/eng/20250311
LC record available at https://lccn.loc.gov/2025010825
ISBNs: 9781541606234 (hardcover), 9781541606258 (ebook)

LSC-C

Printing 1, 2025

to Millie and Cooper
always listening

"For my part," said Deronda, "people who do anything finely always inspirit me to try. I don't mean that they make me believe I can do it as well. But they make the thing, whatever it may be, seem worthy to be done. I can bear to think my own music not good for much, but the world would be more dismal if I thought music itself not good for much. Excellence encourages one about life generally; it shows the spiritual wealth of the world."

"But then if we can't imitate it? — it only makes our own life seem the tamer," said Gwendolen, in a mood to resent encouragement founded on her own insignificance.

"That depends on the point of view, I think," said Deronda. "We should have a poor life of it if we were reduced for all our pleasure to our own performances. A little private imitation of what is good is a sort of . . . preparation to understand and enjoy what the few can do for us. I think Miss Lapidoth is one of the few."

"She must be a very happy person, don't you think?" said Gwendolen, with a touch of sarcasm, and a turn of her neck towards Mrs Raymond.

"I don't know," answered the independent lady; "I must hear more of her before I said that."

—George Eliot, Daniel Deronda

CONTENTS

Chapter 1—...READY FOR IT 1

Chapter 2—DEBUT 17

Chapter 3—FEARLESS 39

Chapter 4—SPEAK NOW 59

Chapter 5—RED 83

Chapter 6—1989 109

Chapter 7—REPUTATION 133

Chapter 8—LOVER 161

Chapter 9—FOLKLORE 187

Chapter 10—EVERMORE 203

Chapter 11—MIDNIGHTS 221

Chapter 12—THE TORTURED POETS DEPARTMENT (THE ANTHOLOGY) 245

Chapter 13—ERAS 271

Acknowledgments 299

Notes 303

Index 327

1

. . . READY FOR IT

WELCOME TO EDINBURGH, SCOTLAND, WHERE TAYLOR is everywhere.

A man in a feather boa plays "You Belong with Me," followed by "Love Story," on the bagpipes beside a crowd of tourists, many in Eras Tour gear: Taylor's face—stenciled, printed, tinted on white pavement—seems to look back with approval. Clear plastic Eras Tour merchandise bags show up everywhere too. A pub in the city center has placed glitter and bangles and Swiftie gear under clear tabletops. A train station near the city center shows, in lieu of the normal Scottish Rail signboard, a sign modeled after the Eras Tour poster.

It's June 8, 2024. Edinburgh's manifestations of Taylormania are only the latest among the splashes she's made as year two of the biggest pop tour in the world rolls on. In Rio de Janeiro, the iconic statue of Christ the Redeemer wears the T-shirt from Taylor's "You Belong with Me" video, projected in lights with faux-handwritten messages. In London, a military band plays "Shake It Off" for the changing of the guard at Buckingham Palace. Not to be outdone by royalty, London's center-left mayor, Sadiq Khan, rolls out a version of the London Tube Map with stations renamed after Taylor's songs: It appears in Wembley Park Station and as a newspaper pullout section. Taylor's tunes, the Swiftie Tube map implies, can find you—or take you—almost anywhere.[1]

This book asks how those tunes, and their creator, got to that point. It began—that is, my Taylor Swift journey began—when I heard "You Belong with Me" in a drugstore in 2009 and got curious about the songwriter. By the time *1989* came out, I was ready to call myself a Swiftie, and by the time of the pandemic albums I wanted to write about her work. Then, in September 2023, a few of my students at Harvard noticed my Swift-themed tote bag and asked if I would supervise a semester-long independent study about Swift's songs. I told them I'd rather teach a course instead. I listed it in the course catalog and expected a few dozen students to show up. Instead, 200 did, followed, from January to June 2024, by reporters who wanted to cover it—TMZ, NBC, NPR, CNN, the BBC, the RTE (Irish public radio), and then others, from Australia, Brazil, Canada, Chile, the People's Republic of China, Ecuador, Finland, France, Germany, Greece, India, Mexico, New Zealand, Norway, Poland, Portugal, Singapore, Spain, and Sweden.

Taylor Swift is a world phenomenon. How did she get that way? This book, like the course that produced it, proposes three answers, which stretch through all thirteen chapters. First, it all starts with the songs. Like the Beatles and Prince, and unlike (say) Sinatra, Taylor got famous by singing the songs that she wrote, both on her own and in collaboration. To understand her we ought to hear her songs as songs: not as if they were poems in printed books, but as lyrics interacting with music.

Second, her songs have worked so well—for so long—because throughout all her changes of style and genre and collaborators, she's been able to stay both aspirational and relatable. She and the characters in her songs present people her fans wish they could be or want to be like. But, even after her ascent to superstardom, she also writes so that we can identify with her: She presents roles, characters, and personae that resonate with many of us, and dilemmas that resemble many of ours. An almost too typical teenage girl, an insecure outsider even when she gets celebrated and welcomed, a beauty icon who knows she tries too much, Swift represents the kind of person that many of us want to be and mirrors the way that some of us already see ourselves. We know she works hard, that she's always been a good girl, that she's tried to please the adults and the audiences around her, and that she has largely succeeded. So. far.

Her music shows how it feels—and here's my third answer—when you can't stop working: when diligence, worldly success, and artistic commitment get you everywhere you've ever wanted to go, and you still want something more. That work ethic, and that attention to what people want (while trying to give us something more), contribute to what my subtitle calls Swift's genius. It's a word more often applied to artistic revolutionaries, to rule-breakers who stand above and apart from the crowd, and (not by coincidence) to men. A versatile creator who understands her audiences; who brings us along with her; who figures out all the rules, then uses those rules to make an art that's many-layered, emotionally compelling, individual, and new: That kind of creator deserves the term "genius" too. And that's the kind that Taylor Swift has become.

What makes her (in that polemical sense) a genius? What makes her music mean so much to so many fans (including me)? My three big answers (along with many small ones) come from listening to Taylor's work and from learning about her life. This book follows that life—her triumphs and scandals, her tours and her relocations, her boyfriends and best friends and colleagues and friends-become-enemies—because that life informs the songs. Ultimately it's not a book about Taylor's life, but a book about the music, the recordings and the performances, that have emerged from that life: Taylor's own versions of Taylor, as heard in those songs.

The songs have a kind of heroic origin story. In Taylor's own telling (from the 2010 documentary miniseries *Journey to Fearless*), she started learning at the age of twelve when, as she put it, "a guy who my parents had hired to fix my computer" saw a guitar in the house and asked, "'Do you want me to teach you a few chords?' I said yes, and that was that.... I was just relentless about wanting to play all the time, songwriting for all my free time." The supposed repair guy that Scott and Andrea hired seems to have been a professional guitar teacher too. Without Scott and Andrea and their wealth and attention, without the family's move to Nashville (see Chapter 2), without Taylor's whiteness, without her photogenic countenance, without her early collaborators (such as Nathan Chapman and Liz Rose), without her willingness to work and learn and study and take direction, both in the studio and onstage, she could not have found success in the same way.[2]

With them, though, her success came from her songs. "It can get complicated on every other level," she said in 2018, "but the songwriting is still the same uncomplicated process it was when I was writing songs in my room." The *New Yorker* critic Kelefa Sanneh, in his majestic survey of American popular music, *Major Labels*, calls Swift "both a brilliant songwriter and a brilliant collaborator." A pop singer who could not please casual fans would run little chance of attracting so many devoted ones: Swift's rise depended not just on the depth of her lyrics (though they helped), nor on her originality (much of which came later), but on her heard-in-the-drugstore, overheard-on-the-car-radio appeal. Nonetheless, the songs and their words reward close analysis: The more attention you pay, the better they get, and the more you can get out of them. Reporters for *Vogue* once asked Taylor, on camera, "If you could teach one subject in school what would it be?" She answered, gleefully, "English!"[3]

She's been the subject of English classes instead, and not only my own. Teachers and readers can learn how those words work so well by setting them next to other English words from other writings, some of them novels, memoirs, and modern poems. I brought some of those novels, memoirs, and poems into the class I taught. Some of them (including novels and poems that Taylor has certainly read) come up in this book. At the same time, this book treats the songs as songs, not page-based poems or speeches or anything else: The way they sound can transform what the words do and say. Before we look at what the words do and what they mean, I want to make sure that we hear the music too.[4]

To take one recent example from the *Midnights* era: "Hits Different" repeats the two-word title phrase four times in each chorus. The song says that the word "love" might be a lie—after all, Swift's friends keep telling her so—but the word, and its hollowness, change as the phrase "hits different" repeats. Its syllables change pitch, up two whole steps, then down two whole steps, then up and down again, as if Swift couldn't figure out whether to believe in love (the upside) or spurn her former belief (the downside). Love and disappointment, in this composition, really do hit different each time, even when the words are the same. And what's true for that song holds for others. To understand why Swift's words hit so hard, and so well, and mean something so different each time, we need to understand how they work in her music.

That understanding requires some slightly technical music-teacherish vocabulary, though I've tried to keep it to a minimum. Most pop music relies on vocal melodies that follow the notes of a major or minor scale. Voice teachers give the eight notes of a scale one-syllable designations: For a major scale, that's *do re mi fa sol la ti* and a higher *do* (as in the song "Do-Re-Mi" from *The Sound of Music*). I use the *do, re, mi* system (also called *solfège*) wherever I can in order to make this book as easy as possible for nonmusicians to follow. Where necessary I also use the names of notes (C, D, F-sharp, and so on) and the chords they make when played together. One chord, for example, is *do, mi, sol* (in the key of C, the notes C, E, and G); we refer to that chord by the Roman numeral I, because it starts on the first note of the major scale. Another chord is *fa, la, do* (F, A, and C in the key of C); we refer to it by the Roman numeral IV, because it starts on the fourth note.

Some chords, such as the major I (also called the tonic), sound stable, or calm, or like "home"; others, like the minor vi (*la, do, mi*), can sound unstable or unsettling, as if they're supposed to lead somewhere else. A series of chords is called a chord progression. In most pop music (and in most classical music written before about 1880), chord progressions end at a stable, "home" place, such as the I or the V (*sol, ti, re*). Modern jazz musicians, contemporary composers, and some pop songwriters (Joni Mitchell; Walter Becker and Donald Fagen; Tori Amos) invent strange or unintuitive chord progressions. Swift mostly reuses simple, familiar ones. Her creative power comes in the melodies, and the arrangements, and the rhythms, and above all in the words—which need all those other components in order to move us as they do.

... READY FOR IT

Some patterns emerge from her melodies on their own. The musicologist Nate Sloan points to one pattern he calls the T-drop: *mi, fa, mi*, and then down to the lower *la*. "Everything you lose is *a step you take*" ("You're on Your Own, Kid"). "You belong *with me-e-e*." Swift uses that drop for dramatic, climactic effect, taking us with her to low points that can precede high points. The big swoop from *mi* down to the low *la* also helps her get the most from a vocal range lower than that of many female pop stars. Hearing these devices come back through her work, we can see how that work holds its words together, how its signature riffs bring us along.

Other effects do show up in the words alone, even though those effects take root and work so well because they're in such catchy songs. Consider all the numbers, and all the ages, that her lyrics specify: Has any other successful pop songwriter used so many? When you're fifteen and somebody tells you they love you, you're gonna believe it. That kind of radiance you only have at seventeen. It's supposed to be fun, turning twenty-one. I don't know about you but I'm feeling twenty-two. I would've stayed on my knees . . . At nineteen (in songwriting, "my knees" rhymes with "nineteen," because heard rhyme for singers is all about vowels). This creator gives numbers for ages, her own and her characters', because she focuses so often, and so closely, on what it means to grow up: for her, and for her listeners too.

That's one reason that fans can see ourselves in her songs. Fans have seen themselves, and their generations, in other songwriters' work, too: Billie Eilish, for example, or Marvin Gaye with *What's Going On*, or Carole King, whom Swift once called "the greatest songwriter of all time." Swift wrote that King's "songs come to you from somewhere else—a loved one, a friend or the radio—and then, suddenly, they are partly ours," and that "her persona on *Tapestry* feels like listening to a close friend intimately sharing the truths of her life so that you can discover the truths of your own."[5]

That quality makes those songs relatable, a word not remotely popular until the 2010s, if we trust Google Ngrams, but a goal, and a concept, that goes back centuries. The literary critic Samuel Johnson wrote in 1779 that Thomas Gray's poem "Elegy in a Country Churchyard" "abounds with images that find a mirror in every mind, and with sentiments to which every bosom returns an echo." The modern literary critic Helen Vendler wrote about her astonishment when she first read the poet Adrienne Rich: "Someone my age was writing down my life." Swifties have felt that way about Taylor's songs since some of us first found her self-titled debut. Many of us, despite her superstar status, hear her latest work and feel the same way. Her self-consciousness about being a songwriter, about putting her feelings into songs—a quality that some skeptics dismiss as contrived—helps bring her closer to her listeners too: As the essayist, editor, and onetime teen celebrity Tavi Gevinson explains, "By pointing to her own authorship, by letting us in on it," Swift "fosters a greater intimacy with her listener than with her male subject," even when she seems to be making love songs.[6]

Taylor would stand out if she could do nothing else. But Taylor, as a songwriter, does something else, just as often, and as importantly. Not only do Swifties, among whom I count myself, feel akin to the characters she creates, and to the versions of herself that she presents in her songs. We also want to be those people. We have looked up to these characters and have seen them as better or more exciting versions of ourselves. Again, other songwriters have pulled off this same feat: Charli XCX, for example. Or Prince, who told us rightly that he was something we would never understand, even if he would also "die 4 u." The David Bowie of "Life on Mars?" remained achingly, sweepingly relatable; the Bowie who became Ziggy Stardust became aspirational. Taylor stands out because, almost alone in her tier, she can do both, often within the same song.

Taylor's earliest commercially released songs paint her as aspirational, too. In "Teardrops on My Guitar," her crush Drew has been dating another, higher-status girl, but at least Taylor, unlike most of us, can make her heartbreak into song. Her supposedly outcast, discouraged, rejected teenage protagonists often sing about problems we might wish we had. Who needs advice, at fifteen (in the song "Fifteen"), about *not* dating the boy on the football team? Who needs advice about what to do when senior guys think you're cute and say they haven't seen you around before? Girls who look conventionally attractive, who can at least compete in the popularity sweepstakes, who belong in the hot guys' dating pool. The same pair—aspirational but relatable, like us but also excitingly not like us—comes out in her later songs about public life: Who needs advice about what to do, and how to handle burnout, when the whole world seems to be watching? A girl, or woman, who's already a star.

Besides making three big arguments about how and why Taylor found such lasting success—she's aspirational and relatable; she makes the words fit the music, and the music fit the words; she depicts her need to be loved, alongside her ambition—this book spends time with individual songs. It's got something to say, not about all 274 (as of early 2025), but about all my favorites and about all the hits, from "Tim McGraw" to "I Can Do It with a Broken Heart," that look like pivot points in her career.

Between the career as a whole and the individual songs come eras and albums. Each chapter has something to say about one of them. *Taylor Swift* launches the teenage star by treating her teenage-girl life as authentic material, the trappings of country music as pastoral conventions. *Fearless* perfects the pairing of the aspirational with the relatable: She's just like you, if you're in her core audience, except that she's got problems you might wish you had. *Speak Now* speaks to that postadolescent question "What's next?" as well as to the post-success question "What now?" *Red* responds with a rush, diving into new musical styles and revving up its lyrical engine to depict headstrong, unwise, disastrous romance along with guitars and fast cars.[7]

The album that Swift described as her own rebirth, *1989*, deploys the self-conscious artifice of 1980s synth-pop to tell us how she's made herself new, how she can live in the present, and pose, and flirt, and pretend, and have fun. *Reputation* draws instead on modern Black pop, on sounds and collaborators from neo-soul, hip-hop, and R&B, to portray Taylor as an empowered adult, no longer a pure, and stereotypically white, girl-child: It's the right place to think about Taylor and race. *Lover* feels now like her only album that doesn't hold together as a whole; its political statements, its efforts to demonstrate joy, and its inward, backward-looking melancholy moments make for rough collisions, taken together, and for plenty of beauties, taken alone. Her pandemic albums, *Folklore* and *Evermore*, treat their acoustic and folktronic atmospheres as alternatives to the chaotic present day, but they work in different ways. The first looks backward, dwelling in teenage pasts and pastorals, while the second asks how, and whether, and when, to escape.

Swift's return to studio pop in *Midnights* put her angst and her meta-angst at center stage: Do I really want all these people looking at me while I process my feelings? What if I do? What if they stop looking? Showing the influence of stars younger than Swift, stars who grew up listening to Swift, it showed us as listeners how to look back on our own roughest moments. *The Tortured Poets Department*, released amid the Eras Tour, considered how much Swift depended on her fandom, on her public life, and on her art, how much she got from chasing the success that American culture asks us to want, even after she had already achieved it. It also framed what many of us have loved, and regretted, and loved again, about falling for the wrong, disreputable, rebellious guy. My final chapter, on the Eras Tour itself, sees what the sets and costumes and performance choices say about the songs Swift offers her fans. That chapter also returns to the joy we can take in a pop hook, a well-turned vocal, a well-launched phrase, the joy that comes from hearing Taylor Swift's best songs even before we know what they mean.

Of course, Swift does more for her songs than just write them and sing them. She said in 2010 that if she had not become a professional musician, she would have gone into "something that has to do with a lot of organization." She would have been "in advertising," she mused, "because you are organizing and creating at the same time." She seems to have learned, eagerly and early, not just how to write and play but how to promote, and how to use social media, and how to keep crews, band members, support staff, and fans on her side. But none of those skills would have worked for her—not nearly so well, and not nearly for so long—had she not continued to write approachable, relatable, singable, and also excitingly aspirational songs.[8]

Taylor's detractors, even when they see those powers, sometimes claim that she only writes songs about guys: either about falling for them, or about leaving them, and condemning them once they're gone. Those detractors are wrong: One of Taylor's earliest masterpieces—a neat way into her gifts—has nothing to do with boyfriends, and everything to do with the way she fuses approachability (she's just like you) with inspiration (if only you could be more like her). That song would be "The Best Day," from *Fearless* (2008). The middle-school Taylor we meet in "The Best Day" had a terrible time with her mean-girl ex-friends, but she also came home to the very best mom she can imagine. That song's musical qualities underline that double aspect too. It starts out so simple that it resembles children's music: A simplified version without a pre-chorus could fit a school sing-along. We can sing along too, as each verse climbs down slowly, one step at a time. "I'm five years old, it's getting cold, I've got my big coat on . . . I'm thirteen now and don't know how my friends could be so mean": *mi, re, re, do, do, ti, ti, la, sol, sol. . . .* Then the song reaches out, and up, and down, until we get her mother's strong support in the chorus's ending, tilting up from *ti* back to *do*: "I had the *best* day with you to*day*." Imagine being held so strongly, lifted up that way.

"The Best Day" also makes a good first case—I used it that way in my class—for Taylor's connections to older literary traditions. Little children (as in the first and last verses of the song) don't know why the leaves change in the fall, but older children do. That's how you know they're growing up, a melancholy experience at best. It's this same experience that animates Gerard Manley Hopkins's 1880 poem "Spring and Fall: To a Young Child":

> Márgarét, áre you gríeving
> Over Goldengrove unleaving?
> Leáves like the things of man, you
> With your fresh thoughts care for, can you?
> Ah! ás the heart grows older
> It will come to such sights colder

By and by, nor spare a sigh
Though worlds of wanwood leafmeal lie;
And yet you wíll weep and know why.
Now no matter, child, the name:
Sórrow's spríngs áre the same.
Nor mouth had, no nor mind, expressed
What heart heard of, ghost guessed:
It ís the blight man was born for,
It is Margaret you mourn for.

Margaret realizes that the leaves change because they will die; we will too. Hopkins laments her loss of innocence and shares her new sense of mortality. ("Ghost" means "spirit" or "soul"; "leafmeal," a word Hopkins coined, means a forest floor of scattered or shredded autumn leaves.) Hopkins relies on a series of couplets, Taylor on verses and chorus and bridge. Margaret doesn't seem to get support from anyone, not even from the poet, who wants to tell her he knows she's going to die! Taylor, on the other hand, seeks and finds support from her whole family, her brother and her dad as well as her mom. She's relatable in her fears at various ages but aspirational in the way that she finds and accepts such reassurance: She's learned things, and one of the things she's learned is that her mom will always show up.

"The Best Day" joins a lot of other Taylor songs in this way: It's simultaneously relatable (we've been there) and aspirational (we wish we were there). This kind of balance carries forward into her pop eras in a way that might seem paradoxical. By the time she created *1989*, Swift's life no longer resembled the lives of her fans, at least not outwardly. As an adult celebrity in New York, writing danceable songs about turning twenty-two and going out clubbing, she could remain aspirational without half trying. But that's only half of her genius. How did pop Taylor, celebrity Taylor, jet-setting Taylor, stay relatable?

Some answers apply only to certain albums. Taylor made *Folklore* while she had to isolate herself during the pandemic months of 2020, when the rest of us had to stay at home too. The Taylor of *Reputation* felt wronged and falsely accused, as many of us have felt at times. But another answer covers her whole career: Even long after her teens, Swift kept evolving, remaking herself in response to circumstance. We associate that evolution, that kind of self-making, with adolescence, with uncertainty, and with vulnerability. Swift has kept up those associations too: She never stopped growing up, if growing up means changing, reevaluating, and rejecting your previous selves. Long out of high school, Swift still feels like "life is just a classroom": Each day our castles fall and we try to build them again. Like Bowie, she won't stay put for more than an album at a time, though her personae, unlike his, insist on their lack of pretense, on their genuineness as versions of her (and therefore potential reflections of us). And those personae show off their troubles alongside their glamour, their contradictions alongside their highest highs. Even her wish to be loved, to give back, to do good (so she believes, at her low points) reflects a "covert narcissism disguised as altruism." Maybe we've felt that way at our low points too.

No wonder Swift's music brings so many people together—literally, at her concerts; metaphorically, through the broad church of her songs. At the same time, she allows, and even encourages, a world within a world, a not-very-secret society in which serious fans communicate through references and quotations. Alex Suskind of *Entertainment Weekly* quipped that Taylor had created a "Taylor Swift Musical Universe," one that's "like the Marvel Cinematic Universe but with more guitars and fewer Stan Lee cameos." Suskind was more right than he knew. I've spent a great deal of my life obsessed with various made-up universes and characters. I found my friends based on those universes, some of them stereotypically nerdy (Dungeons and Dragons), some prestigious but limited in their reach (the poetry of John Milton), some defiantly Not for Everyone (1980s indie rock). Most people didn't care for, or care about, these things.[9]

Swifties are different. As I became one—or learned to call myself one—I discovered a fandom hundreds or thousands of times bigger than any prior fandom I had known. *Paradise Regained* stans were out there somewhere (if you love that poem too, please get in touch). But Swifties were everywhere. Many of them—by contrast with, say, indie-rock obsessives, or John Milton super-fans—knew how to act and seem, if not to feel, at home in modern social life, especially girlhood and womanhood, the demands and delights of which have remained among Taylor's favorite topics since "Our Song." (No one I've met by playing Dungeons and Dragons has helped me learn to layer blush over foundation, but more than one Swiftie has.) We may, or may not, crave social acceptance, but we don't, as Swifties, give up on it, or spit on it when it comes. Many of us really do feel like we belong at the high school football game, or the office party, or the hen party. Many others have learned—are still learning—how and when we might want to fit in.

And Swifties were—are—the opposite of exclusionary. Taylor Swift fandom, by being uniquely expansive, has also become uniquely welcoming. The music avoids the trap of generic celebration and bland inclusion because it's so specific, and so often angst-driven, and so articulate, in the feelings that it presents. But the fandom itself (from what I've seen) rarely tries to keep anyone out. Indeed, you might get—or make—another friendship bracelet each time you bring someone in.

Those links show how many of us see ourselves in her songs, how many of us feel like—but also wish we could be more like—her.

Relatable, singable, changeable, aspirational, communal, emotionally available: All those terms apply to Swift's catalog. All help explain her success. But that success also reflects a ton of work: not only writing and rehearsing and singing and posting on social media and dressing up and dressing down and planning and executing world tours, but also writing songs about and through that work, writing songs (and essays, and a few poems) about the drive for attention, affection, approval, and conventional success that made Swift the star she became. No wonder, then, that Swift can seem both ambitious and insecure, at once delighted by her chosen art form and helplessly driven to pursue it. She can't help wanting everyone to like her. She blows up or melts down or fights back (in song) when not everyone does. And then she gets back to work trying to please us all. That's the paradox of the good girl, of the Type A personality, of "growing up precocious" (as she put it), and taking the advice of the adults to heart. If we do everything right and work hard enough, we tell ourselves, we can feel good about ourselves; we can feel loved. How much work will it take? Who knows? Best to keep at it. Many of Taylor's fans have felt that way too. Her way of portraying ambition as insecurity also runs through all her eras. Those portrayals, too, let her fans see our lives in what she can do, and in what she has done.

2

DEBUT

TAYLOR SWIFT'S MYTHMAKING STARTED EARLY. So did her hard work. She entered the world of popular music through a clearly marked door labeled "Country," and she had to look the part for that side of the house. At the same time, she had to present herself as an almost normal teenage girl, one who understood her first faithful listeners as least as well as they understood themselves. The girl who sings on *Taylor Swift*—Swifties call that first album "Debut"—resembles many other girls, living out common (though hardly universal) teen experiences. She's an earnest, hardworking, flawed role model, in her romances as in the rest of her life. Sometimes guys want to date her; sometimes they just like her as a friend. She wants us to see ourselves as her friends too, even though she knows we'll never meet. We might wish that we could be (even) more like her—especially once we remember that she writes the songs.

Those songs, in turn, place her clearly, almost aggressively, in Nashville, fit for Nashville-centric stages and country radio in the late 2000s, where (unlike on Top 40 radio, and despite the recent example of LeAnn Rimes) teenage girls were hardly common. Taylor's uniqueness there didn't hurt. But it would be wrong to call her choice of country insincere. Up through her twenty-first birthday, country was the music she wanted to make. It was the music that shaped her, and that she in turn reshaped.

Her family helped to shape her too. Scott and Andrea Swift welcomed Taylor—on December 13, 1989, as Swifties know—into the world in West Reading, Pennsylvania, then into a comfortable home on a fifteen-acre Christmas tree farm in Wyomissing. Her brother, Austin, arrived in 1992. Scott—like his father and grandfather—worked for Merrill Lynch as a stockbroker and financial adviser who ran his own division, the Swift Group. Andrea worked as a marketing manager before becoming a full-time mom. From childhood Taylor saw herself as a performer: comfortable onstage, in front of a microphone or a camera. In 2004 she modeled for Abercrombie & Fitch.[1]

The earliest public recordings of Swift singing anything give her performance, age twelve (some sources say eleven), singing "The Star Spangled Banner" before a Philadelphia 76ers game. She strains for the notes but she hits them, and she's got the volume: She's also earnest. She means it. Apparently she had sung the anthem in public before, at age nine, at a Minor League Baseball game, after the scheduled singer failed to show. In *Journey to Fearless*, the authorized 2010 documentary miniseries, Swift explains that singing the national anthem in Philadelphia "was my first huge crowd experience—then I was addicted." So—with support from her parents—she did it again. "It occurred to me that the national anthem was the best way to get in front of a large group of people," she explained later to *Rolling Stone*. "So I started singing the national anthem everywhere I could."[2]

But she wanted to sing country. Maybe because she loved LeAnn Rimes; maybe not. Swift told one interviewer in 2010 that she knew she wanted to sing, and to sing country, "the first time I saw Faith Hill on TV in her video for 'This Kiss.' I was about 9 years old." Accounts of Swift's early years make clear how well her parents supported her goals: She told them she wanted to be a famous singer, never the other way round. Before starting eighth grade, she recorded with producer Steve Migliore in Philadelphia and attended the Britney Spears Camp for the Performing Arts in Cape Cod, with Britney herself in attendance. Of course her parents paved, and paid, her way.[3]

For many country artists, and their listeners, country means authenticity: the real reflection of tradition-minded lives in some version of southern rural America. Some country artists remind us that they come from that authentic place. Sometimes they don't need to tell us: We already know. But Swift came from nowhere near there: not the South, not blue collar, not an especially rural environment (Wyomissing functions as an upscale suburb of Reading, Pennsylvania), nor a rural family. Her grandmother Marjorie (of the song "Marjorie") trained as an opera singer, then became a beloved TV host in Puerto Rico. Andrea Swift's favorite band was Def Leppard; Scott and Andrea seem to have raised Taylor on 1970s singer-songwriter fare. What could country music mean for her?

One answer might lie in the power that it gave songwriters, as against arrangers and performers. Another might come from literary tradition: Country, in Taylor's early work, means pastoral. Literary critics use that term for the rural space (sometimes based on a real place, sometimes not) where poets have set scenes since ancient Greece. Pastoral poets portray shepherds (the term comes from "pastor," which then meant "shepherd"), gardens, villages, maidens, and idylls, all of them simpler and more joyful than the troublesome urban present from which they escape. Alexander Pope deployed its attractions in his long poem *Windsor-Forest* (1713), comparing his English scene to "the Groves of Eden":

My humble Muse, in unambitious strains,
Paints the green forests and the flow'ry plains,
Where Peace descending bids her olives spring,
And scatters blessings from her dove-like wing.

The great modern poet William Butler Yeats employed pastoral, too, envisioning a mythical Ireland where (to quote one 1899 poem) "my lost love came stealthily out of the wood / With her cloud-pale eyelids falling on dream-dimmed eyes." John Denver (who grew up in Roswell, New Mexico, and Fort Worth, Texas) went all pastoral in his 1970 hit "Take Me Home, Country Roads." In each case, pastoral means a purposefully made-up rural retreat, a simpler, happier place to live. Pope used pastoral to imagine an England and a world at peace, Yeats to present the purity of lovelorn yearning, Denver to imagine familial warmth.[4]

At worst, pastoral falsifies and condescends. At best, it both imagines a happy escape and gives poets metaphors. Country music and its tropes count as pastoral when they're consciously adopted and artificial: Loretta Lynn (a Kentucky coal miner's daughter) and George Strait (raised on a cattle ranch) do not use country music in that way (nor do they sing about modern teenage life). The music that other performers took on as a natural fit for their own upbringings gave Taylor a set of

DEBUT

tools, and tropes, and sounds, that let her sing about something else: about popularity and unpopularity, about frustration and ambition, about romance and alienation, in the lives of suburban and exurban teenage girls.

Taylor spoke to those lives not least because she described, and remembered, feeling left out and unpopular. And she was telling the truth. Her middle school drew its students both from affluent, leafy, largely white Wyomissing and from less privileged West Reading. Swift, in biographer Chloe Govan's summary, "not only stood out for her singing voice, but also lived in a palatial home," with an elevator and an indoor pool. She also stood out as a young performer at Berks Youth Theatre Academy, the region's leading children's theater, landing roles that might have made her peers jealous even without her wealth. She played Maria in *The Sound of Music* and Sandy in *Grease*, where she sang the Australian character's parts with a southern twang. "Taylor had this idea that there was a conspiracy to push her out of [her local children's theater] to make way for the less popular children who wanted her roles," one unnamed friend of the family told Govan. "Some of the moms . . . didn't want her around."[5]

How did Swift move from children's theater to teenage writerly prowess? Swift herself describes a trip to Nashville at the age of eleven, when she gave record company executives CDs of her karaoke demos: After they rejected her, she concluded that she'd have to write her own songs. The "computer repairman" showed up after that. And then, by Andrea's telling, Swift never stopped writing, or singing, or feeling left out in middle school. She knew what she wanted—a country music career—and she could not get it in Wyomissing. So Andrea and Scott Swift took their whole family (along with Scott's work at the Swift Group) to Hendersonville, Tennessee, near Nashville, in order to bolster Taylor's musical goals before their daughter began eighth grade. She had financial advantages, and parents willing to use them to build her career, but not the insider connections of a second-generation Hollywood or Nashville star. "There would always be an escape hatch into normal life if she decided this wasn't something she had to pursue," Andrea told *Entertainment Weekly*. "And of course that's like saying to her, 'If you want to stop breathing, that's cool.'"[6]

Her first Nashville show survives only in photographs. Behind a red-and-white banner that reads "Taylor Swift," a fourteen-year-old Swift and her four-piece band take the stage in front of a body of water, before a few dozen onlookers, at the Nashville Rubber Duck Race, a fundraiser for the Boys and Girls Clubs of Tennessee. Swift and her band played before, or after (she later told talk-show host Graham Norton she couldn't remember which), the ceremonial dropping of 10,000 rubber ducks in the Cumberland River: The first duck to float to its goal won the sponsor a prize. It's quite the metaphor for America, where competition rules, and even a duck flotilla yields only one winner. But it's also as earnest an image as a young singer can get.

Taylor took songwriting lessons from adult hitmakers, first with Robert Ellis Orrall (who had written hits for Shenandoah and for Lindsay Lohan), and then—every Tuesday, after school—with the Nashville talent Liz Rose, already a hitmaker for Bonnie Raitt and Gary Allan. Rose told the online platform Taste of Country in 2014 that "with Taylor, it really was *editing*," because writing with Swift was "unlike the way I've written with anybody else before or since" (emphasis in original). Rose continued, "I meet a lot of young girls that think they can be Taylor if I help them out, and I have to say to them, 'These are Taylor's words. There was no magic fairy dust around me. Taylor knew how to write a song at 13.'" Rose also introduced Swift to the then-unknown studio engineer Nathan Chapman, who would craft the sonic envelope for much of her first four albums: sharp guitars, the crystalline twang of a mandolin or a banjo, and the absolute clarity of Swift's voice.[7]

Based on demos from her early work, Taylor got a development deal—a "we might sign you later; stick with us" contract, in effect—from RCA at age fourteen. Such deals could end with nothing, or with an album of songs selected by managers and written by Nashville professionals. After a year she refused to renew. "I walked away because I had the feeling that I was not going to be able to record my own music that I had written," she explains in *Journey to Fearless*. "I wanted there to be something that set me apart. And I knew that had to be my writing." She put that writing on display again at a songwriters' showcase, apparently arranged by Orrall, at Nashville's famed Bluebird Cafe; there she earned the trust of Scott Borchetta, a former Universal Music executive, who asked her to join his new label Big Machine.[8]

Taylor Swift showed how—with support from Borchetta, and her parents, and Rose, Chapman, and Orrall—a girl could become, simultaneously, a country songwriting powerhouse and an ideal-typical American teen. She had just the look for it, too: As the fashion scholar Sarah Chapelle writes, Taylor's debut look "spelled it out for everyone ... sundress + cowboy boots = teenage girl + country star." Swift showed everyone she meant country, as well as teenage, in her first single, named after (though not quite about) the country star "Tim McGraw." Entering a space dominated by older men, without a rural backstory, Swift established her bona fides not just through her sound, but also by name-checking McGraw, a name that country listeners (but not Top 40 pop fans) would recognize: The business scholar Kevin Evers even calls the song "a Trojan horse," designed to get Swift through the gates of country radio. Her song about McGraw's songs points hard to southern rural whiteness: blue eyes, Georgia stars, a Chevy truck, back roads at night, and "the moon like a spotlight on the lake."⁹

McGraw's own hit "Something Like That" (1999) remembers a county fair at the end of summer, when he or his character was seventeen: "I worked so hard for that first kiss, / and a heart don't forget something like that." That's pastoral. But it's not Taylor's version. "Something Like That" treats youth at the county fair as pastoral, modern southern life as the real thing. Taylor's debut, beginning with "Tim McGraw," reverses the pattern: Country life, rural America, gives her a set of pastoral tropes, but as for the teen years? She's genuinely living those. "Tim McGraw" gives country radio listeners—especially younger, female ones—something to recognize immediately, a version of feelings they can understand. It's also meta: a country song about hearing the right country song. Sometimes that song already exists.

At other times, Swift intimates, you can write it yourself. The apex of meta-songwriting on Swift's debut came with "Our Song," not the first hit with a title of that kind (consider Elton John's "Your Song"), or the first country song about writing a country song (see Alan Jackson's "Talkin' Song Repair Blues"), but the first that many Swifties would encounter. Pastoral signals crowd the lyrics: roses, and screen doors, and most of all the amens, for a God-fearing good girl who says her prayers at night. Many Swifties believe "Our Song" and "Tim McGraw" address a particular senior from Henderson High whom Swift dated or just crushed out on. "Tim McGraw" evokes her nostalgia when he moved away, but "Our Song" opens up a romance as it happens. "We don't have a song," she complains (twangily), unless "our song" lies in the ambience of screen doors, slow telephone conversations, and other acoustic byproducts of youthful courtship.¹⁰

DEBUT

For another girl, those non-songs might suffice. Not for Taylor. She's not only his girlfriend: She's a songwriter, and if they don't have a song, she'll grab a pen and an old napkin (pronounced spondaically, so that "napkin" rhymes with "cap when"). New fans might come for the love story, for the screen doors and the trucks, and for the feeling, both shy and exciting, "that I didn't kiss him when I should have" (better to stop short than go too far: She's a good girl). Those fans can then stay for the writerly empowerment (especially if they skip the disturbing video, which looks like an homage to the movie *Heathers*: An immaculate, straight-haired Swift reclines on AstroTurf, then reappears in a prom dress). If you see yourself in this version of Taylor Swift—the one in the song, not the one on the screen—not only can you imagine yourself with this affable, reachable boyfriend, but you can imagine yourself creating art about your life: You might see yourself writing songs.

Especially if you're a girl. Women have made country music since before country existed as a commercial category, but we've never been a majority: The former Spotify data guru Glenn McDonald writes that even in 2024, "mostly, on country radio, you hear men." Swift's diaries—excerpted, in facsimile, inside deluxe editions of *Lover* (2019)—confirm the dilemma: Visiting Capitol Records at age thirteen, Taylor heard "that country is directed to 35-year-olds. Radio just doesn't play teens." Teen girls who did make it in country had to perform songs by Nashville professionals, carrying them with distinctive vocal flair. Like Rimes. Or like Tanya Tucker, whose 1974 *Rolling Stone* cover profile called her the "Teenage Teaser," praising (accurately) her voice—"low, brassy and vibrating"—alongside her Elvis-like "stage presence," making her "all things to all people." (Tucker still has that voice: See, or rather hear, her albums with Brandi Carlile.)[11]

Women who wrote their own songs (even Dolly Parton) took longer to rise. They had to establish country bona fides, and then to write as adults. Swift, by contrast, treated country as a set of tropes, and teen social problems as her lived reality—hardly a new dilemma in rock or pop, by 2005, but new to the Nashville scene. We can hear that life in "Teardrops on My Guitar." The arrangement folds in a kind of inside joke, since the instruments that track Swift's vocal line are mandolin and banjo, not guitar. The song also leans on pedal steel: a guitar, but not the one she cries on. We can feel ourselves into this situation, friendzoned by the boy of our dreams. But we can also aspire to Taylor's reaction: driving or riding around, coming home, picking up our guitar and turning our sadness into these midtempo hooks, stretched to fit over Chapman's instrumentation and Eric Darken's brush drums.

"Teardrops" remains a signal of Taylor's debut era: On the Eras Tour in Nashville, night one, she introduced it with a monologue. "I have people here who were friends with me and welcomed me into my school in eighth grade," she told the audience at Nissan Stadium, "and who would tell me to keep going when I played them my songs, so it just makes me want to play something that I wrote when I was in school." This piano version of "Teardrops," with no guitar, had the Nashville crowd singing along for the entire first verse, going quiet for the highest note in the chorus ("*rea*-son"), then joining back in. The chorus wraps itself up comfortably in three low notes, like a sad girl rolled up in a duvet: "You're the song in the car I keep singing, don't know why I do" (*do-re-mi, do-re-mi, do-re-mi-re, re-do-re-mi-do*). The song comes from experience that feels personal, but it works because so many of us have found our best selves in its melodies too.

In "Mary's Song (Oh My My My)," the pastoral tropes and country signifiers take over the song, even though it's based on a real-life couple, "a perfect example of forever" (as Swift has said). You could play it on a contemporary Christian station, since it describes the story arc to which conservative families (though not only those families) aspire. "I was seven and you were nine," the girl in the couple remembers; they grew up together, played kiss-chase, starting dating seriously, fell in love, married, raised children, and grew old together in their hometown. "Our daddies used to joke about the two of us / They never believed we would fall in love." The melody line nods to Train's "Drops of Jupiter," the 2001 pop hit that Taylor would later cover onstage. This couple grew up near a creek; he drove a truck. They fought and got over it. Now here they are, supported by sweet electric guitars and an arpeggiating mandolin. "Mary's Song" portrays the happy ending promised by the rhetoric of compulsory heterosexual monogamy, the message that says we should save ourselves for marriage (to the opposite sex) and then settle down and own a home. The problem with such rhetoric is not that it never works out, but that other happy endings are possible: That particular ending cannot fit us all.[12]

Country tropes and teenage feelings, girls who could be us and girls we might wish we could be, come together again in Taylor's first great revenge song. "Picture to Burn" has a mildly infamous history: The first released version warns her ex that she'll tell all his friends he's gay. The version now on streaming replaces that lyric, but otherwise it's the same anthem, led by a speedy descending violin. Carrie Underwood's "Before He Cheats" stands behind the composition narratively, if not musically: Underwood's 2005 megahit (written by Chris Tompkins and Josh Kear) has Carrie keying his car and trashing his reputation while showing that she hasn't left him. Maybe Carrie's stuck with him. As for Taylor? She's done: The only "match" they made ends with his portrait in flames.

In the video Taylor spies on her ex alongside her real-life bestie Abigail Anderson. Then she torches both his picture and his "stupid old pickup truck you'd never let me drive." (The high school boy who apparently inspired the song became a Nashville firefighter.) An early performance practically vibrates with the intensity of her attention—not so much to his cheating heart, though, as to the audience that needs to hear her message: You don't have to stand there and take it. You can get out; you can be like her. You can—while respecting traditions of country music—burn your antagonists down.[13]

Swift did not grow up country, but she knew the heritage. An essay she wrote at the age of eighteen about Brenda Lee saw print in a 2017 collection of essays about female country stars. After watching Lee sing "Someone Loves You Honey" on a videocassette, Swift wrote about how Lee "could create classics and break down barriers no matter what genre," and about how she "mastered the sound of heartbreak so flawlessly that she made audiences not only identify with her but believe her." Swift continues, "I watch the look on her face as she ends her song and first hears that applause. There's a reason she's been able to move people to their feet for almost sixty years." It sounds like aspiration as well as ambition: When the young Taylor reaches that age, maybe she, too, can have the "class and composure" to keep all those listeners on their feet.[14]

Taylor Swift follows a template that Swift saw in Lee, finding and holding and standing with her audience. The album takes up country arrangements, country settings, and even namechecks country songs in order to fit firmly into a commercial radio genre. The album also uses country as pastoral, a set of familiar symbols and tropes for Taylor's core subjects: first love, teen ambition, teen nostalgia, teen angst. Her songs about those subjects fit the music to the words—that's why the words work. And they make her both relatable (as listeners we feel we are like her) and aspirational (we want to imagine we are more like her, feeling that moonlight on that lake, picking up a guitar to write our own song).

Swift's essay on Lee also underlines Lee's hard work: She wasn't born able to sing that way—she learned it, because she wanted it. The Taylor Swift of *Taylor Swift* wants it too: We can hear, in other songs, her own role as a performer, a people-pleaser, driven both by her wish to follow the rules and by her own persistent artistic ambition. That ambition makes songs such as "Our Song" possible—it's one of the things that "Our Song" is about. But that ambition also leaves her vulnerable. What if she fails? What if people think she's fake? Swift told *Entertainment Weekly* that she wrote "Tied Together with a Smile" about a girl at her school, a "beauty queen, pageant princess," "gorgeous, popular": "I wrote the song the day I found out she had an eating disorder." Swift would later develop disordered eating herself, on the *1989* tour, under pressure to hit her choreography, fit into costumes, and look her best under lights.

Yet "Tied Together with a Smile" does not address disordered eating directly: It's about beauty and the pressure to perform—what the sociologist Erving Goffman calls, in his 1956 book of that name, *The Presentation of Self in Everyday Life*. Social life, for Goffman, requires "impression management," curating and maintaining how we appear to others: trying to stay beautiful, to sound good, to show people what we think they want to see. For some, it comes easy; for some, it hurts more. And if we look past our "techniques of impression management," says Goffman, "each performer tends to wear a single look, a naked unsocialized look, a look of concentration, a look of one who is privately engaged in a difficult, treacherous task." That's how the friend in "Tied Together with a Smile" looks to Taylor—at risk, and coming undone. The pre-chorus evokes the sexist double standard, not as something to fight against, but as something that girls just have to acknowledge. "Giving it away" leads into a rhyme on "not his price to pay," which Taylor repeats, stretching "pay" from a single held syllable into a four-note trill. Taylor won't think about sex that way later on.[15]

She will, however, keep thinking about the performance of selfhood, about exhausting yourself (as in "Castles Crumbling," or "Anti-Hero") so you can show people what they want to see. The girl in "Tied Together with a Smile" resembles a sheaf of grain, or an old-fashioned doll, liable to fall apart when her ribbon is pulled. If "pay" gets four notes, ending on a step down, "undone" gets all of seven, taking more than a measure to stretch and hold its emotional world. "Tied Together with a Smile" is, in other words, a song about becoming, as Swift would put it much later, a pathological people pleaser, someone who can even do it with a broken heart. No wonder its almost stately progress leans on instruments that Swift herself does not play: a fiddle and pedal steel. If she's going to tie things up neatly and get to the end of the song, she's going to need help.

As much as the girls on *Taylor Swift* need other people—especially other girls—they need some ability to call their own shots, to find, as she put it, "A Place in This World." Sometimes they need more independence from boys. And sometimes they do not yet know they need it. "I'm Only Me When I'm with You," cowritten with Orrall, stands out musically because it represents Taylor's first pure guitar-pop—its pace and instrumentation place it closer to, say, Blink-182's "All the Small Things" than to most of the Shania Twain catalog. The words, set beside her later lyrics, stand out too, and not in a good way: She practically celebrates codependent toxicity. To say "I'm only up when you're not down" is to confuse romance with a lack of boundaries, to let your boyfriend's depression eat you alive. "My first boyfriend would make subtle suggestions," Swift told an early interviewer, "like 'I like your hair straight'... [s]o I'd straighten it all the time. Or he'd say 'You look good with a tan,' so I was tanning every day. It hit me that I didn't want to be the version of myself that he approved of, so I had to end it."[16]

"I'm Only Me When I'm with You" shows how it would feel not to end it. What if you could become exactly the person your boyfriend wanted? What if you could make him happy that way? We can hear Taylor stepping away from the tropes and rules and powers of country instrumentation, country tropes, country songwriting, in this number, while remaining both aspirational and relatable, ambitious and vulnerable: As much as it points to a kind of romance she'd reject, it also points forward to the rock-oriented, *Red* part of her career. And it points to a kind of romance, a destructive codependence—reliance on someone else's mood for your own; the feeling that you're incomplete without your boy or girl—that too many of us have often known.

That kind of codependent romance colludes with the pressure Swift chronicles in other songs to be beautiful, to be perfect, to be the person that friends, teachers, and mentors want to see. It's a kind of pressure only rarely described in earlier generations' songs, because it comes out of a beauty myth and a sense of romance and an educational system that only developed in recent decades. It's also a kind of pressure that contemporary poets describe. Robyn Schiff, for example, compares her younger self, pushed to excel, to bits of fired clay: "The pressure that / made them makes more of them than it makes of / me," she writes. "Out of proportion, out of the quarry... I feel a great pressure." Swift has felt, and accepted, that pressure too.[17]

What could make somebody want so much to fit in, or work so hard to look right, and follow all the rules, even to the point of falling apart? What could make somebody (especially somebody young) feel like all that effort was never enough, like so much depends on how other people feel? You might feel that way if you've already felt excluded, ignored, rejected, left out, making any sense of inclusion more precious. The earliest songs that Taylor chose to preserve describe those feelings—another key to her appeal, since her kind of teenage girl outsiderhood (unlike, say, Britney Spears's, or Tori Amos's, or Bikini Kill's) did not require open rebellion, or contempt for the popular kids, or a way to live without adults' dumb rules. No matter how much she accomplished, or how far she could go, she began as an outsider, just like you, and still feels like one deep inside. Maybe you can be like her (and succeed, later) in other ways too.

Taylor's earliest recorded songs about feeling left out, dependent, and excluded tend to be Orrall cowrites. Others include "A Place in This World" on *Taylor Swift*, "Invisible" on the deluxe edition of the debut, and "Crazier" on the soundtrack to the *Hannah Montana* movie. "Invisible" goes out of its way to stack up polysyllables and half-rhymes: beautiful, miracle, unbelievable, invisible. "Crazier" stands out for its sonic choices, made to support a singer's long notes: Every line ends with a liquid (*l* or *r*), a nasal (*n* or *ng*; "ground" sounds like "groun"), or an open vowel ("believe" sounds like "belee"). All three songs' lyrics suggest a writer who has felt unseen, overlooked, insubstantial, looking at high school dating life from the outside.

In that way they point back to the oldest song on *Taylor Swift*, "The Outside," which Taylor penned in middle school. "I was writing from pain," Swift told *Entertainment Weekly*. "I was taller, and sang country music at karaoke bars while other girls went to sleepovers. Some days I woke up not knowing if anybody was going to talk to me that day." The *Lover* diaries record its composition, on Valentine's Day: "It's about being left out in the cold. . . . I don't know if it'll go anywhere but it made me feel better." "The Outside" became an Eras Tour surprise song in Tokyo, night three, a passionate piano version suggesting Swift's continuing connection to her lonely thirteen-year-old self. With its range of exactly an octave, the song seems designed for other lonely kids who might sing along in their own rooms. The chorus also contains a puzzle. If Taylor has always felt this lonely, why does she say that she's never been on the outside? Wouldn't "I've *always* been on the outside" make more sense? Maybe not, given Taylor's happy childhood and her effortful focus on future success. She might belong outside a middle school social group that never wanted her anyway. She might leave Pennsylvania and become famous—and popular—beyond her bullies' craziest dreams.[18]

That's what she did. And it took—along with her musical talent—constant promotional effort. She visited radio station after radio station to talk to DJs. She shared her work aggressively on then-new social media, especially MySpace. She performed, showing off her music and herself, even when she wasn't on any stage. One entry in 2006 from the *Lover* diaries shows Taylor's—and Andrea's—ambition and drive:

> Today was great. I got up early and went to Love Shack, a studio downtown with Mom. There I had an ISDN phone interview for Westwood One radio, then one for NASCAR radio, then we broke for lunch, then went to Sirius Radio and that went amazing. Then an interview at CMT radio. Then went to the label to label envelopes of singles. . . . Then answered like 100 emails over MySpace. Then my friend called me and said they heard "Tim McGraw" on the radio! . . . I'm so happy.

What stands out, now, about Swift's promotional tactics? Her energy, and her packed schedule, and her level of adult support. What stood out at the time? Her use of social media, especially MySpace, the barely or badly regulated pre-Facebook site whose users could easily put their own music online. "MySpace is one of the main reasons I'm here," Swift told *Entertainment Weekly* in 2007, adding that the website was "pretty much a younger thing at the moment." Few major-label pop stars, and even fewer country musicians, at that time, used social media in that way. The puzzles and Easter eggs on *Taylor Swift*, the physical album, made sense (and promoted further engagement) without the internet. But MySpace helped turn individual interest into a real-time community: the first Swifties. "I spend so much time on MySpace," she confirmed for *Billboard*. "I upload all the pictures, I check the comments. . . . It really is important to me . . . when someone comes up to me and says 'I'm your friend on MySpace.'"[19]

Swift did not just act like her new fans' new best friend; thanks to her offline image, and to the material in the songs she wrote, she made herself plausible in that role. Jon Caramanica of the *New York Times* observed the growing community in his otherwise damning-with-faint-praise review of *Taylor Swift*: It is, he wrote, "essential to her self-presentation that there is no barrier between her and her songs, and their listeners, the consumers." She dove hard into the kind of self-promotion that turned songs into sales, feelings of solidarity into commercial transactions. She knew, and chose, that kind of marketing. It worked. *Taylor Swift* sold modestly at first, but as fans contacted the stations that played it, the debut picked up commercial momentum, and it went triple platinum by the time *Fearless* came out. She clearly enjoyed—indeed threw herself into—promotion. And yet, Andrea told *Entertainment Weekly*, "the happiest I ever see her is just after she writes a killer song."[20]

DEBUT

Not all those killer songs got commercial releases. Taylor (and her team) chose songs for *Taylor Swift*, and for the promotional singles, based on how well they set her up as accessible, admirable, and a potential best friend, both a country star and a teenage girl. Some of the best of the rejected rest—the ones that would not fit her image—pop up and then disappear regularly on YouTube and Spotify: Presumably Team Taylor's legal eagles get them taken down. Among those rejected songs, the finest in terms of songcraft must be "Dark Blue Tennessee." One version uses only piano and vocals; another adds pedal steel and heavy strings. In it a man pines for an ex-lover "just seven miles away," believing she's left town. He writes her, in the last verse, a "goodbye note," likely a suicide message, in "such sweet sorrow." It's beautiful and affecting: It's also a song nobody would place on a first album meant to show off a fresh teenage voice.

"Just South of Knowing Why," which Swift recorded (but never released) with a full rock band, also works on its own terms, and also could not have fit on *Taylor Swift*. A road song, a drive-away-from-your-problems number, with an appropriately driving beat, it might have worked on *Red*; it would have stuck out, in a bad way, on an album whose principal songwriter made a point of being barely old enough to drive. "Sweet Tea and God's Graces," another unreleased early song, presents the opposite problem. Built around a four-chord loop, co-written by Liz Rose and Brian Maher ("Mary's Song"), it's over-the-top and implausibly retro, as well as effortlessly pious: The lyrics invite us to "love like a sinner, lose like a winner," and "get by on sweet tea and Jesus." Another song left off the debut album proper, "I'd Lie," did find commercial release, as a digital download extra with some CD versions of *Taylor Swift*. Its jaunty attitude and teenage setting fit Taylor's early persona. So would the passenger seat where she places herself—perhaps the same seat as the one in "Our Song." But it's no wonder that Swift left it off the album, because it paints her as a conscious schemer, someone who feels she has no choice but to deceive.

Swift managed her image, and shaped her fan base, through what she left off *Taylor Swift* as well as through what she put on. She shaped that image again through her choice of live covers. As much as *Taylor Swift* established her firmly and clearly in the realm of commercial country, those earliest covers point to larger ambitions. At the KAT Country outdoor festival in California in 2007, Swift—in her signature sundress with cowboy boots—told listeners that "one of the cool things about being able to play guitar is being able to play what you want. You can play songs that you wrote, or you can play songs that other people wrote. Or you can play this." She then launches enthusiastically into a sped-up acoustic version of Beyoncé's "Irreplaceable," known to even the most casual listeners by its opening words: "To the left, to the left, in a box to the left . . ." She's announcing her startling goals by setting herself beside Beyoncé: an artist who might take over the wider world. If you don't think she can do it, if you're not on her side, as Beyoncé says, "you must not know 'bout me."

Other covers speak to the side of Taylor that can't stop trying hard and seeking approval: an outsider, just like us, even when standing in spotlights. Recorded while on tour for *Fearless*, a version of Tom Petty's "American Girl" became a digital-only single in 2009. You can still hear it now on fan-circulated videos, and it's beautiful but jarring, fuzzy and urgent, the closest to punk rock Swift has ever come. The nineteen-year-old Swift takes up Tom Petty's (or rather his character's) complaint about the endless chain of American "promises," each leading to the next, fulfillment nowhere, certainly not in the arms of a man who's gone. The songwriter and critic Scott Miller wrote that Petty had "captur[ed] a girl's . . . 'one desperate moment' of unrequited love, with a vague hint she might jump off a balcony." Jumping, a Swiftie might say, from a very

DEBUT

tall something, knowing that she can never be satisfied. No wonder a younger Swift selected the song. And no wonder the thirtysomething Swift of the Eras Tour, having gotten all the things fans might think she wanted, still would not stop chasing her very American promises.[21]

Lore around *Taylor Swift* emphasizes her hard work to break into the industry, her hours and weeks online, and the time she spent answering physical mail and meeting local DJs. That lore isn't wrong. But the songs got big not just because of what happened around them, but also because of what happens within them: country signifiers aplenty, treated as pastoral delights; the authenticity of youth; a teen who understood teen experience from the inside as well as the outside (or "The Outside"); a songwriter who understood how to be aspirational and relatable, how to come across both as a peer and as the next great country star, seeking a spotlight where she might feel comfortable, ready to invite new people in. *Taylor Swift* gave her, to quote her, a place in this world: a place on the country charts, a fan base to start with, a recognizable image both visually and psychologically. It also gave her a recognizable sound, at home on commercial country radio, electric and acoustic guitars at hand, mandolin, banjo, and fiddle in reserve. Glossy, imperfect, both vulnerable and confident, Swift's debut told fans both what she hoped to become and what she hoped she could do. And then—with *Fearless*—she did it.

3

FEARLESS

ALL TAYLOR'S ALBUMS BELONG TO ONE story: the story of how she can stay both accessible and aspirational while drawing on her own life, keeping her songwriting fresh, and reflecting on her never-ending work. Each of Taylor's albums tells another story of its own. For *Taylor Swift*, it was the story of how she learned to place herself—a suburban girl with teen problems, not a rural adult—within country music traditions. On *Fearless*, it's the story of how Taylor Swift, the ambitious teen who hoped to make it in Nashville, became TAYLOR SWIFT, the international, unignorable superstar. It's the first album that gave her a national, and then an international, headlining tour. And it's the album that made her commercially powerful, big enough to make decisions for herself that most young stars see adults make for them.

Fearless made Swift the youngest Grammy winner for Album of the Year, and it appears to have won the most awards (up to that point) in the history of country music. It's the first album that she wrote partly on tour: Some of the songs, she's said, came to her in hotel rooms, after she opened for bigger country names. It's also the last album to reflect Swift's experiences as a "normal" teen, a student at Hendersonville High in ninth and tenth grades. She completed eleventh and twelfth grades through the Christian distance-oriented program Aaron Academy because she wanted to stay on tour. In other words, the Swift of *Fearless* had the unusual experience of leaving high school while still a teenager. No wonder the ninth-grade crushes the album describes seem—and seemed, at the time—so real.[1]

The album made Taylor a national star, and fast. But it did not—it could not—establish her staying power: In retrospect, it threatened to do the reverse, since so much of her success seemed to rest not just on her songwriting but on her public (and authentic) persona: naïve, teenage, trusting, much like her fans. Her duet version of "Fifteen" at the 2009 Grammys (her first time performing at the ceremony) paired her with Miley Cyrus (born in 1992), known for her own portrayal of a teen pop star in *Hannah Montana*. Watch the duet today, and Taylor stands out for her friendly professionalism, switching her long-lashed, welcoming gaze between Miley (as if to support her) and the audience (as if to support us all). Swift sounds like she remembers being fifteen; Cyrus, who gets the emotions but misses some notes, sounds like she still is.

And yet "Fifteen" represents—better than any other single Taylor Swift song—her ability to present, to stand for, to speak for, an ideal-typical, just-like-you-but-better American suburban high school girl, someone who could both stand for, and stand with, her listeners. That's how *Fearless* made her an international star: It's the first thing she did better than anybody had ever done it before. "Fifteen" opens element by element, first a guitar, then a mandolin, then the bass, then the vocals: "The morning of your very first day." Drums come halfway through the first verse, in time for the chorus: "This is life before you *know* who you're *gon*-na *be*." Swift dives down a fifth, *do* to *fa*, then picks herself up. She's inviting us to sing along, and at the same time she's telling us—if we're in high school—what to expect, like a trustworthy, more experienced companion, what the poet Allen Grossman calls a "hermeneutic friend." Hermeneutic friendship is what you get from works of art that promise to take your hand, to serve as an intimate guide: They seem to know you well, even if their real-life creators died before you were born.[2]

And hermeneutic friendship describes—at least as well as that better-known word "parasocial"—what Swift at the time believed she was doing. "My main goal is to never alienate my fans," she told a college newspaper before *Fearless* came out. The "you" in "Fifteen" is a prior version of her, so that she seems to be speaking to her own earlier self, even as she gives advice to you. William Wordsworth did something similar in "Lines Composed a Few Miles Above Tintern Abbey" (1798), addressing his younger sister:

> Thou art with me here upon the banks
> Of this fair river; thou my dearest Friend,
> My dear, dear Friend, and in thy voice I catch
> The language of my former heart, and read
> My former pleasures in the shooting lights
> Of thy wild eyes. Oh! yet a little while
> May I behold in thee what I was once,
> My dear, dear Sister! And this prayer I make,
> Knowing that Nature never did betray
> The heart that loved her.[3]

It's quite the display of confidence: He believes in her more than he believes in himself. And Swift—in a more accessible, less spiritually involuted way—believes in you, and in a future where you'll do greater things. At the same time she appreciates the weirdness and the glory and the excitement of being fifteen. All the songs in the lyric sheet to *Fearless* hid a message in seemingly random capital letters: The one on "Fifteen" says, "I CRIED WHILE RECORDING THIS." The song portrays a difficult age—you don't know who you're supposed to be!—but also an aspirational one: If you are going to be a high school freshman, it's probably less awful to be the girl the senior guys see and crush out on (even though age-gap relationships are sketchy), less awful to be that girl than to be someone other girls shun.

Wordsworth turned to his sister, Dorothy, both a real person and a stand-in for readers. Swift turns to her "best friend Abigail," her real-life friend Abigail Anderson, last seen in the video for "Picture to Burn." She wrote the song for Anderson, and then asked for, and got, her permission before recording it. You can see Anderson's photograph again in the video for "Fifteen (Taylor's Version)." But most of the people in this song aren't that specific: They're "I" and "you." If you inhabit a pronoun in this song you get to be scared and unsure of yourself and worried about your decisions and their consequences for your reputation, but you also get to be popular and pretty. And you get to grow up far enough to inhabit not only the "you," but also the "I" and the "mine" and the "dreams of mine" in this song.[4]

As we now know, Taylor has not only realized those "bigger dreams of mine" but also managed to date the boy on the football team. Her point—a point that emerges on *Fearless* and propels itself all the way through the rest of her work—is that it's fine if you fall hard for boys (as long as you tell your friends about it). At the same time, you should try not to give "everything you have" for any boy who wants you: not your virginity, to be sure, but (more important) not your friendships, nor your ambitions. The mandolin line in "Fifteen" gives the low vocals in the verse a ceiling to play against. It's also the sound of uncertainty, high or low, not knowing where you belong. Taylor's lyrics let us ride with that uncertainty: Credulous high school first-year girls need not reject, or disbelieve, senior boys—we can go on those dates and feel like we're flying! At the same time we can remember how credulous we've become, swept away in his passenger seat: You might be flying, but he might be lying. And, if we have not gone out on that date yet, we can vicariously enjoy the experience (which also reminds us not to give it all away).

"Fifteen" also downplays Taylor's difference from us. Almost nobody, as the song states, knows their life goals at fifteen. Taylor Swift, however, seems to have known—and, with help from adults, she got there. We can imagine getting there too: The song includes a prediction in the bridge (you're gonna look back) and then a time jump, so that Taylor is looking back at herself in the past, as well as looking back at us. Other relatable pop stars—who wrote their own songs, too—turn up earlier in rock history. Perhaps the most important is Buddy Holly, who, as the eminent rock critic Greil Marcus once put it, both "looked like an ordinary teenager" and "on the radio came across as one." Swift aspired to become, and did become—through country music, for girls, and then through other kinds of pop—what Marcus said Holly became: "a mythic figure you could imagine talking to. One you could imagine listening to what you had to say."[5]

At the same time, Swift became someone that girls, in particular, might *want* to be: a trustworthy friend a bit more worldly than you, and maybe with a cooler wardrobe, too. Even in her days as a too-tall outsider, Swift must have known that she *could be* pretty and popular (remember her tryout for Abercrombie & Fitch). Skeptics might say she was singing only for girls who could literally resemble her. More generous listeners would say instead that her genius, once again, mixes representation and aspiration: If you feel like an outsider, and she resembles you (on the inside), maybe you can be more like her (on the outside). The Swift of *Fearless* made her personality, her accessibility, her openness to fans—both in her songs' personae and in her conduct outside them—part of her art.

She did not, though, disguise its artfulness: Fans could see that her singing, and touring, and recording, was work. The great English songwriter Tracey Thorn opens her book about vocal performance, *Naked at the Albert Hall*, by observing that non-singers sometimes think singing comes naturally. "We have the same body as the singers we are listening to, we come tantalizingly close to being able to do what they can do," and so we feel close to singers in a way that most of us cannot feel close to, say, clarinetists. Because your voice comes right from your body, using the same equipment you use for speech, "someone not liking your voice . . . can feel very much like them not liking *you*" (emphasis in original).[6]

No wonder, then, that Swift might feel crushed when her voice seems to fail. Such things have happened: In 2010, a duet with Stevie Nicks at the Grammy Awards went seriously awry when Swift sang Nicks's "Rhiannon" off-key. Scott Borchetta defended Swift with an op-ed in *The Tennessean*, blaming the problems on a monitor glitch. The botched duet nonetheless inaugurated a friendship: Nicks wrote a poem for the physical copies of *The Tortured Poets Department*, and "Clara Bow," from that album, would namecheck "Stevie Nicks in '75."

What made Nicks a model? Not just her songwriting, though that too: "Rhiannon" and "Edge of Seventeen" unveiled a consistent persona—witchy, arcane, enchanting, lacy, Gothic—though not one that brought her especially close to fans' lives, in the way that Swift's *Fearless* persona could do. Thorn warns against asking a singer "to carry the make-believe elements of her job," her stage persona, "into real life." And yet it's an ask—a demand—that Swift wants fans to know she understands, a demand she does not exactly refuse. Rather than show us everything, and rather than turn us away, she will show how her music reflects her real life and her real feelings, but on her own terms.[7]

Fearless is an album about how you, too, can be a teenage girl who wants to date guys, and who has a shot at popularity, and at getting the guy in the future, whether or not you're popular now. It's also an album about how to do romance right and how to do it wrong, and there's no better instruction manual here than "You Belong with Me." The introduction, again, establishes genre: one riff twice on a banjo, two repeated key notes, and then the voice. The verses set the scene: high school, afterschool phone calls, yearnings. Then the chorus hits like a playground rhyme, as if Swift wanted to drive her rival away.

Instead, she's trying to persuade a boy. She's also advising all the girls in bedrooms, looking at lyric sheets, or hearing the radio in a car. That chorus introduces (as we saw in Chapter 1) what the musicologist Nate Sloan called the T-drop: down and then down, *fa, mi, la*; "*see*-ee-ee." That drop sets up the chorus as a recovery, a step back up: What can't you *see*? That you belong with *me*. Not *to* me, because no one belongs to anyone: That's the wrong way to imagine romance. *With* me, because I'm a better friend. Love between Taylor and this guy should follow directly out of their friendship. It should be "e-e-a-sy." It should already feel right.

Alas, the video for "You Belong with Me" undermines every scrap of advice in the song. Instead that video shows what the scholar Ilana Nash calls a chrysalis moment, "the carefully manipulated scenario in which an adolescent female is shown crossing a threshold of sexual maturity." As in *Pretty in Pink* and *She's All That* and countless earlier films, the glasses must come off for the kiss to come next. The video even adds slut-shaming: At the prom, the wrong girl wears red and shows off her belly button, while Taylor wears white and looks both starstruck and demure. In the song, by contrast, the problem with tight clothes and heels has nothing to do with sexual availability: The rival cannot feel comfortable, in those outfits or in her body. She's not comfortable with herself, and so the boy doesn't feel comfortable with her. He'd feel better, more at home, with a sneaker-clad, unreconstructed Taylor instead.⁸

If "You Belong with Me" had never existed, "Love Story" would stand out as the big hit from *Fearless*. For some Swifties it still does. It's also a starting point for high school teachers: Its speedy, excitable verses find Swift playing Juliet to her lover's Romeo, enduring their families' disapproval. "It's one of the best love stories ever told," Swift said of Shakespeare's original. "But it's a tragedy. I thought, why can't you make a happy ending and put a key change in the song and turn it into a marriage proposal?" The propulsive vocal melody, duplicating the guitars, carries us along and upward to the most common key change in modern pop music, a whole step up (so that *re* becomes the new *do*). It's a modulation so common that internet haters have given it a derogatory name: the "trucker gearshift," almost always used to elevate a mood or signal a happy ending.⁹

Here the gearshift suits the way Romeo pulls out a ring: the happiest, most conventional, fairy-tale ending the song can manage, whether or not you see the song's Juliet (to quote Kristen Hé, writing for *Billboard*) as a woman freed from male authority, "in control of her own narrative." Taylor would use the trucker gearshift again, to indicate recovery after heartbreak, in "Mr. Perfectly Fine," a vault track from the *Fearless* era, and much later in "Getaway Car." This first big occurrence shows fans how she controls the narrative in the song. In 2010, Swift said, "I wrote 'Love Story' about a guy I never ever kissed in 25 minutes on my bedroom floor." Taylor-as-Juliet, after the key change, believes in the fairy-tale ending: Her father has given permission, and she's got a white dress, but she's also giving her beau enthusiastic consent. And she's making another literary reference: "I was the scarlet letter" means both that his family first disapproved of her, and (if we take the allusion to Nathaniel Hawthorne seriously) that everyone knows she's had sex. Virginity and inexperience no longer look like requirements for the fairy-tale ending she craves.[10]

Throughout *Fearless* you can hear teen empowerment happening musically as well as lyrically. You can also see Taylor—still in her teens—treating her previous songs as a career to which she already wants to respond: That's what happens in "Forever and Always," with its multiple T-drops. The verses include multiple stops and false endings, as if the song could have ended some other way—for example, like the happy ending in "Love Story." The two songs have similar tempos; similar insistent, straightforward, eighth-note beats; and similarly compressed vocal range in the verses, hammering a repeated note. "Love Story," though, repeats *do*: "We were both young . . ." "Forever and Always" begins in a less settled way, emphasizing *re*—"I be-*lieve* it *was* a *Tues*-day *when* you *caught* my *eye*." The song cycles through the hope and disappointment that come with an unreliable, high-stress romance, without a key change or a final happy ending. It's a song Taylor might have written for Abigail to sing to the guy who dumped her in "Fifteen," or to the jerk in "Picture to Burn."

In fact, it's about Joe Jonas. *Fearless* in part records, and in part caused, Taylor's first big life transition: from ambitious Everygirl to pop celebrity. That transition also changed her dating pool. When the songs on *Taylor Swift* and most of *Fearless* addressed real boys, they were teens from Hendersonville High. During the summer of 2008, however, she began dating the middle Jonas brother—as far as observers know, her first celebrity boyfriend. "Forever and Always," a late addition to *Fearless* (Taylor had to book another session on short notice to record it), describes their breakup: Swift said as much on Ellen DeGeneres's talk show, where she also dragged Joe for breaking up over the phone. (Jonas later maintained that she ended that phone call, and he wrote an answer song, called "Much Better.") Swift even did a video bit on MySpace (still available via YouTube) with a Joe Jonas doll: "This one even comes with a phone. So he can break up with other dolls." She then lifted up a Taylor Swift doll: "Stay. Away. From Him."[11]

Other parts of *Fearless* also work to make Taylor's persona seem continuous with the real Taylor behind the songs: admirable, but still much like us. We've seen how "The Best Day," a song for her mother, resonates with literary tropes that go back centuries, but Taylor's own stories about the song emphasized her real-life memories instead. The second verse stems from Taylor's months as a middle-school social pariah in Wyomissing. She told the whole story to *Philadelphia* magazine in 2008: "My friends . . . ditched me and talked behind my back, which is cool—I'm over it. One time I called them and said, 'Hey, do you want to go to the Berkshire Mall?' They all gave me excuses and said no. So I go to the mall with my mom, and don't you know, we run into *all* of them. Together. Shopping. My mom could see I was about to cry, so she said, 'You know what? We're going to the King of Prussia mall,' which was the mecca" (emphasis in original). Taylor told another interviewer during the *Fearless* era that she recorded the song without telling Andrea: "She didn't have any idea. . . . When she finally got it, she just started bawling her eyes out." Swift later took the song out of her live performances, the interviewer wrote, "because it would prompt her mother to break down in tears every night."[12]

When Taylor began to chronicle middle and high school experience—tracking girls who felt weird, but not too weird—she knew how to do it, while showing her pop-star life at the same time. She felt shunned, a total outsider, in Wyomissing. In Hendersonville, though, "I just loved school," she claims in her documentary *Journey to Fearless*. "All the kids were really nice! I wasn't weird. For the first time." Either she grew into social skills, or her new context—suburban Nashville—found aspirations to stardom almost normal. That documentary mostly shows how hard she worked to keep one foot in teen normalcy and the other in the expanding world of stardom that backed up the songs. Part of *Journey to Fearless* shows Swift making the rounds of major-label record publicity on a one-day trip to New York City: *Good Morning America*, MTV, WPLJ 95.5 FM (at the time, an adult contemporary station), and *Late Night with David Letterman*. Rushing from studio to studio, she looks both exhilarated and exhausted. She returns to Hendersonville on the same day so she can buy her own CD when it goes on sale, at midnight, at Wal-Mart.

Teens and tweens from the 2000s had already seen a girl stay normal and do normal high school things while becoming a rock star. But that girl was fictional: Miley Cyrus's character Hannah Montana, in the hit TV show of the same name, which ran from 2006 to 2011. And Hannah Montana, like Peter Parker, struggled to keep the two sides of her life distinct, even wearing a (silly) disguise (a blond wig). Swift presented herself, with reason, as the real thing, without a secret identity: both Everygirl and Living the Dream. On the first day of the tour, in Nashville, Swift says, in *Journey to Fearless*, that she's been "dreaming about headlining since I was four": Seeing the stage "felt kind of like being dropped off on the first day of school." Arena crowds familiar with *Taylor Swift*, the documentary confirms, can already sing along with "Our Song."

Journey to Fearless shows us what kind of pop icon Swift aspired to be. Her song "SuperStar"—left off the original thirteen-song pressing of *Fearless*, but added later—tells us what kind of stardom she planned to avoid. The girl in "SuperStar" (restyled "Superstar" on the 2021 re-recording) wishes that she could meet her pop idol. Instead she pretends to do so, talking, or singing, to the picture on her wall. It's the kind of one-way, unacknowledged relationship that Swift and her fans might have seen in boy-band fandoms, the kind described in older songs about boys looking at sexed-up photos (such as Pete Townshend's "Pictures of Lily"). The star in Swift's song (presumably a young man) smiles, and "all the girls in the front row sing your name": "I'm no one special, just another wide-eyed girl / Who's desperately in love with you." Swift stretches out the first syllable in "desperately" as if to stress the futility. He will never care about her.

It's the kind of parasocial relationship that Swift worked hard to avoid. She wants her fans to know that she cares about them, even though she will never meet most of them. She wants us to feel like she hears us. And her relationship to her audience—by contrast with boy-band fandoms—does not seem sexual. Her most enthusiastic fans want to be her friend—and, for the space of a song, she is their friend. We can ride, as it were, in the back of the car as Swift rides in the passenger seat in "Fearless," or learn how to dance from her in a storm in her best dress: We can experience her first kiss ("It's flawless, it's really something") even before we experience our own. She might show us how to feel fearless too.

FEARLESS

Journey to Fearless does not only show what kind of show, what kind of persona, Taylor wanted to put on. It also bears witness to her exceptional work ethic, alongside her attention to coworkers, collaborators, and fans. We see how Taylor and her team select dancers, a choice that happens to put people of color onstage beside this white singer and her white (or white-passing) band. Swift says nothing on camera about those demographics. She does, however, talk about her responsibilities as an employer: The *Fearless* tour is "providing jobs for about 150 people," including bus drivers and promotions managers, and Swift wants to notice them all. The same tour inaugurated "T-parties," where tour employees picked out individual superfans from the audience and brought them—along with their parents, if needed—backstage. The T-parties look forward to the private concerts and other invitation-only events Taylor hosted around subsequent album releases. But the parties—as shown in *Journey to Fearless*—also cast her as a children's entertainer, with the relentless, exhausting positivity required for anyone who makes a living, in real time, entertaining the under-twelve set. If Swift ran out of energy, or positivity, for the T-parties, night after night, that exhaustion never appeared on film.

And yet the tour, as a whole, does look exhausting. Stage business includes a bit where the star left the stage, raced through an underground tunnel, and reemerged, in her words, "in the back of the arena," near "what you used to think were the worst seats in the house. See what we did there? Ha! Switcheroo!" Swift sounds positively giddy about a move that can bring more of her presence, more of her personality, to more fans. "Going out into the crowd," Andrea Swift explains in *Journey to Fearless*, "for Taylor, is what she needs to do to feel that connection to the audience." The "switcheroo" required Swift and a few of her band members to make their way under the seating, across the arena, which took a few minutes (at least), and fans needed something to watch without Taylor onstage.

What they got was a short comedic film called *Crimes of Passion*, in which Swift's supposed targets came forward. "I was the very first victim of a Taylor Swift song," confesses the real Tim McGraw. A boy named Neil says that she took advantage of him so that she could rhyme on his name. It's funny. It works. And it shows the author of "Our Song" already asking the question that all artists concerned with autobiographical raw material must ask sooner or later: Am I making art about my life, or living my life for the sake of my art? Devote yourself enough to autofictional creations and you may find the question unanswerable, as the poet James Merrill did in a sonnet within a longer poem about youthful operagoing:

> What havoc certain Sunday afternoons
> Wrought upon a bright young person's morals
> I now leave to the public to condemn.
>
> The point thereafter was to arrange for one's
> Own chills and fever, passions and betrayals,
> Chiefly in order to make song of them.[13]

Journey to Fearless suggests that Swift really did gain, from touring, the kind of energy that other pop musicians find themselves using up in order to tour. "We just decided to keep looping around the world," Taylor tells the camera after she, and the band, and her parents, decide to book more concerts. "Every night I go out there and sing songs I have written to girls who are just like me, and they're singing the words right back." It's safe to say that the Swift of *Fearless* looks happy, that she seems to love what has become her more than full-time job, and that—having written (by her account) half the songs on *Fearless* during downtime in hotel rooms on her previous tour—she never stops working. She has had her "normal" first loves already; she's made songs of them.

A skeptic might say that this version of Swift embodies the nonstop work ethic of twenty-first-century capitalism: Never stop gigging in the gig economy; never stop trying to make yourself more commercially viable. Become a commodity; never look back. As the business writer Dave Pell objects, in our "always-on marketplace" of an online culture, "everything about you is priced to move."[14] That's how Swift lived for years at a time, starting when she left high school to go full-time on the road. And yet a more generous reader could see Swift's career not as capital's apex but as its antidote. What does she do, in her songs, on the road, in each of her choices, but tell fans that we ourselves matter, that each of us merits attention, whether or not we get famous ourselves? What does she do—when she sings about her own angst—but show that she shares our dissatisfactions?

The scholar and social worker Olivia Ordoñez writes that "although Swift lives *with* so much that . . . most people will never have—wealth, fame, poetic sensibility, racial privilege—she lives without the ability to be satisfied." That lack keeps her relatable, at least, to those of us brought up in achievement culture, with AP tests and beauty myths and stacks of extracurriculars, or with loaded-up resumés and work-from-home, twenty-four-hour expectations, perhaps with dependent care stacked on top. She knows that we know that she knows how hard she works. It's as if she had to work as hard as anyone, ever, just to keep up with what she expects from herself.[15]

That knowledge began in *Taylor Swift*; it came on full display with *Fearless*. And it animated some mashups on the Eras Tour. Lyon,

France, night one, brought "Fifteen" into a piano mashup with "You're on Your Own, Kid," stitching her insecure past to her present self. That version stays faithful to the *Fearless* hit until Taylor gets to "In your life you'll do greater things than date the boy on the football team," and there you can hear that she knows that we know that she's dating the guy from the Chiefs: She almost cracks up as the audience sings along. Then she begins the bridge from "You're on Your Own, Kid": "The football team, from sprinkler splashes to fireplace ashes . . ." She's been through so much, chose to put herself through so much, searching for "greater things," and she still needs friends like Abigail, and friendship bracelets. We do too.

"Fifteen," and "You Belong with Me," and "Love Story," and "Forever and Always," each in its own way, put forward Taylor's version of aspirational youth. A few other songs on *Fearless* invite us instead to delight in, and to see ourselves in, Taylor's adroit and playful songcraft. She wrote "Hey Stephen" about her crush on another songwriter, Stephen Liles of the band Love and Theft. No wonder, then, that the song flaunts its clever construction. The irregular bass line seems to anticipate what the vocals do, staying a beat ahead. Swift's lyrics play around too. After rhyming "Stephen" with "believin'" and "deceivin'," Swift rhymes "kiss you in the rain, so" with "look like an angel," taking advantage of the way liquid consonants—*l* and *r*—can stretch out as if they were vowels. Then she vowel-rhymes "alone now" with "come out." The song concludes with yet more meta-songwriting: All those other girls are beautiful, but none of them would "write a song for you." Only a few girls could put sounds together this way—the craft, as much as the crush, becomes the point.[16]

Fearless aspired so much to lifting listeners up—and to letting us feel seen—that it nearly left out a fine song about feeling let down. During years when network TV could make a musician's career, *Grey's Anatomy*—a show Taylor watched (she would name a cat for its star)—put "White Horse" into Season 5, episode 1. Apparently Swift had planned to omit "White Horse" from *Fearless*: "I really felt like we had the 'sadness' represented," she explained. "If it wasn't going to be on the show, then we weren't going to put it on the album." And yet it became a track five: the slot that, as fans came to believe, represents a special place of intimacy and confession. Swift does not only reject the man who thought he would sweep her away. She does not only tell him that she's not a princess (having recently written, or planned to write, "Today Was a Fairytale"; having asked her Romeo, in "Love Story," to pick out a white dress). She also tells him, anomalously for a country audience, that she's leaving their small town: Once she gets away (presumably in a motor vehicle, not on a horse), she may find somebody else who can treat her well.[17]

She might, on the other hand, find someone wild and free and bad for her. Her windswept, anthemic "The Way I Loved You" introduces the Taylor Swift who can't help falling for a glamorous chaos agent, a man (to quote Frank O'Hara) "as handsome as his character is bad": the first of the ultra-hot, bad-for-you boys portrayed on later records, from *Speak Now* all the way to *The Tortured Poets Department*. Too many of us know the feeling: the contrast between the "good" and boring boyfriend and the wild, exciting one. Swift and coauthor John Rich frame both the "good" boyfriend and the exciting bad boy musically. The verses introducing the too-perfect guy move to an almost military rhythm, with prominent drumrolls and banjo plucks. The beats—like the good-boy boyfriend's phone calls—arrive exactly when you'd expect them. The chorus feels louder, whether or not it is: It's more fluid, with much more guitar, like the ease and the "roller coaster rush" that Swift shared with the wilder guy.

Except perhaps for "Hey Stephen," with its standout bass line, the songwriting on *Fearless* shows less musical range than the compositions on any later album. And that makes sense, given the career shape Swift sought back then: She was pursuing not a range of characters and styles but a particular archetype, the not-quite-popular-yet, hopeful high school girl, and a particular moment for radio hits. The multiplatinum success of *Fearless* might look now like Swift's own tribute to the Nashville songwriting process, to what the critic Kelefa Sanneh once called "a city of perfectionists, stuffed with great players and great writers, working within the same narrow parameters, all trying to solve the same puzzle: how to write the perfect song." On *Fearless* they did it: "they," here, meaning mostly Swift and Liz Rose.[18]

Fifteen years after *Fearless*, while writing this book, I visit Nashville to see the Taylor sights, and to learn what I can about how she found her success. My host takes me first to the Bluebird Cafe, in the suburban strip of Hillsboro Avenue, with its faded awning and its tiny parking lot. From the outside it could be a dive bar or a barbecue joint. Inside, it could be an extraordinarily popular barbecue joint, with tables and benches close together (I wonder about the fire code), and a merch counter (I buy a tank top that says "BLUEBIRD"). Three professional songwriters sit in the middle of the café, each with a mic and an acoustic guitar: They take turns performing, showcasing their art, for a town where a big payday still means selling a song to a star, not becoming one.

Tonight's performers—Maia Sharp, Dean Fields, and Jay Knowles—chat on-mic about who else has performed the hits we are hearing.

"My buddy and I wrote this one together," Knowles says, in his beardy, fine-grained baritone. "And Alan Jackson recorded it. He's pretty good at singing country music." Garth Brooks got signed after playing here in 1988. The place has since shown up in a Bruce Springsteen song, and in a Foo Fighters song, and in the TV series *Nashville*. A hit Bluebird song must describe someone else's life, not just the life of the songwriter. Otherwise who else would choose to record it? Before about 1965, almost all pop songwriting worked in this way, and openly: It's the world that produced Carole King. But it's not the world that produced other women in pop and rock music known for their self-expression, from Tori Amos to Lana Del Rey. Nor is it the world of Disney teen-star machines, based in Los Angeles with outposts in Stockholm and London—another form of stardom that Taylor, presenting herself as a songwriter first and foremost, and presenting herself right here, managed to avoid.

After the Bluebird, my host takes me to the opposite of the Bluebird: downtown Nashville, Broadway east of Fifth Street, with its choking, beery crowd of cowboy hats, satin sashes, new-bought boots, and hen parties. Johnny Cash (or his estate), Jason Aldean, and a dozen other stars have lent their names to clubs with neon and rope lines and cover bands pumping conflicting versions of greatest hits. We find a singer in a Second Avenue bar, a beautiful, powerful alto who turns Tracy Chapman's "Fast Car" into an anthem with Indigo Girls overtones, then does similar work on "Before He Cheats." We notice her name, Josée Champoux (pronounced "shampoo"). Then we move back to Broadway to Miranda's, the three-story hen-party-oriented bar named for and owned by Miranda Lambert, where we find a freewheeling singer with a pencil mustache, a technically gifted, metal-loving guitarist, a bored-looking bassist with a beard the size of my head, and a drummer who rocks a sombrero. The dance floor loves them. The singer—who looks alarmingly like Taylor's notorious ex-boyfriend Matty Healy—leads the crowd in a Zach Bryan number, then gets everyone singing "Don't Stop Believin'," waving arms and shouting the outro.

Not-Matty-Healy asks the ladies to move to the front, and we do, and my host correctly predicts the next number: "Love Story." We sing the chorus and lift our fingers and open our palms to the sky, and we try to pretend to kneel when the singer gets to "he pulls out a ring." I can't hear the vocalist well, and the drummer's about to lose the beat (on the next song he does), but that's not the point. The point is the crowd, and the crowd is the song, and I realize that maybe Fifth and Broadway, not the Bluebird, is the final destination and the highest goal for the songs that they sing at the Bluebird: "Love Story" has entered the stratosphere of songs, and poems, that "everyone" knows, like "Don't Stop Believin'" and Robert Frost's "The Road Not Taken" and Michael Jackson's "Beat It." Frost—who sometimes seemed to hate his audience as much as Taylor loves hers—once said that an artist's "utmost ambition" was "to lodge a few poems where they will be hard to get rid of": "Love Story" has now been thoroughly lodged.[19]

4

SPEAK NOW

WHAT DO YOU DO ONCE YOU'VE reached your life goals? What if you've reached them at age nineteen? On *Fearless*, Taylor Swift gave the world her first star persona. On *Speak Now* she extends it and reacts to the ways in which the world sees her. It's aspirational, but not, like *Fearless*, in framing teen problems that many teens wish they had. Instead, it's aspirational in that it imagines chances for us to talk back, to have do-overs, to reengage with the moments of truth we wish we could relive. Here, the players are famous, the stakes are higher, the high schools show up only in rearview mirrors, and Swift shows us wounds that no one could dismiss as puppy love. *Speak Now* hits back, as it looks back, at bad actors, at men (not boys) who have hurt Swift. It shows how friends—and fans—can come together and help one another. And it sets an example: It asks us to raise our own voices.

Speak Now also showed what Swift could do on her own. All the songs on the original release of *Speak Now* credit Taylor as their only author. The *Speak Now* tour also showed off how she could play her own instruments: not just acoustic and electric guitar, but banjo guitar, ukulele, and piano. In 2010 Taylor claimed that cowriters simply weren't available, because she wrote the songs on tour: "I'd get my best ideas at 3 a.m. in Arkansas, and I didn't have a co-writer around." Swift later admitted, however, that she had eschewed coauthors in order to show that she didn't need them. "When I was eighteen, they were like, 'She doesn't really write those songs,'" Swift told *Rolling Stone* in 2019. "So my third album I wrote by myself as a reaction."[1]

That show of independence seems aspirational, too. What young adult does not want to show independence? At the same time, the songs remind us how much her music still involves collaboration: It's not like she's producing and engineering her own tracks, much less playing her own bass and drums. Nonetheless, a lot of those songs depict her alone. And a lot of them show her looking back in order to look forward—back at the teenage life she is already expected to represent, and forward to the adult life that other people now expect her to live. "You deserve to look back on your life," the album's insert booklet said, "without a chorus of resounding voices saying 'I could've, but it's too late now.' . . . If you know how you feel, and you so clearly know what you need to say . . . I think you should speak now."[2]

What kind of stories does Taylor tell when she speaks? They are stories about young people becoming adults, professionally and socially and romantically and even economically, stories about entering a wider, riskier, more consequential world. Literary critics call that kind of story a Bildungsroman. The album also promises a Künstlerroman, the story of how a young person becomes an artist.

And it yields songs about going back, fixing mistakes, and trying again. "Sparks Fly" does so musically, with its stops and starts and announcements: "Drop everything now!" The title track plays on language conventionally used in Christian weddings, from the 1549 *Book of Common Prayer*: "Should anyone present know of any reason that this couple should not be joined in holy matrimony, speak now or forever hold your peace." In real life, almost no one ever speaks at that moment. Many otherwise traditional Christian weddings exclude it. But in Taylor's song, the familiar words go back to the past to create another future: If we look back in the right way, and speak about it at the right moment, we can write another story.

"Speak Now," the song, makes a kind of do-over, or sequel, to a story in which the boy picks the wrong girl. "Mine" makes a kind of do-over, or sequel, to a song (or an album) about first love (by the water, as in "Tim McGraw"). The bridge looks back to a later, pivotal moment in their romance. Then, in the third verse, the radio-friendly, four-chord power pop song soars toward the couple's future, away from the waterside town that shaped their youth. The song can't be autobiography—nobody sensible sees Scott Swift as a "careless man"—but the self-portraiture feels real: This careful, dutiful daughter, reliant on her familiar scenes and musical structures, still wants to get swept away.

"Never Grow Up" is an obvious sequel, too. It follows "The Best Day," instrumentally, rhythmically, and lyrically. You can play the songs simultaneously (one of our students did it for me). Taylor made them into a lovely mashup near the end of the Eras Tour in Vancouver, night one. But "Never Grow Up" ends up sadder, because it's written from farther away: Swift no longer takes a child's point of view. First she sings like a parent to a baby. Then she gives advice to somebody who's fourteen, a sequel of sorts to the thirteen-year-old in "The Best Day." Be nice to your mom, she says (remembering her own mom). "Don't make her drop you off around the block; remember she's getting older too" (one of our own teenagers literally insists that we drop her off around the block: She's ashamed that her mom gives her rides).

As in "The Best Day," "Never Grow Up" places teenager and mother in the second verse, father and little brother in the bridge. And, as in "Fifteen," Swift switches from second person to first person for the last verse. That last verse ends "early," so to speak: Where you might expect a final line, you hear just a guitar loop, as if Taylor knew that she, and you, the listener, have not yet written the lines that say how this next, more consequential chapter of your life will go. The hidden message for "Never Grow Up" in the lyrics booklet reads, "I MOVED OUT IN JULY." She literally did: out of her parents' house in Hendersonville into an apartment in downtown Nashville, in a modern concierge building called the Adelicia.

You might not be moving into the Adelicia, but you, too, might imagine yourself moving out, heading off to college or to the big city: away from whoever made you feel bad in your teens, like the point-of-view character in "Mean." Addressed overtly to generic bullies, "Mean" also follows up on Swift's botched awards show performance alongside Stevie Nicks. Hearing her go out of tune on TV, some older male critics (notably a journalist named Bob Lefsetz) made fun of her voice. As much as the song faces down Swift's own detractors, it reaches out to her listeners. How many of us, at any age, have faced an opinionated, mansplaining blowhard? How many of us have imagined leaving that blowhard in the dust?[3]

"Mean" comes close to bluegrass—Swift's only pre-pandemic song to do so. That arrangement lets Taylor share the spotlight with one of her closest friends on tour, the fiddler Caitlin Evanson. But the bluegrass feel and the video—on a hokey-looking 1970s-vintage stage set, with hay bales, like something from *The Muppet Show*—make another point: Taylor plays old-timey music in order to speak to old-timey, ornery adults. Bullies who peaked in high school will stay stuck in small bars, and in sets from their own long-ago youth, while Taylor and her allies move on. Again, she treats the elements of country music as pastoral conventions, not as lifelong signs of authenticity: Her authenticity comes from teenage life. In Taylor Swift's music—as against so many earlier country songs—it's okay to leave your small town. You don't even have to miss it.

Tracks like "Mean," looking back, worked to build listeners' confidence. But *Speak Now* also registered other desires, and other requirements, facing women and girls, among them the obligation, if not the desire, to stay beautiful, sweet, nice, and soft. Sarah Chapelle, the world expert on what Swift wears, notices that the outfits for *Speak Now* had girlier, softer looks: flowy dresses, long tailed gowns, some in pastel shades of purple or yellow. Responding to the claim "that a teenage blonde could not possibly be in charge," as Chapelle put it, Swift "rerooted her image in soft girlish femininity." Those outfits call out not just sexism, but also what the trans activist and cultural critic Julia Serano calls femmephobia: "dismissive or delegitimizing views of people who express femininity." Think about pantsuits as symbols of women's power, then think about what that symbolism implies about women, or girls, in flowy skirts. "It takes a certain level of confidence to rock a tailored take on a menswear suit," Chapelle writes. "But there's something even stronger about taking a pink A-line skirt and matching top and making it your Boss Outfit." Girl power and girlishness might go hand in hand.[4]

Besides striking back at the people who doubted her chops, and establishing girliness as power, *Speak Now* looks back at other stories, scandals, and memories from the *Fearless* era. Taylor's romance with Joe Jonas left at least one trace on *Speak Now*: "Better Than Revenge," a kind of manifesto for the man-eating, rivalrous, antihero Swift had begun to learn how to pretend to be. The track offers windmill guitars, crunchy distortion, and an unusual focus, not on the man who left her, but on the girl whom he chose: "She thinks I'm psycho 'cause I like to rhyme her name with things." As in a proper punk-pop song, there's no pre-chorus, only a chorus that ends on the title. And, as in earlier work, the song becomes aspirational not just because it turns loneliness into angry energy, but because it boasts about her songwriting (rhyming) prowess. The 2010 version explicitly attacks her rival for "things that she does on the mattress": The re-recording changes that line to a figure of speech about a flame and matches, because Taylor has realized that slut-shaming hurts everyone, and because—as she put it in 2014—"no one can steal your boyfriend from you if he doesn't want to leave." Yet the bridge, the core of the song's aspirational energy, stays unchanged—in it, Taylor promises that she, the songwriter, "will always get the last word."[5]

Still in her teens when she became world-famous, Swift would face the kind of public scrutiny that comes to A-list adults (as when Lefsetz and company attacked her voice). She would also date men who shared the celebrity spotlight. Swift's role in the romantic comedy *Valentine's Day*—shot during the summer of 2009—paired her with Taylor Lautner, the bushy-eyebrowed hottie soon to achieve shirtless, lycanthropic fame in the *Twilight* films. *Valentine's Day* represents a road not taken for the still-teenage star—what if she had tried harder to make it in film?—as well as a look at who Hollywood thought she could be: a bubbly, outgoing blonde who carries a giant stuffed polar bear to high school and explains to a local TV reporter that she's definitely not a cheerleader ("I'm on the dance team"). Swifties know the movie for its delightful signature song, "Today Was a Fairytale," apparently written in 2008 and re-released only as a vault track on *Fearless (Taylor's Version)*.

We also know the film as the start of the real-life love story around Swift and Lautner, who kissed for the cameras before they dated backstage. Spotted together through the fall of 2009, the pair were clearly an item (nicknamed T-Squared) by the time Swift hosted *Saturday Night Live* that November. She wrote and sang her own opener: "I like writing songs about douchebags who cheat on me / But I'm not gonna say that in my monologue!" It's a letter-perfect example of what rhetoric experts call apophasis, raising a topic or making a statement by claiming that you have no plan to raise it ("I come to bury Caesar, not to praise him"). Swift goes on: "If you're wondering if I might / Be dating the werewolf from *Twilight* . . ." Then silence. The whole thing (you can watch it online) shows Taylor's apparent comfort with fame and attention. It's also hilarious—the audience loves it.

Swift seems to have broken up with Lautner in December 2009, on or around her twentieth birthday: That ending inspired one of her strongest, most sympathetic breakup songs, "Back to December." The song fades in, instrument by midtempo instrument, as Swift describes meeting a former flame: "small talk, work and the weather." His "guard is up," and no wonder. The girl in the song broke up with him, suddenly, cruelly, and wishes either that she could date him again or else that she could have ended the romance in a way that respected his uprightness, his devotion, and his value as her hot friend. Swift described the song as an apology: It's the first in her catalog to cast her as the guilty party.

And it's a beauty, not just for its directness, not just for its use of seasonal cues (summer, fall, winter; what about spring?), but for its vocal melody. Verse and pre-chorus rise only a third above *do*, but drop a full fifth below it, so that she's literally under the (notes for) "weather." The chorus then leaps, and stays, almost entirely above that same *do*, peaking a fifth above it (on *sol*). The past, remembered, lifts her up; the present day brings her down. If only she could go back to the D in December and make it the start of a climb, not the end of the fall.

Swift's fame was what she wanted, what she worked for, but it came with a cost she could never have expected: one that would affect her moods, and her songwriting, all the way through the next decade and a half. On September 13, 2009—after she had started writing *Speak Now*, but before she had finished recording it—Swift won an MTV Video Music Award (VMA) for "You Belong with Me." Accepting the award on live TV from its paired presenters, Lautner and the Colombian pop star Shakira, Swift began her speech: "I sing country music so thank you so much." Then the hip-hop titan Kanye West leapt onstage. "Yo Taylor. I'm really happy for you," he announced. "Imma let you finish. But Beyoncé had one of the best videos of all time." By the time Ye had finished his own mini-speech, the auditorium was resounding with boos.

The VMA incident made international headlines. President Barack Obama called West a jackass. Katy Perry reacted concisely: "F*** you Kanye. It's like you stepped on a kitten." Ye already had a pattern of storming, interrupting, and inserting himself into awards shows, among them the 2004 American Music Awards, the 2006 MTV Europe Music Awards, and the 2007 VMAs. You might think Swift must have known in the moment that most of the viewers were taking her side.[6]

You would be wrong. She thought they were booing her. Video clips of the incident, easy to find on YouTube, remain hard to watch. Receiving the statuette before West appears, she looks awestruck, glad to be there, perhaps fighting impostor syndrome. After he comes into view and begins to tell her—and the crowd—just what he thinks, she stands motionless, stunned. Behind her, Lautner also looks frozen: He said later that he thought West was performing "a practiced and rehearsed skit," and that he wished he had chosen to intervene.[7]

The experience left indelible marks both on Swift's sense of herself and on the way the listening public saw her. In 2015 a reporter who interviewed her said Swift considered the interruption "the most consequential accident of her professional life." "When the crowd started booing," Swift had said, "I thought they were booing because they also believed I didn't deserve the award. . . . I went backstage and cried, and then I had to stop crying and perform five minutes later. I just told myself I had to perform, and I tried to convince myself that maybe this wasn't that big of a deal." But it was. When Swift later renovated her Nashville penthouse, she hung a photograph of West's interruption above her fireplace, right next to her 2009 VMA statuette, as if to remind herself that she had lived through it. By then she had made her public embarrassment into a launching pad, a basis for her own art, in performances and in songs that invited us as her fans, again, to see ourselves in her.[8]

Swift made the incident into the last punchline for her opening monologue-song on *Saturday Night Live*. Slowing down, winking (as seen in the video clip), she sings to the crowd: "You might be expecting me to say / Something bad about Kanye," "how he ran up on the stage / And ruined my VMA monologue." She looks down in mock dejection, bats her eyelashes, and resumes her chirpy pace: "But there's nothing more to say / Cause everything's OK / I've got security lining the stage." Two cast members show up with black suits and earpieces, Secret Service–style. Then Taylor gets to the end of the bit. "We have a great show. Kanye West is not here. Stick around." She gets a laugh, but it's a nervous laugh: Does she feel threatened for real? Should she feel threatened? As a young white woman nervous about her critical reception, famously upstaged by an adult Black man whom critics regard (with reason) as a genius, how should she feel? Should she even show how she feels?

It's a question that seems to have vexed her for years, and it generated more than one musical answer. Swift put one track that appears to address West on *Speak Now*, premiering the song at the 2010 VMAs. "Innocent" begins with exceptionally noisy drums, almost like radio static or crowd noise, as if Taylor had to work to sing through it. It's addressed to anyone who "lost your balance on a tightrope," then "lost your mind tryin' to get it back." This song, too, looks back on a childhood lost: "Wasn't it easier in your lunchbox days? / Always a bigger bed to crawl into."[9]

Every song on this album feels like a sequel to something, and every song imagines a possible future. This one appears to imagine a future for West: "Who you are is not what you did / You're still an innocent." The meditative song in a minor key ends its chorus on the root of the relative major: It ends up calmer, or happier, than the opening might lead us to expect. But it also ends up condescending: Why should this young white woman treat this confident, famous Black man like a child? The scholar Shaun Cullen has argued that the contretemps, and especially the "Innocent" video (where Swift herself appears as a fancy hostess), "proves West's point about the inherent racism of the media industry." Arrogating to herself the right to decide how and when to forgive, Swift made herself a vehicle for white privilege. But if "Innocent" represented the wrong thing to say, and the wrong way to say it, what would have been the right one? Should Swift, could Swift—who drew her songs from the most stressful parts of her own life—have simply and silently moved on?[10]

Not all the album's backward looks turn painful: Some give unalloyed delights. "Enchanted" records an encounter with Adam Young of the bedroom-pop-electronic band Owl City: "Wonderstruck," a word in the song, is also the title of an Owl City track. The booklet's hidden message spells out "ADAM." According to Young, he and Swift exchanged emails for months—he was hoping for a collaboration—before Swift stopped writing back. Somewhere out there is a universe where Taylor did work with Adam Young, where her turn to introspective bedroom electronica took place not in 2022, with *Midnights*, but ten years before. In our universe, we have the song "Enchanted," another example of Swift's skill at building up a vocal melody. The verses move up and down one whole or half step at a time, carefully, tactfully . . . until Taylor leaps all the way up from *do* to *sol*, on "meet." It's a ride we can take with the singer, a pure uplift, as it looks back on a purely enchanting evening with a literal aspiration: a breath of fresh air.[11]

Taylor wanted to call the whole album *Enchanted*, but Scott Borchetta overruled her: "We were at lunch, and she had played me a bunch of the new songs," he remembered in 2010. "I looked at her and I'm like, 'Taylor, this record isn't about fairy tales and high school anymore. That's not where you're at.'" It's easy to see why Borchetta rejected the title. But why would Taylor request it? What's special about the song that would merit unusual attention, keeping it in the Eras Tour set when nothing else from *Speak Now* stuck around?[12]

One answer might come from Emily Nagoski, a psychologist and expert on sex and sexuality who, in her 2024 book *Come Together: The Science (and Art!) of Creating Lasting Sexual Connections*, distinguishes between desire and pleasure. The former, the most common topic for love songs, moves people forward and onward, as a melody or a harmonic progression can move a song toward an end it has not yet reached. "Desire is forward movement," Nagoski writes, "exploring to create something that doesn't currently exist. . . . Desire is motivation toward a goal." Pleasure, on the other hand, exists right now, enchanted and satisfied, even wonderstruck, by what already is: "Pleasure is stillness, savoring what's happening in the moment," rather than trying to "pursue something different." "Enchanted" stands out—among Taylor's songs up to this point—for its expression of pleasure: the critic Annie Zaleski calls it, delightfully, a "pastel-tinted fantasy." This night, right now, already feels flawless. Even the doubt she feels (is he dating someone?) gives her pleasure, "dancing around all alone." Its major chords and reverberant textures encourage us to join Taylor in having fun, right now, just feeling good about being around a person—a musician—who turns her on.[13]

But "Enchanted"—again—feels like an exception. Most of the album looks back as well as forward, at desires alongside regrets. It's an album about revisions, sequels, consequences, memories, second thoughts. Taylor encourages friends and guys and listeners and musicians to see her as she wants to be seen, and not as others have seen her; the rebel (and not the good girl) in "Mine," the success (and not the bullied victim) in "Mean," the triumphant suitor (and not the abandoned lover) in "Speak Now," the ex who has owned her mistakes in "Back to December." She also—as our hermeneutic friend—asks us to support her, and to imagine that she will support us, when somebody has behaved badly or done us wrong.

SPEAK NOW

John Mayer seems to have behaved badly indeed. The virtuoso blues, folk, and rock guitarist, born in 1977, tweeted, in the summer of 2009, that the eighteen-year-old singer should join him in recording a song he just wrote. The two became friends, then collaborators, that fall, recording Mayer's "Half of My Heart." That duet sounds now like a seduction in progress, now like a prediction of disaster: "Half of my heart's got a right mind to tell you / That half of my heart won't do," Mayer intones. "Down the road later on / You'll hate that I never gave more to you." Swift sings backup, mostly: "Ah, ah, ah," and one line of her own.

Swift and Mayer seem to have started dating, or doing something like dating, over the winter of 2009, ending things in the spring of 2010, in time for "Dear John" to become track five on *Speak Now*. At 6:45 (Taylor's Version) or 6:43 (original flavor), "Dear John" was the longest song Taylor had released up to that date. It's also her first song to use waltz time (3/4), though "Last Kiss" (also on *Speak Now*) uses 6/8. None of her other arrangements, and few of her rhythms, sound anything like "Dear John," which sounds instead, and pointedly, like Mayer. The shiny electric guitar licks point to his blues chops. The stately tempo, the largely acoustic instrumentation, and especially the waltz time, echo Mayer's first number-one chart hit, "Daughters," from *Heavier Things* (2003), which won Mayer a Grammy for Song of the Year (beating out, among others, Tim McGraw). Mayer's song has not aged well: "Boys would be strong and boys soldier on," he sang without irony, "but boys would be gone without warmth from a woman's good, good heart."

By the time she wrote "Dear John," Swift wanted boys like that gone anyway. She also (to judge by her own words) wanted girls her age to stay away from men nearly old enough to be their fathers. Her lyrics offer a guided tour into, then out of, the kind of unequal, exploitative romance that many girls and young women experience. At first it seems wonderful, the more so the more the adults in her life object. "They said run as fast as you can," which made her—of course—run the other way, toward him.

A man in his thirties—especially a charismatic, powerful one—should know better. "Don't you think I was too young to be messed with? / The girl in the dress cried the whole way home." Swift buries the rhyme on "dress" and "mess" midsentence, so that we notice what follows, too, learning where and how much she cried. Now that she's gone, Swift goes on, her ex will "add my name to a long list of traitors who don't understand." Swift emphasizes the vowel rhyme in "name" and "traitors," setting both syllables at the same place in the measure: If we see ourselves in the song, getting out of a toxic relationship now or in our own pasts, we might see our names on that list. Sarah Chapelle remarks on how the last chorus in "Dear John" "quietly switches from 'I' to 'you'"—it's the older man, not the girl, who "should have known."[14]

Again, when Swift sings about men, especially bad men, she's often singing to, and for, other women, and she's usually giving advice. The literary critic Arielle Zibrak writes that as a reader of romance novels, a viewer of "trashy," soapy TV, she has sought a "place where we contend with the fraught desires of female heterosexuality without the oppressive presence of their objects." Warning other girls about men like Mayer, sharing with other girls the unstable excitement along with the lousy outcome, Swift's music inhabits that place. New friends who say all their old friends keep turning against them, a new romantic partner who believes all his bitter exes just don't understand, should raise red flags, though there's no reason to think that a nineteen-year-old who has just met her guitar hero should know as much.[15]

Unless, perhaps, she has heard songs like "Dear John." Swift told Lizzie Widdicombe of *The New Yorker* in 2011 that intense identification, relatability, and connection made for "the best musical experience": "Hearing a song by somebody singing about their life, and it resembles yours so much that it makes you feel comforted." Not only seen: comforted—even protected, or warned. That's why so many Swifties find "Dear John" so meaningful. Most of us know at least one young person—usually a woman—who has entered an unwise romance with an older, more powerful man.[16]

It's easy to see what could make the song relatable. But what—if anything—might make it aspirational? For one thing, Taylor's apparent triumph. She stopped playing his game, she walked all the way home, she wrote "Dear John," and now she's "shining like fireworks over your sad empty town" (a reference, perhaps, to Mayer's real hometown, the fabulously wealthy but anodyne Fairfield, Connecticut). Swift has become—or will become—bigger than Mayer: She's already emotionally healthier, and if she keeps on writing songs about exes, at least she doesn't manipulate them, withhold affection, or "change the rules every day."[17]

Moreover, she's able to write about getting out. "There is no intimacy without vulnerability," runs an oft-seen quote from the popular psychologist Brené Brown, and Swift's vulnerability here, and throughout *Speak Now*, becomes a kind of intimacy with—a way to share trust with—her fans. Her waltz-time catharsis becomes our education; we might wish we could conclude these sorts of relationships as powerfully, as helpfully, as "Dear John" seems to have done. Mayer recorded his own apparent response to "Dear John" three years later, "Paper Doll," from *Paradise Valley* (2013). The catchy soft-focus pop number appears to ask Swift why she didn't "fall" farther for Mayer, while berating her for acting like "22 girls in one / And none of them know what they want." Swift's song "22" appeared on *Red* (2012). Of course she didn't know what she wanted. He was a grown-ass man. She was nineteen.

"The Story of Us," placed later on *Speak Now*, returns to the Mayer debacle in its lyrics, and to "Forever and Always" in its sounds. The song arose after the split, when Swift encountered Mayer unexpectedly at the CMT Music Awards in the spring of 2010. She told her mom, after the unpleasant encounter, "It was like I was standing alone in a crowded room." Its catchy pop-punk makes uncommon use of full stops, false endings, short rests, and instrumental dropouts, as if to mimic Taylor's own nervous uncertainty: It even ends (as if to make sure) with "The End." Swift has never stated directly that either song addresses Mayer. A "Dear John letter" (the term dates from World War II) could be a letter breaking up with anyone. And yet the music, and the words, leave little doubt.[18]

When Swift performed "Dear John" on the Eras Tour (Minneapolis, night two), she prefaced it with a lengthy explanation, telling her fans she had moved on, and that we should too. It's as if she had always addressed not Mayer, but the girls and women who might be listening: not the problematic man, but her allies, the Swifties. Looking back in order to look forward, making an album from memories and second thoughts, Swift often seems to know she's setting an example for her fans. Sometimes she knows she's bringing us together around common (relatable, if you like) dilemmas: how to apologize to an ex, how to warn others about red flags.

Sometimes she's looking right at us. The connection she's built, over three albums, with her listeners becomes the de facto subject of "Long Live." "I've loved my fans from the very first day," Swift told the website Popsugar after *Speak Now*. "But they've said and done things recently that make me feel like they're my friends—more now than ever before." She expects that connection to stick around, too, as the exhilarating array of verb tenses and moods in "Long Live" suggests. "I said [past tense] remember this moment [imperative] / . . . our lives / Would never be the same [the future as seen in the past; a past conditional] / . . . If you have children [conditional future], . . . / Tell them [conditional imperative] how the crowds went wild [past] / Tell them how I hope they shine [future]. / . . . One day, we will be remembered." The future will see the present as the past.[19]

Swift has said that she wrote the song for her touring band—the "thieves in ripped-up jeans" with whom she could travel, if not "rule," the world. The hosts of the great podcast *Taylearning* suggested recently, and very credibly, that Taylor might have believed, when she wrote the song, that the *Fearless* era could be her peak. And yet the song came to stand for her future instead, and for her expanding fan base: Once it found its way through the world, its sense of community came to represent not her collaborators but her fans. The song promised—and still promises—that Swifties might give one another what the psychologist Devon Price calls "expansive recognition," a sense of commonality that "declares that our battles are only won when we realize they are shared." You're not the only girl ("Fifteen" told us) who felt used by the guy on the football team. You're not the only one who got bullied in "Mean." And you're certainly not the only one who's ever felt like you're standing alone in a crowded room.[20]

Expansive recognition, Price continues, counteracts isolation, self-hatred, and shame. It "encourages us to . . . reveal our pain, and to name when we are overwhelmed, so we can seek out the support we deserve." Hearing Taylor's music, even at a concert, can seem like a one-way transaction—we listen, she speaks. In fact, though, even imagining that more people out there can see us sympathetically, or share our dilemmas, might help us live more deliberately, connect with real-life friends, and seek emotional repair. That's what Price (quoting other social psychologists) calls "*perceived* social support" (emphasis in Price). And it's one of the things that all those friendship bracelets mean: Taylor Swift's music, expensively produced and bearing the marks of its singular writer, nevertheless helps show us what we too can do.[21]

A 2010 video for "Long Live" shows Taylor on the roof of a bus with her fans, as if they belonged together, as if they could support one another emotionally far beyond the length of the shoot: It's what the late cultural critic Margaret Rossman, writing about the community of Swifties, called "a joint girlhood space." The end of the 2023 movie release *Taylor Swift: The Eras Tour*, when "Long Live" plays over the credits, feels like a sequel to that video, or else like one more of the many fan-made videos that have circulated since: Rather than watching Taylor, moviegoers see more of her fans, enthusing together over what they, and we, just saw. Not only (these audiovisual moments show) has Taylor trained us to see ourselves in her, to see ourselves as more like her: She's also showing us that we constitute a community, that we can be celebrities to ourselves. The word "we" occurs nineteen times in the lyric sheet, the word "I" only nine, including the line "I had the time of my life fighting dragons with you." She did. We did too. She will, and we may, once again. She's looking back in order to look forward, and she's bringing us along as she moves ahead, away from her teenage triumphs, into her public adult life.[22]

The vault tracks from *Fearless (Taylor's Version)* largely validate Swift's—and her team's—decisions as to what ended up on the album: Most just seem weaker than what the original album contained. The vault tracks from *Speak Now (Taylor's Version)* instead show Swift's expanding narrative range. It's easy to think she left them off the album not because she thought the songwriting inferior, but because they might have discomfited her label, made the record seem less unified, or alienated her youngest listeners. "Timeless" returns to the country twang, and to the nostalgic, monogamous fidelity, celebrated on earlier albums, dialing up the literary specifics while flaunting elaborate rhymes: "We would have been timeless," "we were supposed to find this." Its present-day love story parallels a couple whose boy is "headed off to war in 1944," a pair of 1950s teens in a driveway, and a pair of star-crossed lovers from the 1500s, described in a book of unknown vintage: as "Long Live" put it, a history-book page.

Other songs—stellar ones—say things about Swift's feelings, in 2009–2010, that might have alarmed fans, had they been heard at that time. After the Kanye incident, Swift feared that the media, and the fan base, that built her up would start to tear her down. "Castles Crumbling" imagines that the teardown has begun—it's a song about feeling, or fearing, that you've reached your peak. Shimmery keyboards underpin Swift's stated fears: not just about losing her fame, but (worse) about losing her friends, such as Hayley Williams from Paramore, who joins her on the vault track's vocals.

And yet, once again, the song also offers a kind of solidarity. "Castles Crumbling" does not just address Swift's actual worldwide (and, she fears, fragile) prominence; it hands a bright mirror to good girls who fear adulthood, to (in the words of the comics critic Dan Grote) "any good overachieving child who dive-bombed after college because there were no more multiple-choice tests to ace." The title line, "I feel like my castle's crumbling down," played in E minor, moves from E (*la*) to G (*do*), down to *la*, up to *do*, back down to *sol*, up to *la*, and then down all the way to *fa*, a minor sixth: Taylor has literally, repeatedly, let everyone down. It's her most direct writing so far about her need to work, her need for attention, her fears about failure, her life as a careful daughter, and the good-girl syndrome that has kept some of us, some of her fans, inside the classroom or the practice room.[23]

If Taylor gives fans succor when we feel most alone, she also shows how durable friendships support her. We can imagine such friendships supporting us too. Musically simple and verbally arresting, "When Emma Falls in Love" might be the sleeper hit from the *Speak Now* vault tracks: The song shows more intimacy, more confidence, in its devotion to one female friend than anything Swift chose to put on the 2010 album. Fans have speculated that she left it off *Speak Now* so as not to boast about her friendship with the actor Emma Stone. This Emma feels everything strongly, gets support from her mom, falls hard when she falls for a boy, and shows endless charisma, just as "if Cleopatra grew up in a small town." She can even reform a "bad boy," though Shakespeare's Cleopatra, corrupting Mark Antony, did the reverse. Taylor might have had this then-unreleased song in mind when she told *Parade* magazine, during the *Red* era, "I think every girl's dream is to find a bad boy at the right time, when he wants to not be bad anymore." And the passion that Emma shows never backfires: Even if she gets hurt, she can love again.[24]

No wonder, then, that Emma proves aspirational for Taylor, almost as Taylor proves aspirational for us: Taylor wants to be, or be like, this Emma. She reinforces that final sentiment—a declaration of loyalty, of friendship, of something that's somehow more—not only by repeating it as the song ends, but by labeling it with an out-of-place chord. "When Emma Falls in Love" consists entirely—verse, chorus, bridge, instrumental, everything—of the four most common chords in pop music (I, V, ii, IV: here, D major, A major, E minor, G major), except on the line "Sometimes I wish I was her." There, Taylor uses a chord

(C major) whose root does not belong in the home key at all. It's the line that stands out; it's the line we take home.

The song now gives obvious fodder for the Gaylors, the contingent of Taylor Swift fans who insist, or believe, that Swift dates or wants to date women. After all, "Do I want to date her or do I want to be her?" remains a common catchphrase in lesbian culture. But nothing in Swift's song, taken literally, supports a Gaylorist reading. Nor does anything else, taken literally, in Swift's life. Despite the many writings (among them a 2024 *New York Times* op-ed) suggesting that Swift may secretly consider herself gay, or bisexual, or pansexual, or heteroflexible, her life as we know it gives no clear support for such theories.[25]

"When Emma Falls in Love" instead illustrates the overlap, and the difference, between romantic affection and erotic attraction: You can love someone, and want to be near them, without ever wanting to kiss them or take their clothes off. "When Emma Falls in Love" may feel vividly real both for lesbians who remember "wishing I was her" and for straight women who wish their own love affairs with men could be as passionate or as promising as Emma's. Taylor's stripped-down arrangement (as if we might sing or play along) invites fans "to fill in the gaps in her story," as Margaret Rossman writes, and to see our friendships in hers.[26]

No sensible user of the phrase "punk rock" would apply it to Taylor Swift, or to her music, or to her clear influences (though the first two Paramore albums come close). And yet this artist who's known fantastic commercial success, who almost defines the 2010s mainstream, here overlaps with the history of punk. In particular, she and her fan communities seem to have brought to a much larger, less confrontational set of women and girls some of the same goals, and some of the same versions of friendships, seen in the 1990s feminist punk rock movement

Riot Grrrl. As Kathleen Hanna of Bikini Kill wrote in her 2024 memoir, Riot Grrrl aimed "to take places usually reserved for men and turn them into expressive spaces for girls and women."[27]

Swift, too, for all her corporate synergies and her expensive production, challenges the barriers and fourth walls that normally separate artist from audience ("the walls we break through"): She, too, gives girls and women space that feels like our own. Like Hanna and other Riot Grrrl leading lights, Swift on *Speak Now* asks us to imagine being like her, and then gives us ways to think we could. During the *Speak Now* era, Swift told Britain's *Daily Telegraph* that "girls come up to me and tell me exactly what's going on in their love lives. They always come out with these bold confessions like 'I'm so glad I'm at your concert tonight. My boyfriend just left me.'" Hanna's memoir described similar effects: Clusters of girls came up to her after each show, often in order to talk about trauma, saying things they could never speak out loud before. During the 1990s, Hanna encouraged women and girls to "draw hearts and stars on your hands," and then to look for other girls with those markings as ways to "strike up a conversation." Swift, in the *Speak Now* era, writing on her own arms, encouraged fans to do it too.[28]

These physical symbols helped to create community. They stood for what the best parts of *Speak Now*, from "Back to December" through the vault tracks from the re-recording, had meant all along: They provided ways to look back at your own life and find that, contrary to expectation, you're not alone, you're not subject to men, and you have some say over what comes next in your own life. Riot Grrrl's core participants, sending photocopied zines to one another and meeting up in basements before the internet, tried to bring the high spirits of girlhood with them into their teenage and post-teenage lives, much as Swift did with the ethos of *Speak Now*. Swift openly sought, and found, commercial success, while Riot Grrrl bands avoided it, or else (like Hanna) approached it with anxious ambivalence. Yet Swift, too—the Swift of hand hearts and Sharpies on arms; the Swift of "Long Live" and "Speak Now," of "Dear John" and "Mean," who also wrote "When Emma Falls in Love"—created communities where girls' bodies belonged to girls, where women's bodies belonged to women, where girls paid more attention to one another than to what men might want them to do. Hearing the songs, accepting Taylor as a hermeneutic friend, we could look back on our lives to look forward, see our future in light of our past, and speak with one another, even now.

5

RED

Is *Red* Taylor Swift's most unified album? Or is it instead a hot mess? Maybe it's both: It feels like a fast, reckless ride. Swift has called *Red* her one "true breakup album," since most of it addresses her romance, and then her split, with the actor Jake Gyllenhaal. It's also the start of her slow-motion breakup with Nashville. Musically it takes her all over the place, with arena rock, country compositions, chirpy Swedish pop with dubstep elements, 1970s-style singer-songwriter ballads, and more. Its sonic variety matches a newly varied, and newly international, roster of collaborators, from the familiar (Nathan Chapman in Nashville) to the then-startling (Max Martin and Shellback in Stockholm and two members of Snow Patrol, a band from Scotland).

And yet, in its lyrics, in tone, in the stories it tells, *Red* has more unity than any of Taylor's albums before or since. No wonder she named it after a single color (perhaps inspired by Joni Mitchell's *Blue*).

As she told *Entertainment Weekly*, "All those emotions—spanning from intense love, intense frustration, jealousy, confusion, all of that—in my mind, all those emotions are red." Elsewhere she said she had made an album about "tumultuous, crazy, intense, insane, semi-toxic relationships," the kind that go "from zero to one hundred miles per hour and then hit a wall and explode." Everything in the album speaks to that feeling—from its sonic variety to its literary references, up to the changes it underwent when Swift re-recorded it in 2021.[1]

Hearing *Red* means hearing the unity in its stories. It means tracing the album's palette of colors, and its flurry of numbers, and its very American focus on driving and cars: the musical rush of the open road, and the lyrical references to automobiles, from the rock-and-roll traditions that Swift evokes and then rejects. Those cars, those numbers and ages, all those colors, the big guitars and the new-to-Swift dance-music moves, build up the heartbreak, the anger, and the emotional vertigo that keep Taylor aspirational and relatable. She's a singer who seems to know what sharp turns and near-crashes we've been through, and who takes us where we wish we could go.

Red once again hits Taylor's career-long goals: remaining close to her fans, exploring her drive for approval and her need to keep working, making music that animates the words. The memoirist, essayist, and dominatrix Melissa Febos has written about the kind of love, or lust, that Taylor labels "red," the kind that, as Febos put it, seems "insatiable because no need could be met—like fire, they grew when fed"; after all, "you can't get enough of a thing you don't need." Red love (or lust or desire) works like an addiction. The more you want it, the more of it you want: Its promised equilibrium, or satisfaction, or calm, or confidence, recedes past imagined horizons, as in a road trip that never ends. The album—whose re-recording (unlike the re-recordings of *Fearless* and *Speak Now*) radically reinvented a signature song—uses its sonic variety to stay with its narrative of dangerous passion. That kind of passion could well scramble our boundaries; it might demand more than one register, more than one kind of music—indeed, more than one version—to get its story told.[2]

If we start by asking what makes love red, we may go on to ask what counts as love. How many things can that word mean? The fiction writer Ursula K. Le Guin once explained the problem from the point of view of a space alien: "When I was on the ship, [a human] told me that many languages have a single word for sexual desire and the bond between mother and child and the bond between soulmates and the feeling for one's home and worship of the sacred; they are all called love. There is no word that great in my language." Love is what the literary critic William Empson called a "complex word" (as in his book *The Structure of Complex Words*): By using it, we imply equations and overlaps and differentiations. We connect the word's meanings with one another, perhaps unconsciously. (To take a less freighted example, because "brave" can mean at once "determined, courageous," "outstanding, notable," and "good, admirable," merely using the word can imply that standing out is admirable or good.)[3]

The word "love" in sexual and romantic contexts (never mind "I love my mom" or "I love jellybeans") implies or can imply some (but rarely all) of these things: a rush of fluttery interest; a desire to spend a lot of time with someone; the feeling you get when you do spend a lot of time with them; the wish to know where they are when they're not with you; jealousy; hope for their happiness when they're not with you; the hope that they'll need you; the feeling that you need them; rooting for them; wanting to smooch them; wanting to go on adventures with them; seeking time alone with them; loyalty; forgiveness; hoping they notice you dress up for them; loving how they don't care whether you dress up; wanting sex now; wanting sex, but not now. Which ones does "love" imply at a given point? It is, as Swift says, like trying to solve a crossword puzzle when there's no right answer. The closer we look at a breakup album like *Red*, the more chances we get to think about how to disentangle, clarify, and unencumber the various things love can mean, and (therefore) the kind of things that make some love feel treacherously red.

We can find those meanings one or two songs at a time. "State of Grace" and "Red," the propulsive tracks one and two, resemble each other in tempo, in texture, and in rhythm. "State of Grace" also uses a ringing, piercing electric guitar technique made popular by the Edge from U2, who, as the rock critic Niall Stokes explains, "used open strings to create a drone-like effect," full of "arpeggios and harmonics touched and left to hang." Swift made "State of Grace" (mashed up with "You're on Your Own, Kid") the guitar surprise song for the Eras Tour in Dublin, night one, playing her most U2-like song in homage to the city that gave us U2. This soaring, traveling, repetitious sound can suggest a spiritual yearning (as in many U2 songs), or an amorous one, or the powerful straight-ahead movement of a fast car, maybe even a new Maserati: Swift, Chapman, and guitarist Paul Sidoti use the effect for all three.[4]

If we see ourselves in this song, we may identify with its almost religious optimism about what new romance can bring. The instrumental lead that follows the chorus on "Red" begins with the same note eight times, like a car horn, or like the low-budget electronic instrument called a Stylophone. It, too, seems to promise a big mainstream rock hit, like something by U2, suffused with optimistic road-trip energy.

Then it breaks that promise. "Red" ends oddly: The Auto-Tuned vocal echoes ("ah-ah-ah") and the electric guitars stop before the banjo does, as if the song, like the ride, really did conclude on a "dead-end street." It's a musical signal that Swift plans to do something new.

Much of *Red* also follows a literal plot: the rise and fall and rise and definitive fall of Swift's romance with a single man. That man (to judge from clues within the songs) seems to be older than Taylor, has a sister, skipped Swift's twenty-first birthday party, and spends a lot of time in London and New York. Taylor-watchers identify him as the actor Jake Gyllenhaal, and the much documented story of their real-life romance makes up what literary critics call the extradiegetic context for the album—the context that exists in the real world, outside the work of art. The diegetic contexts, those created inside the work, include things like the road and the scarf we imagine when we hear "All Too Well": They show how speedy, scarlet, crimson, burgundy, fiery romance speeds up, slows down, takes a curve, or goes off a cliff. The journalist Courtney Conley made a list of "Taylor Swift's Lyrics on Dating Bad Drivers," finding some on every album, though it's *Red* where they stand out. As much as it's an album about colors (red, blue, gray) and numbers (like 22), it's also an album about riding in cars: about motion, and change, and travel, and acceleration. This story of love that's red asks us to think about wrong turns, U-turns, missed stop signs, and perilous choices, about how time speeds up or slows, like an automobile, according to that unsafe driver, the heart.[5]

Those rides led to new destinations, both geographical and musical. Swift began making *Red* with her usual producer, Nathan Chapman. According to Scott Borchetta, who was then still a friend, Chapman himself recommended that Swift pursue "a pop sound." Swift then asked Borchetta to call the Swedish hitmaker Max Martin, known for his work with the Backstreet Boys and Britney Spears. Martin said yes, and Swift's sonic world broke open. Their three collaborations became three of the first four singles from *Red*. "We Are Never Ever Getting Back Together" (known to Swifties as WANEGBT) hit the charts first, but "I Knew You Were Trouble" comes earlier on the album (track four), perhaps because it leads so well into her new sounds. Choppy guitar riffs introduce verses with words, textures, and attitudes that would have fit the pop-punk snottiness of (say) "Better Than Revenge." The electronic glides, sudden drops, and guitar-free moments of Martin's dance-pop and dubstep come later, as the chorus launches itself into international space. In the bridge, Taylor takes the story backward—you never loved me or her or anyone—while the instruments, Beatles-style, run backward, too. It's as if Swift wanted to extricate herself at once from her ex, from her guitar-based earlier hits, and from her habit of falling for the wrong guy.[6]

Red takes a reckless car ride away from Nashville, but it does not proceed in a straight line. Sometimes it doubles back, or makes right turns. One of her first outings with Martin and Shellback, "22" feels closer to Swift's other songs than the two other Martin/Shellback numbers do, less like a cocreation than like something Swift handed them almost complete. It's got Easter eggs, too, not only the reference to Swift's heartbreaking twenty-first birthday (discussed later in this chapter), but also the spoken aside "Who's Taylor Swift anyway? Ew," mixed low in the second verse: another sign that she could leave the old "Taylor" behind. On the 2012 recording of "22," the verse, with its booming kick drum, acquires a raw 1970s-style sound: We could almost be hearing Cheap Trick. "22 (Taylor's Version)," with its shinier, processed guitars, makes the song more fun, more like a night on the town, the sound of a girl who knows who she wants to be.

If Taylor means to show the whole course of a red love, she has to represent the fast drive, and the crash, and the aftermath of the crash. And Taylor seems aspirational, in those moments, because she survives that crash: She can walk away and tell her former man that they are never, ever, ever getting back together. "We Are Never, Ever Getting Back Together" supposedly began when someone asked Taylor, in the recording studio, whether she and an ex (likely Gyllenhaal) had reunited (other versions of the anecdote have Taylor overhearing a conversation about someone else's breakup). The stops and starts in the song mimic the false endings in the relationship. Percussion changes from a bassy kick drum to an obviously synthetic WHACK, like a whip crack and a snare drum together. The four even quarter notes of the pre-chorus bass line vault into two quarter notes, then two quarter rests: yet another part of the song that (like this relationship) stops and starts and stops and starts.[7]

Then it gets weird: It amounts to quite a ride, with dance-club-style drops and then (for the first time on a Taylor Swift record) a record-scratch sound. These effects remind us that songs tell stories in time. Minutes elapse while we hear and feel the song, and perhaps see our own feelings in it; days or weeks or years pass in the story that the song tells. Swift, Martin, and Shellback's post-production effects, their record scratches and overdubs and backward instrumentation, remind us that we're hearing about something that already took place; we're not live at the breakup as it happens. Instead Swift has written and packaged a story to show her fans.

That anti-live, confected, glossy sound, the sound of Martin and Shellback and the early 2010s charts, sets Swift's work apart from the lo-fi, live-sounding music that her ex prefers, from (as she put it) "some indie record that's much cooler than mine." Taylor called WANEGBT "the opposite of the kind of music that he was trying to make me feel inferior to." In launching international, high-gloss pop—with a producer known for launching boy bands—Taylor was also making a point about taste, and girlhood, and prestige, a point against what with-it critics call "rockism": the assumption that music made to sound live, with electric guitars, predominantly by white men, would always mean more, and last longer, than music reliant on electronics, and studios, and (by implication) girls.[8]

Really there's no one serious way to write songs, and every way of writing implies a way of feeling: Speedy, high-energy songs with guitars, about falling for a guitar-mad guy, swerve hard, in the course of the album, into bouncy electronic pop songs about getting out of his life, and getting him out of yours. And, in a delightful paradox that would continue to pop up in Swift's career, her new sense of autonomy required not absolute independence but new coauthors and collaborators. The journalist John Seabrook, an otherwise thoughtful observer of the music business, seems to have missed the point when, in 2015, he wrote a book on producer-led pop, focusing on Ke$ha, Katy Perry, the not-yet-disgraced Dr. Luke, and—more happily—Max Martin. Seabrook called Swift Martin's "ultimate collaborator: an artist strong enough to stand up for her vision, but canny enough to appreciate his genius," adding, "Still, for the first time Swift's hit songs sound like anyone could have sung them. The singer-songwriter . . . was gone." But Swift never wrote songs to highlight her voice. The point (as she told *The New Yorker*) was for her to deliver her own lyrics. When her personality and her goals changed, her genres, and her production styles, would too.[9]

If *Red* holds so many breakup songs, what makes the album—or those songs—aspirational? How could you elevate yourself or your mood by listening to them over and over again? For some of those songs the answers seem obvious: "We Are Never Ever Getting Back Together" has Taylor doing the breaking up, declaring her wants, and making her own decisions. Its stops, starts, and emphatic thumps mimic the good feeling of getting somebody who's bad for you out of your life. Other breakup songs on *Red*, equally invested (as Swift has said) in a love that feels red (dangerous, perilous, zero to one hundred), treat the end of that love in ways that glamorize, glorify, render dramatic, the version of Swift that lived it. Her tragic, sad love—in a slow waltz time—stays beautiful.

To see how they work, and how they invite us in, we need more of the real-life story behind much of *Red*. Taylor and Jake Gyllenhaal, whose sister Maggie is also a movie actor, started dating no later than the fall of 2010, when journalists spotted them at an apple orchard in upstate New York. If they hooked up earlier, no one who knows will say. Swift and Gyllenhaal seem to have stayed together for several months after the orchard sighting, despite his transatlantic acting commitments. Then he didn't show up at her twenty-first birthday party on December 13. She apparently felt crushed. Her dad noticed. She then decided that Gyllenhaal wasn't for her.

As with almost everything else in Swift's personal life, she wrote about it in ways that would keep some of the story private, some of it decodable with effort, some of it public and clear. Swift flat-out told a journalist in 2012 that "The Moment I Knew" remembers her real-life twenty-first birthday party, her "worst experience ever," when her boyfriend never showed up. Again, what's relatable also becomes aspirational: What if your own worst experience ever involved your movie actor boyfriend failing to fly in for your birthday party? "Come Back . . . Be Here," with its "taxicabs and busy streets" and its trips to New York City, connects its longings to the distances traveled, and to the neatly layered vocal melodies, oscillating between two notes in the verses ("said it in a simple way," "4 a.m. the second day"), then running anxiously four steps up and four steps down for the bridge.[10]

"All Too Well"—track five (a place of honor) on the 2012 release—now occupies a special, and slightly confusing, place in the story of *Red*, and in the story of Taylor's whole career, because the ten-minute version of the song—written along with the rest of *Red*, but recorded only for *Red (Taylor's Version)* in 2021—says so much more about how Swift sees her romance with Gyllenhaal, and so much about how she sees her life. The ten-minute "All Too Well" is also the only song *not* on an original album that showed up in the regular Eras Tour set list: From Swift's point of view, that's the version she wants us to hear.

It's also her masterpiece, in the first, now obsolescent sense of "masterpiece": the single work that demonstrates how a young creator (sculptor, painter, composer, etc.) has mastered the whole of her art. Even the first, shorter, less ambitious version of the song suggests, self-referentially, that we think of a "masterpiece" (though "you tore it all up"). It doesn't make sense to think about *Red* at length without considering Taylor's ten-minute version. Nor am I the only fan who thinks so: In his ranking of Taylor's songs, Rob Sheffield places "All Too Well" (in all its versions together) at number one. And when I asked the students in my course "Taylor Swift and Her World" to nominate the single song that summed up her gifts, they seemed to agree. Most of her radio hits, beginning at "Our Song," received multiple nominations. But "All Too Well (10 Minute Version)" proved the runaway winner, with more than thirty votes (the runners-up got fifteen and fourteen). For her verbal powers, there's no better place to dig in.[11]

The ten-minute version—which, again, she clearly wrote in 2012, along with the rest of *Red*—works as a masterpiece in part because it contradicts most people's intuitions about how long pop songs can be. Many rock, funk, and R&B tracks last this long or longer, but they're not constructed like pop songs; they've got multiple parts like classical music suites, lengthy instrumental passages and solos, or improvisational sections. Led Zeppelin's eight-minute "Stairway to Heaven" has all three. Some neo-folk songs are this long too, but they repeat themselves, with musically identical verses and choruses and nothing in between, as in Bob Dylan's almost nine-minute "Lily, Rosemary and the Jack of Hearts."

"All Too Well (10 Minute Version)" does none of those things. Instead it stretches out a whole pop structure—verse, pre-chorus, chorus, bridges, instrumental interludes—until it justifies its ten-minute length. It's not so much an alternative to the original as its fulfillment, the long and exciting drive from start to finish that the 2012 version should have become. The long version, like the short one, introduces the idyllic autumn start to a romance: opening a door, scenting the air, introducing the red scarf. Both versions set a seasonal scene, both outdoors and in; both versions give us a house that felt like home (but wasn't home), along with—of course—an automobile ride. Two minutes into the ten-minute version we hear the first words not in the original: "And you were tossing me the car keys, 'fuck the patriarchy,' / Keychain on the ground." Taylor gets aggressive, faster, about the competitive energy in this relationship, even when it was still going well. Would Big Machine Records have permitted Taylor to say "fuck the patriarchy" in 2012? None of her first three albums included swear words: This segment from the ten-minute version has no counterpart in the three-minute hit.

All these lyrics, new and old, intensify the sense that *Red* (2012) already gave—a romance defined by acceleration, movement, unpredictability, and an ultimately deceptive sense of breaking free, as well as by traveling in fast cars. The memory of those car rides dwells in her, has shaped her, still excites her, even though the romance has "long gone." And it's all red: the autumn leaves, the scarf, the ex-boyfriend's cheeks when he came in from the cold. The song amounts to a masterpiece not just in how images move within the restricted space of a pop song, but also in rhyme and off-rhyme and consonance. "Gaze," "upstate," "place," and "days" shift as if each word sought, but couldn't quite settle into, its perfect rhyme. "Asked for too much" chimes with "tore it all up"; "break me like a promise" matches "name of being honest" (notice the *t*'s in the first pair, the *b*'s in the second).

The ten-minute version piles on additional sonic effects. The "archy" in "patriarchy" half-rhymes with "car keys." The "ain" in "chain on the ground" sets up an echo with the "ays" and the "in" in "always skippin' town." These devices might come off as not much more than basic competence in hip-hop, where rapid off-rhymes across lines are what we expect. In Taylor's kind of pop song, though, where everything has to fit a melody, and verse-chorus patterns aren't optional, it's bravura technique. It carries her anger forward, too. That's one way the song stays relatable: It's as if we rode, with her, in the back of the car, as if we attended that ill-fated party.

Again, the original short version makes the emotional connection that Swift needs, but the extended version does it better, because it says more. It asks us to try on Taylor's points of view at several moments, times, and scenes—in the cold air, on the road, with a "MAPLE LATTE" (the hidden message in the 2012 lyric sheet), and then at his sister's house, "in the refrigerator light," then running the red light—through more full rhymes and vowel rhymes: gaze, upstate, place, days, same, grave, shame, frame. At the party, in the ten-minute version, Swift shifts to her dad's point of view. "It's supposed to be fun, turning twenty-one," he tells her, and that's the moment we know the romance has crashed for good. What's aspirational here? A parent who gives good advice. Would your dad say as much to you, if your twenty-first birthday crashed and burned?

That moment in the ten-minute version about Swift's twenty-first birthday also hooks back up to all the numbers elsewhere on the album—twenty-two (years), eight (months), "4 a.m. the second day"—to tell us that we've got a coming of age gone wrong. "You get older but your girlfriends stay the same age" echoes an infamous line from the 1993 film *Dazed and Confused*, where Matthew McConaughey's character talks about dating teenagers: "That's what I love about these high school girls, man. I get older. They stay the same age." "Men who serially date significantly younger women," writes the essayist Jill Filipovic, "are not looking for equal partners"; they're "looking for someone who will admire them, who they can mold, and who will make them feel sophisticated and important." That's the dynamic that Taylor rejects, both in "Dear John" and again in other postmortems on age-gap relationships, starting with "All Too Well" (even in its short version) and extending all the way to "The Manuscript," from *The Tortured Poets Department*.[12]

And that rejection means a lot. It's a model for listeners, another way some of us might see ourselves in the songs. And it's a shot across the bow (at the least) against all the elements in American culture that have encouraged grown men to chase teenage or nearly teenage girls. As of 2025, it's not hard to find (once you look) pop songs by big-name artists about problematic, or predatory, older men. Yet almost all those songs, and all the hits, postdate "Dear John," and postdate the first version of "All Too Well." And most of them come from artists younger than Swift: Phoebe Bridgers ("Motion Sickness"), Demi Lovato ("29"), Billie Eilish ("Your Power"). "All Too Well" got there first.

Of course, "All Too Well" finds models outside recent music (consider the modern dancer Isadora Duncan's famous red scarf) as well as within it. The environmental journalist Nina Nowak suggests Carly Simon's "You're So Vain" (1972), with its "apricot scarf" and its vanished naiveté. That hit topped the list of five favorite songs that Swift gave the editor Melanie Dunea in 2010. Swift later called "You're So Vain" "the best song that has ever been written." But the problem in "You're So Vain" is not an age gap; it's a Hollywood personality issue. The story in "All Too Well" is age, as well as crazy red feelings, and time.[13]

We might see ourselves again, and admire Swift's insights, once we understand how "All Too Well" handles time, both the time that it takes to hear or perform the song itself, and the months or years that the song describes. The three-minute version of "All Too Well" envisions time passing: that fall, that drive, that sense of home, back then, not like now. The long version also leaps from autumn to winter, from changing leaves to a December birthday party to snow in Brooklyn. On the one hand, this version of Taylor feels stuck in the past, forever (turning) twenty-one. On the other hand, she's lost the innocence of her past self, along with the scarf. It's the worst of both worlds, both ephemeral and enduring. Sarah Chapelle, the fashion and clothing expert, even sees "All Too Well" as the scarf's own story, "from its cozy coil around Taylor's neck," to the boyfriend's sister, "to its eventual residency in the ex-boyfriend's own drawer," where it reminds him of innocence lost.[14]

The ten-minute version plays with time—takes us along on its ride—not only in what it says, but in how Taylor sings. "The idea you had of me who was she" and "some actress asking me what happened" take up nine syllables each. Each phrase takes up one 4/4 measure. But "charmed my dad with self-effacing jokes," also nine syllables, takes two measures—twice as long—to sing. In other words, the song displays, in its sounds, the same effects that the lyrics invite us to hear: Sometimes time flies, and sometimes it slows us down, so much so that we feel paralyzed by it. Exploring both the speedy forward motions and the post-crash paralysis in a red love. "All Too Well (10 Minute Version)" sets up, and contrasts, six timelines at once: (1) the pace of the song as we hear it, speeding up and slowing down over ten minutes; (2) the moments painted so vividly in her words; (3) the story of the relationship month by month and day by day; (4) the lifetimes, birthday to birthday and age to age, of Taylor and boyfriend and his sister (who still has the scarf); (5) the time Taylor has spent looking back on her now-finished romance, in order to write the song; and (6) the cyclic changing of the seasons over the course of each year. Most of these timelines also show up in "The Moment I Knew," a song that becomes a kind of pendant to, or detail from, "All Too Well": the birthday party, the moments ticking by, the hours when he didn't show, and the call, sometime later, all laid out at one stately, heartbreaking pace.[15]

That attention to time passing makes both these songs not only romantic (that is, about romance and breakups) but also capital-R, lit-crit-style Romantic. Time in nature normally moves in cycles. The leaves change, the snow in Brooklyn comes down, every year. We, however, get older. We cannot make the leaves or the years or the moments stay. And that contrast links Swift's masterpiece to older masterpieces in other genres: for example, John Keats's ode "To Autumn," which ends with an orchestra's worth of words for sound:

> Where are the songs of Spring? Ay, where are they?
>   Think not of them, thou hast thy music too,—

> When barred clouds bloom the soft-dying day,
>   And touch the stubble-plains with rosy hue;
> Then in a wailful choir the small gnats mourn
>   Among the river sallows, borne aloft
>   Or sinking as the light wind lives or dies
> And full-grown lambs loud bleat from hilly bourn;
>   Hedge-crickets sing; and now with treble soft
>   The red-breast whistles from a garden-croft;
>   And gathering swallows twitter in the skies.

"Full-grown lambs" are sheep, but newly so: like humans who have just turned twenty-one. Helen Vendler says that "To Autumn" frames the passage of time against the limits of art, which cannot revive a life or a love: "The day dies, the season ends, the vistas end in horizons and skies, the fruits end in oozings." Or in maple lattes.[16]

I do not want to claim that Swift has read Vendler's *The Odes of John Keats*, though she has probably read the odes of John Keats. Nor do I mean that "All Too Well" is somehow the equal (whatever that would mean) of "To Autumn": poems for the page and songs with lyrics and music, in our time, are different entities, whose words do different things. I do mean, though, that the words and music of "All Too Well," even in its three-minute but especially in its extended version, echo Keats's accomplishment. Taylor's move from autumn to winter, past the red scarf and the red lights and the refrigerator glow, takes the willing listener on a musical and emotional journey not wholly unlike the reconciliation, the moving on, in Keats's last ode.

Taylor's Romantic side, in this sense, predates *Red*: It inhabits "The Best Day," and sneaks into "Never Grow Up." But *Red* brings it out. "State of Grace" and "Treacherous," "Begin Again" and "Starlight," are unquestionably romantic—about romantic love—as well as Romantic, songs about longing and time and change, connecting the present to the past, and wondering whether the future can measure up. The English professor Betsy Tontiplaphol gets even more specific about how and where and why Taylor gets Romantic. In her view, Swift matches the late Romantic poets and novelists known as the Biedermeier generation, who focused on nostalgia, disappointment, homeyness, and familiarity as balms for the passage of time. Those poets (Alfred, Lord Tennyson, for example) hoped their readers would feel recognized, supported, and seen. They tried, we might say now, to remain relatable. And they succeeded: Tennyson's long poem *In Memoriam* became a Victorian best seller and made him Poet Laureate of the United Kingdom. It's also the source of a very *Red*-relevant line: "'Tis better to have loved and lost / Than never to have loved at all."[17]

Romantic nostalgia extends all the way through *Red*, inviting us to join Swift in her melancholy, her backward looks, as well as in her jarring, jaunty, risky accelerations. That nostalgia extends to the few songs that describe non-Gyllenhaal romances. The introduction to "Starlight," another U2-ish song with guitar licks, evokes glamour as it moves through generations: The "best night, never would forget how we moved" comes first for a couple who met in 1945, then recurs for couples up to the present day, as Swift asks each one, "Don't you see the starlight? / Don't you dream impossible things?" The song derives from Swift's time dating Conor Kennedy. Its hidden message, "FOR ETHEL," namechecks Ethel Kennedy (1928–2024, Conor's grandmother). And it contains other Kennedy-clan Easter eggs: Robert F. Kennedy himself (1925–1968, Conor's grandfather, and the president's brother) liked to quote George Bernard Shaw's line "I dream things that never were and say 'Why not?'"[18]

That starlit, or floodlit, energy extends to other songs about romances now ended—each one red, exciting, unstable, in its own way. The romance in "Holy Ground" blessed the lovers so well that Swift still feels energized, sanctified, lifted up, even after the breakup. Again, lyrics emphasize motion and speed, "faster than a green light." That excitement comes through in the way the accompanying music moves: Kick drums and floor toms, right on the beat, propel the verses steadily, like a car motor, into the chorus, where the whole programmed (but live-sounding) rhythm section pauses, as if to lift Swift and her ex "above" that beat. One alternate version of "Holy Ground," unreleased but available online, makes it into a full-on rock song, electric guitars screaming, squealing, and wailing away. This drama, this red electricity, this rise and fall, become aspirational too: They seem preferable to the more pedestrian lives, the less exciting hookups and breakups (or, worse yet, loneliness), that most of us have known.

If *Red* is an album about time and change and autumn, it's also an album—and "Holy Ground," and "All Too Well," and "State of Grace," and "Red," are songs—about cars, and driving, and wrong turns, and going too fast. What pickup trucks were to *Taylor Swift*, and to commercial country generally in the years when Swift emerged, speeding passenger cars are to *Red*, and to the rock-and-roll traditions that she must (as it were) drive through on her multiyear journey from Nashville twang to Stockholm pop. Novels and poems about cars are as old as cars (look up Rudyard Kipling's 1904 volume *The Muse Among the Motors*), but cars for young people, cars as all-American, emerge in the 1920s. They show up throughout specifically American culture by the 1950s, the decade of interstate highways, of suburban expansion, of

Jack Kerouac's *On the Road*. Some critics pick Jackie Brenston's "Rocket 88" (1951), about a popular Oldsmobile, as the first rock song. Countless automotive rockers followed. Almost all of the cars were American, and most of them were driven by men—Jan and Dean's "Little Deuce Coupe," Jonathan Richman's "Roadrunner," Prince's "Little Red Corvette" (another red ride).[19]

For Swift, on *Red*, cars mean not only journeys and sexual excitement, but also attempts at autonomy: Who gets to drive? Who's in the passenger seat? The scholar Michael Bull writes that cars have become metaphors for "individualism and private property," for "the romantic imagery" of "individual freedom." He adds that cars with sound systems—radios, CD players, digital audio systems—let us further control our experience of space and time: "The privatized aural space of the car becomes a space whereby drivers reclaim time, away from the restrictions of the day." Like the red kinds of love, cars let us think we can go faster and farther, and experience the world more powerfully, than we could without these accelerating machines. That's why some of us love them. That's why, sometimes, they crash.[20]

And sometimes, we decide to get out and walk. The non-deluxe version of *Red* ends with "Begin Again," and with instrumentation that breaks slightly new ground. The bridge introduces the rich bleat of an accordion, a decidedly non-rock instrument, associated with sidewalks and cafés and Europe rather than the open road. Swift underlined its café connotations with a Paris-themed video, then with a TV performance seated on a stool, wearing a "French" striped shirt, accompanied only by an accordionist. The love that this song describes is not about speeding cars, taking dumb risks, or driving across America. It's not all-consuming. It happens in a café, not in a speeding Maserati. And it points to a boyfriend able to meet you where you are and happy to do so. Taylor and her new flame connect not through flaring, uncontrollable passion, but via shared interests—James Taylor records, for example—and day-lit joy in one another's company. They can afford to take it slow.

Nor do they care much about who else sees. Jake Gyllenhaal's apparent desire for privacy, his ambivalence (despite his movie career) about fame, was one of the things that torpedoed his romance with Swift. "If you care about privacy to the point where we need to dig a tunnel under the restaurant so we can leave?" she later complained, "I can't do that." The *Red*-era slogan T-shirts—brought out again for "22" on the Eras Tour—point to her growing fame too: "NOT A LOT GOING ON AT THE MOMENT" (meant ironically); "EW WHO'S TAYLOR SWIFT ANYWAY" (quoted from "22," another dig at indie snobs, who resented her fame). Some of us don't want extreme fame, or constant attention. Some of us run from those things if we get them: That's the idea behind the song "The Lucky One." The song may address Kim Wilde, the LA-based star who sang "Kids in America," then switched careers to become a gardener; Swift also samples Wilde's "Four Letter Words." The lyrics reflect on Swift's own choices too: Almost all her references to Los Angeles end up wary or negative, and Swift never tried to live there. Nor (after *Valentine's Day*) did she pursue larger roles in feature films.[21]

On the other hand, she never considered rejecting a pop career. Her ambition, her wish to be seen, to keep going, has always won out. Wilde, or whoever "The Lucky One" addresses, is not only *not* Swift; she's someone who Swift temperamentally could not become, because Swift (like it or not) requires companionship, reactions, other people's approval, an audience. Wilde isn't lucky because she got out: She's lucky because she *could* get out, because she doesn't need what Taylor needs. And the way the chorus to "The Lucky One" repeats its title—three lines in a row, expanding the word "one" on the third try until it takes in at least five notes—underlines Swift's disbelief. She could never become a gardener, stop the car, stop driving, or abandon her drive for attention and artistic success. Instead, she could set up and pull off the Eras Tour.

Taylor's ambitions helped her open doors for listeners who wanted to be more like her. Some of those listeners became younger singer-songwriters who emulated her path: They, too, began with Nashville country and moved on—Kacey Musgraves into softer folk sounds, less Grand Ole Opry than NPR; Maren Morris, erstwhile "Lunatic Country Music Person," into full-on dance pop; Kelsea Ballerini, into both. All these artists, early in their own careers, recorded songs ("Tim McGraw," "Dime Store Cowgirl," "My Church") about how they grew up on country music and would never leave it behind (and then left it behind). Their success caught Taylor's eye: She invited Morris to join her on one vault track from *Red*. The best of those tracks—discussed in this chapter's last section—return to the album's premises: red love, moving dangerously like a speeding car; Swift herself reflecting on how time moves on; and Swift as a public figure, changing and growing away from Nashville, showing her masterful, newly expanded range.

"Ronan"—the first "new" song on *Red (Taylor's Version)*, released as a benefit single in 2012—shows that range, though it can be hard to see through the tears. "Ronan" responds to Maya Thompson's *Rock Star Ronan* blog, which chronicled her son Ronan's diagnosis and treatment for the brain cancer neuroblastoma. Ronan died in 2011, just before he would have turned four. Swift, who had read the blog, invited Thompson to see the *Speak Now* tour in Glendale, near Phoenix, where Thompson lives. The following year, Swift completed the song, which lists Thompson as a coauthor, then called Thompson in person to tell her about it, obtaining permission before releasing the single. "She took my words and tweaked them in the most beautiful way," Thompson told *USA Today*. Swift has since performed the song three times: once at a 2012 Stand Up to Cancer benefit, and twice when Thompson attended her shows. You can search Thompson's blog for phrases that Swift chose to use: You'll find surprisingly few—not "plastic dinosaurs," not "army guy," not even "kitchen floor." Taylor did not adapt Thompson's words so much as she turned the story that Thompson told into a Taylor Swift song. She did, though, use Thompson's account of Ronan's last day: "I grabbed my baby boy and whispered in his ear that I loved him, but it was time to go, so he needed to come with me. I kept saying, 'Come with me, Ronan. Let's get out of here.'"[22]

As much as Swift makes the music fit the words, and makes the words reach out to us, most people will not find directly relatable—will not see our own lives in—this mother's experience of her small child's death. Many more people might recognize the experience of trying, and failing, to care for self-harming peers. One of the few songs Swift has never performed onstage, "Forever Winter," speaks to a friend (widely believed to be the late Jeff Lang) about his life-threatening mental health problems: self-isolation, self-loathing, acute depressive episodes, and apparent self-harm. The arrangement builds to an elaborate mini-orchestra, with horns and pedal steel, as if to offset the stark isolation the friend has made for himself. That same arrangement heightens the contrast in the final chorus, where almost every instrument except the voice drops out. It's one of Swift's least aspirational compositions: Who would want to feel this way? Instead, it bets all it has on its solidarity not with the depressed person, but with his would-be carers, allies, and friends. Who will take care of these caregivers? runs the Latin proverb. *Quis custodiet ipsos custodes?* We may not, but Taylor will.[23]

Who will take care of Taylor? Who can understand her own struggles, not just with red love, with relentless sexual passion, with unsafe driving, but with the up-and-down road that might be her whole career? Who will look after her—or after any of us—once our struggles no longer seem exciting, shiny, brand new? The vault track "Nothing New," a duet with Phoebe Bridgers, suits Bridgers's melancholy, intimate vocals so well that it sounds as if Swift wrote it for her. In fact, Swift wrote it—in the same years she wrote *Red*—with an earlier template in mind. She composed the song on an airplane over Australia, intending a musical homage to Joni Mitchell, on an Appalachian dulcimer that (if we trust the *Lover* diaries) Swift picked up in homage to *Blue*.[24]

"Nothing New" asks what will come next in the speedy, audacious ride of Swift's own career, and whether she's already past her peak, likely to get supplanted by an even younger singer with "the kind of radiance you only have at seventeen." The poet, cultural critic, and actor Amber Tamblyn, who became a well-known TV actor by age twelve, wrote that during her early years in Hollywood, "My responsibility not just to my craft of performing but to the performance of youthfulness was reinforced constantly." Such messages, Tamblyn went on, place women like her in a "tenure of self-torment that teaches us that nothing we say, do, weigh or want is ever right." If you're twenty-two, you can't literally be seventeen, and if you're in an entertainment industry—in Hollywood, Nashville, Manhattan, or London—you may cry yourself to sleep about it. Swift's song title, placed at the end of the chorus, ends on *do*, the home (or tonic) note ("thing new"). The dejection that Swift anticipates, growing into a less remarkable, less remarked adulthood, feels (at least to her) musically inevitable, like the passage of time, or like coming home.[25]

Maybe youthful stardom amounts to a fast, unreliable car ride, just like red love. Maybe young stars should prepare to hit a wall too. Swift might have lost a fight with her label had she, in 2012, insisted on releasing a song about drinking to excess, or about how old she had begun to feel. Like "22," "Nothing New" addresses adulthood—but very much unlike "22," "Nothing New" explores disillusion and fear, as Swift wonders whether she's already lost her beginner's luck. And—as Swift admits in her duet—after midnight, when she's had too many glasses of wine (or liquor), that's what she thinks about. Not the loss of one or another boy, but the extinction of her talent, or the collapse of her career: the moment when, having been famous but lost her shine, she can no longer go anywhere fast.

And that's how "Nothing New" fits into the other argument I have been pursuing about Swift's view of her own career: Anyone who's had early success—even winning a high school basketball game or a TV quiz show, or getting elected prom queen—might find it relatable too. If you find yourself caught up in a love that feels red, or a career that feels like a rocket taking off, you might enjoy it. You might, or might not, try to drive that speeding car; you might want to take your companion—or your duet partner, if he's Ed Sheeran in the vault track "Run"—and run, as fast as your motor will let you run. But you should also know that your love, and your career, can crash. You might try not to stake your whole being, your entire life story, or even your whole birthday party, on one accelerating romance, or on your sudden, Nashville-based fame. You might want to learn to see yourself, and to find strength, elsewhere, or imagine another kind and color of love. That's "Begin Again." It's the advice underneath "Nothing New." It's the advice you might take after all the excitement of "State of Grace" and "Red" and "All Too Well" and "Treacherous." It's advice Swift tries to give herself after romances crash, and advice she can barely take in when contemplating not her love life, but her life as an artist. And it's the advice—don't bet everything on one boyfriend; enjoy the moment; learn to drive your own car; don't rely on just one life goal—that Taylor tries out, electronically, synthetically, excitingly, on the international pop album that comes next.

6

1989

FOR ANY SERIOUS ARTIST, ANYBODY WHO organizes their life around making art—whether it's poems or pop music or sculpture—changing the kind of art you make may feel like becoming a different person. Taylor Swift's fifth album represents that kind of change. The passionate journeys of *Red* led her all over the place, but they kept her connected to teenage experience, to first love, to innocence and the loss of it, to guitars either electric or acoustic or both. *Red* also showed her as geographically restless: going out, living as an adult (turning twenty-two), leaving the South, the land of Nashville country (as she had promised she would do in "Mean"), but unlikely to tell us where she's going.[1]

Swift's fifth album says where. It shows Taylor remaking herself as thoroughly as she can, announcing that she—not her family, not any single genre, not Nashville, not teenage life—can take charge of her sounds. It shows how challenging, anxious-making, and uncertain attempts to remake yourself can be. It shows—or tries to show—how to enjoy a quarter-life crisis, a romantic, embodied, erotic life that need not put her on one clear path: how to live in the moment and not depend on a guy. It asks us to empathize not with teenage concerns, but with the life of a glittery urbane celebrity. And it shows how this reinvented, New York City–based, pop-oriented, pleasure-loving, fantastically privileged version of Taylor remains not only someone her listeners might want to be, but someone in whom we might still see ourselves.

The album also holds together new and semi-new teams of collaborators, consistent in their glossy sonic direction. It marks the return of Max Martin and Shellback, world-famous then and now for boy bands and chart pop (Martin chose not to return for Taylor's Version). The OneRepublic bandleader and TV-song-show pop professional Ryan Tedder worked with Swift for the first time, as did the English electro-pop maker Imogen Heap. Taylor also brought in Jack Antonoff for the first time on an album, though Swift and Antonoff had already worked together on "Sweeter Than Fiction," written for the soundtrack to *One Chance*, a 2013 biopic about the British opera singer Paul Potts. Most of the music in *One Chance* comes from opera: "Sweeter Than Fiction" has nothing to do with bel canto. Instead, its flat, layered textures presaged the turn to synths on *1989*—if not for Swift's distinctive voice, "Sweeter Than Fiction" could pass for a 1980s hit by Orchestral Manoeuvres in the Dark.

Electronics-led production fit the new Swift, the newly emancipated, non-guy-dependent, cosmopolitan figure she hoped to be. The pop musician and gallery artist Laurie Anderson has said that she likes the feeling of transformation that heavily processed vocals give, since they keep her "a little bit removed," adding, "I didn't have to always be myself, which can be pretty tiring." Taylor's processed vocals never go as far as Anderson's charades, but neither do they sound like the Bluebird Cafe: The vocals sound sometimes distant, tinny, multitracked (so that Swift became her own backup singer), and sometimes Auto-Tuned, as in the chorus to "Welcome to New York," or the start of "Bad Blood." If earlier hits, like "Love Story," imagined that teen romance might—naturally—work out, the hits from *1989*, self-consciously artificial from their slick surfaces to their digital cores, promised that you too could move to the city, reinvent yourself, and go out on the town with your new best friends.[2]

Swift has said that electronic pop songs simply came to her, in place of the country she had been writing, just as the album's title came to her on the night after *Red* failed to win a Grammy. "I came home from the Grammys and . . . invited my friends over and decided to play them what I thought were the strongest songs and we got in this discussion about how without even realizing it I had started to incorporate Eighties synth-pop elements," Swift has said. "I knew I was switching genres, starting over." Having already made a guitar-based masterpiece, Swift turned, sonically, to the years of her own childhood, and to the years before that, so that she could find her own future.[3]

Her new sound required a new scene in a new place: No wonder the album opens with "Welcome to New York." Swift's New York City includes, even flaunts, clichés. It's what you see if you move there with confidence, glamour, and money, the New York that for centuries has welcomed the rest of America as a place for reinvention, for ramping things up, for amplifying ambitions, escaping earlier selves. Other country artists—such as Steve Earle on 2007's *Washington Square Serenade*—had also moved to Manhattan from Nashville and loved it, but they had kept making country, or Americana. Not Swift. "Everybody here was someone else before," Swift chants in a monotone over a throbbing dance beat, textures musically unthinkable on any earlier album (even *Red*). Her line celebrating same-sex affection ("boys and boys and girls and girls") is almost a throwaway, one among many examples in a list of ways that New York welcomes you—though the gay-positive history of club music, from Sylvester to Erasure, would not have been lost on Swift, nor on Ryan Tedder, who cowrote the song, and whose own early life (evangelical Christian schooling; Oral Roberts University) would not have welcomed queer love.

Taylor told fans just what she was trying to do, as if she meant to set an example. "I was born in 1989, reinvented for the first time in 2014," she said on Instagram in 2023 to mark the release of *1989 (Taylor's Version)*. Back in 2014 she told *Billboard* that the album showed her "starting over." The Nashville establishment seemed to agree. Soon after "Shake It Off" dropped, the Country Music Association (that is, its social media manager, maybe an intern) tweeted "Good luck on your new venture @taylorswift13! We've LOVED watching you grow!" The CMA soon tweeted a palinode: "We will never, ever, ever say goodbye to @taylorswift13."[4]

About half the songs on *1989* address Swift's romance with Harry Styles, at the time the most famous member of the world's most famous boy band, One Direction. The aspirational part here should go without saying: How many people, in the mid-2010s, imagined dating Harry Styles? But how could this new Taylor stay relatable? The author of "All Too Well" could speak to the rush of a first serious romance, to the feeling of post-teenage uncertainty, to the perils of dating older guys: familiar terrain for many. But the coauthor and lead performer on "Shake It Off" owned a fancy pad in New York and a mansion in Los Angeles, dated the planet's most crushable young man, and made music that put its glossy, confident artificial surfaces first. What could she still hold in common, emotionally and practically, with most of her fans?

The album itself proposed an answer: Like many of us, she can't and won't stop working. Like many of us, she seeks, and needs, attention, and she'll exhaust herself in order to get it. Like many of us, she needs a stable romance much less than she needs an innocent vacation, a night with her besties out on the town. And if you want, or crave, or need—as Swift did, and does, and says she does—attention, validation, and praise, that craving can feel similar whether you're meeting five fans or fifty thousand. Swift has said over and over how much she loves meeting her fans, and how much she likes being on tour: the hand hearts, the thrown hats, the friendship bracelets. She seems to be most herself—and she says so—when she's her professional self, an artist making her art. As early as the *Speak Now* tour Swift told the Nashville *Tennessean*, "I don't know what I'm going to do when I'm not on this tour anymore. . . . I love the schedule. I love the crowds. I love the feeling you get when you walk off stage and it was a good show." Speaking to the United Kingdom's *New Musical Express* (*NME*), during the *1989* tour, she went further: "I don't want this tour to end. Ever." And while accepting a *Billboard* music award before *1989* came out, Taylor thanked her fans by saying, "You are the longest and best relationship I've had." It sounds like a joke, but it wasn't a joke at all.[5]

Her effortful demonstrations of joy—on the album and during the tour ("There's nothing I would change about my life!" she told *NME*)—seemed serious too, as well as sincere. At the same time, she kept some things private. It's one of the rougher ironies from this era: Swift was rehearsing, recording, and promoting songs about how well her new life worked, and about how she'd taken control of that life, at the same time as she struggled with disordered eating. The Taylor of the documentary *Miss Americana* (2020) shocked some fans when she described her disordered eating during the *1989* tour, with its tight-fitting costumes, challenging choreography, and constant scrutiny of her every move. Pictures she saw as unflattering, Swift said, "would trigger me to just starve a little bit. . . . I thought that I was just supposed to feel like I was going to pass out at the end of a show, or in the middle of it. I thought that was just how it was. . . . I did exercise a lot. But I wasn't eating." Swift described some combination of anorexia, orthorexia (an unhealthy fixation on healthy food), and compulsive exercise: all problems that classically afflict perfectionists, workaholics, good girls who crave praise and fear disapproval.[6]

On the one hand, the Taylor of *1989* keeps on announcing how much she has changed: She lives in New York, she's a pop star, she's dated (and now she's done with) Harry Styles. On the other hand, she's clearly the same person as the girl who sang "Our Song," the same writer who understood the perfectionism she chronicled in "Tied Together with a Smile": a girl who yearns for attention, and for connections to fans, and for control over her destiny. "When I was a little kid," she told Scott Raab of *Esquire*, "my friends were watching Disney Channel, but I was watching *Behind the Music*," figuring out how celebrities "lost their level of self-awareness. . . . And I never wanted to make that mistake." She never wanted to lose control.[7]

The Swift of "Shake It Off"—and, perhaps, the Swift we hear on other parts of *1989*—may be showing us how she'll never lose control. She's also advising us not to lose ourselves: She's proud and confident enough to shrug off other people's disapproval, in a way that she had never quite done before. Swift says she told Martin and Shellback that she wanted "drums that make even the person who's having a terrible night at the wedding" exclaim "Oh, it's my song!" Together they crafted music for any number of weddings, a song about pride in yourself that nearly begs you to dance along. "Shake It Off" boasts—all new to Swift's work—a horn section, a neo-soul beat, and a somewhat perfunctory rap break, performed by Swift herself. It is, among other things, a song about how previous versions of Swift—versions influenced almost entirely by white-coded genres, including Nashville country, 1970s singer-songwriters, anthemic guitar rock—did not find, in those genres, the resources she wanted or needed to grow, nor to show grown-up joy. Starting with "Shake It Off," she found those resources in the joyful, contentious sounds of R&B, disco, 1970s soul, and hip-hop. And she tried to learn, from their models of community, defiance, and resilience, how to accept seeming failure—how to reject perfectionism. She would have far more to say about her whiteness, and her relationship to Black music, with *Reputation* (and so will I).[8]

"Shake It Off" begins that conversation while inviting us to focus on other things—on her capacity for joy, on her willingness to try new things, even on how well she can fall on her face (not least by rapping, badly). That's what happens in the video, where we see Taylor at barre, trying, and mostly failing, to learn ballet, a white-coded form. We then see Taylor surrounded by Black dancers and actors, who perform hip-hop moves that Taylor can't match. As she put it, in the video "there's ballet dancers, breakdancers, modern dance, twerkers—and me, trying to keep up with them, sucking." The biographer Caroline Sullivan sees a clear moral: "It's more important to dance with your whole heart, however clumsily, than to be the best." It is, if you like, a song with a particular message for her white listeners (most—but not all—of Swift's audience): Be prepared to recognize where you need help, where you'll never excel, where mere adequacy, or cross-cultural competence, might be your only goal.[9]

This album sounds like a self-remaking—in genre, in attitude, in musical texture—but it's also a series of dares. Can Taylor Swift do something she's never done before? Can she learn in a space where she'll never be a wunderkind, or a first-of-her-kind, or an ingenue? "Blank Space" can feel like a series of dares as well, laid out not only for Swift but for her future lovers, and for her listeners as well: Can we, do we, imagine she's really that confident, that callous, that much, so much? It's got few or no guitars until the chorus hits, and the drum hits sound nothing like live drums. It exists on the edge of Eurodisco playlists. Bring your passport! And it invites you to spend some time in Taylor's new international world—a world that's maybe scary, like adulthood, as well as alluring, and expensive, and silly. If it's aspirational, too, the aspiration is to let yourself be ridiculous, let yourself act out.

"Blank Space" imagines Taylor stringing man after man along, taking them too far, seizing the moment, and then throwing each man aside. The song's unusual (it's tempting to say experimental) construction connotes excess too: The chorus lasts twice as long as it normally "should," thirty-two measures instead of sixteen, with couplet rhymes that double back on themselves: *flame, pain, insane, game; far, scar, insane, name*. A rearranged version of "Blank Space" performed on the *1989* tour begins with a couplet taken from the middle of the recorded version: "Boys only want love if it's torture / Don't say I didn't warn you." The couplet then becomes a chant, while the audience starts in on call and response (for example, "Sydney! Syd-NEE!"). Taylor isn't warning herself, or warning boys: She's giving advice—and a warning—to her friends in the crowd, all 76,000 of them. The "Sydney!" chant then became an Australian meme, replicated on TikTok and replayed at the Eras Tour, an homage to the goofy excess already pulsing inside the song.[10]

Swift has said that she meant "Blank Space" as a kind of parody: What if she really were, or pretended to be, the serial dater, the "man hater," the "psychopath," that the tabloids thought they saw? "Half the people got the joke," she told *People* magazine. The song won attention not just because it's one of the catchiest pop songs ever composed but because it's unusual thematically and emotionally. A woman invites a guy to become the next contestant on her reality show. Try to date her, and *you* could go down in flames. But Taylor herself? She'll be fine. She'll even have fun. Again, it's aspirational as well as over-the-top: What if you, too, could try on these kinds of poses? But it's also, covertly, relatable, for anyone who's ever been called a man-hater, or a serial dater, or been accused (perhaps by a toxic boyfriend) of choosing career, friends, and hobbies over true love.[11]

The self-reinventing, self-remaking, self-cleaning Swift of *1989* also remakes her own voice, not just with electronic processing but with rhythmic choices anathema to folk, country, or straight-up rock. Again, she's giving her fans an example: Maybe you can change how you come across, too. The musicologist Matt BaileyShea has noticed these moments on *1989*. For example, in "Wildest Dreams," Swift sings, "Say you'll see me *a*-gain," where spoken English would require "a-*gain*." "The eccentricity of the accent," BaileyShea explains, makes these vocals sound "*different* from normal speech" (emphasis Bailey-Shea's). In "Bad Blood," the normally unstressed "it's" hits extra hard: "*It's* so *sad* to *think* about the *good* times." Such changes can stretch one word to the length of three, or jam a phrase into one note: Taylor—and not the language she inherits—has taken charge of how she sounds.[12]

This virtuosic play with spoken against sung accents also generated the twenty-first century's most famous misheard lyric, or mondegreen, in "Blank Space": "All the lonely Starbucks lovers." No less an authority than Andrea Swift claims she once thought "Starbucks lovers" was the real lyric (the term "mondegreen" derives from a misheard English folk song: "Lady Mondegreen" for "laid them on the green"). Why the common mistake? Swift sings "*long* list *of* ex-*lov*-ers," though spoken English requires a "*list* of ex-*lov*-ers." BaileyShea explains that listeners "assume, unconsciously, that 'of' must not be the correct word," because it's accented, "so they link it with the end of the word 'list' to create the syllable 'stuv,' and then link *that* with 'ex-lovers' to create 'stuv-ex lovers,' and since they know that 'stuv-ex' is not an English word they imagine a likely replacement." Starbucks lovers. Lonely ones, too, since the "st" in "list" gets reassigned to "Starbucks," leaving "*long* li," which we recode as "lonely."[13]

The Taylor of *1989* may love Starbucks, but she no longer seems lonely. She's putting her life together herself, synthesizing it, if you like, and so she's using a lot of synthesizers. She's going out dancing, so she's making dance music. She's living for the moment, so she's making pop songs that stay in the moment, rather than trying to live inside a romance plot, or moving up a relationship escalator. The journalist Amy Gahran introduced the term "relationship escalator" in 2012 for the set of expectations most of us have acquired as to how romantic relationships "should" progress: first dating and getting to know you, then snuggles, then more dates, then sex (if sex has not come earlier), then an exclusive commitment. Shared living quarters. A ring on it. Probably kids. An escalator goes up whether you pay attention to it or not, and whether you choose it or not. And once you get on, it's hard to get off.[14]

Much of what's aspirational, what's an example, in *1989* implies alternatives to the relationship escalator. "Just because someone is cute and wants to date you," Swift told *Cosmopolitan* magazine at the time, "that's not a reason to sacrifice your independence." Nor do you have to eschew sex and romance. You can date, or cuddle, or have sex, without committing yourself to a narrative. Rather than inhabit somebody else's story, you can live in the moment, in style. And, if you're Swift, you can do it while flirting with, or dating, Harry Styles, who has—like the man in the song "Style"—green eyes, and James Dean–level good looks, and slicked-back hair, and a preference for tight plain white T-shirts.

The genius of "Style"—what makes it an aspiration, even a piece of advice, and not just a boast—comes from the way it implies that its romance has no particular destination: not up an escalator, not on a red road in a speeding car, not toward any commitment more serious than hanging out and looking good. This couple will never go out of style, because they're performing as timeless, basic style icons. They're having fun, they're confident, and they don't need to take their relationship anywhere it hasn't already gone. In the same way, Niklas Ljungfelt's guitar part (composed before the lyrics) sounds full of vigor, but goes nowhere: The six-stringed instruments play licks and do tricks while the throbbing bass and keyboards propel the song. It's not a rock move, nor a country one. Instead it's classic disco, as in, say, Nile Rodgers and Chic. The song never swerves from its midtempo beat, the kind you nod along to without trying, and—melodically, harmonically—it barely changes. Even the vocal melody hammers repeated notes: "James Dean daydream look," "out of style," "go crashing down," "the lights are off." There's no progression, no story—there need not be.[15]

What's the opposite of "style"? Substance. Or story, or things that happen one after another, or plots that lead somewhere. "If you don't have a story you can still have a style," writes the literary scholar Jeff Dolven. "It may not always be yours to choose [where] you go," but "you can go and you can be there in your style." Style, and stylishness, might prove especially appealing if you don't want to pick a direction, or make a commitment, or change. Stan Lee of Marvel Comics fame supposedly said that he wanted to hook readers in via "the illusion of change": Heroes like Spider-Man would seem to develop from issue to issue and yet stay the same. In the same way, "Style" does not have to take us anywhere in particular, to tell any story or go anywhere, because Taylor and her partner feel excited, and delighted, and fulfilled in the moment: They want to stay the same. Again, she's writing against the relationship escalator, the idea that every romance must become a love story with the same shape as "Love Story," even while she's still writing about romance.[16]

She's also writing about glamour and privilege. *Red* still let fans imagine that the outward circumstances of Swift's life—the car rides, the older boys, the twenty-first birthday parties—might resemble our own. With *1989*, in songs like "Style" and "Welcome to New York," Swift can no longer invoke that kind of resemblance. Instead she shifts to what the literary critic Arielle Zibrak nicknames "RWPFs": Rich White People Fictions, like *Sex in the City* or *Gossip Girl*. The Swift of *1989* not only led, but sang about, the New York City lifestyles we see in RWPFs on TV. Consuming an RWPF, we know that we cannot—but also like to imagine we could—live that life. And as Zibrak explains, "Escapism is not all the RWPFs offer." Their aspirational fantasies hint at "why most of us have not had access to the amount and kind of love we crave. The reason this fantasy is so compelling is because it's partly true. Though not a guarantee of all the love and happiness I desire, my life would be easier if I were richer and whiter. . . . Acknowledging that [fact] in a backhanded way lets me off the hook." Swift—unlike, say, Carrie Bradshaw from *Sex and the City*—seems to know it.[17]

1989

As with so much of this album, the aspirational aspects, the ways we might want to live out this song, seem obvious. But what makes (for example) "Style" relatable (for fans who find it relatable)? If anything, it's an undertone of anxiety: Can we really go on this way? That kind of fear takes over on the magnificent and jittery "Out of the Woods," which also apparently represents Swift's first foray into track-and-hook composition, writing lyrics and melodies to a preexisting backing track by coauthor Jack Antonoff. The repeated title, rushed and almost spit out, implies repeated answers: No, we're not out of the woods, and we will not be out of the woods until I stop feeling compelled to ask myself, or ask you, again and again, whether we might be out of the woods. It's also a phrase you might use about a patient in a hospital, one who had twenty stitches: Are they in mortal danger? Or are they out of the woods? The tom-toms, mechanical drum-machine hits, and drones almost push Taylor's vocals out of the mix. No wonder she had to move the furniture to dance; no wonder the trees, closing in, resembled monsters—too many of them approached her, too fast.

They approached her beau, too. Styles in the early 2010s wore a necklace with a paper airplane charm. Swift at one point wore that necklace too: thus the paper airplanes in the song—"Your necklace hanging from my neck"—and the spectacularly grotesque mondegreen it spawned, "Your neck was hanging from my neck." Again, part of Taylor's genius involves turning the accoutrements of fame, the troubles that come with having paparazzi follow you everywhere, into relatable, empathetic dilemmas. We don't face internet hate campaigns; Taylor and Harry have. We don't need to take private jets for safety reasons; Taylor Swift does (see Chapter 13). We can, however, feel—as the Taylor and Harry of *1989* feel—overwhelmed, unjustly treated, harried and hassled, betrayed.[18]

With so many songs that ask us to live in the moment, to dance right now, to shake it off, *1989* resists the same escalator that a song like "Love Story" embraced. Not that Swift exactly abandoned "Love Story." The *1989* tour reimagined that *Fearless* gem with an electronic keyboard, drum-machine handclaps, and sound-effect bell trees. There's a guitar for a moment, but only a moment: She has reinvented herself, and she has reinvented her iconic song, the only pre-*Red* element in the *1989* tour's set list. "We Are Never Ever Getting Back Together" also got a total renovation on that tour: hard rock, almost metal, with squealing and growling guitars all the way through. The splendid aggression must have shocked concertgoers—there's nothing else in that set remotely like it. These remakes show that Taylor, along with her band, can sound new: that she can remake herself radically, that her style (as Dolven would put it) is an embodied choice.[19]

Singers, and female singers in particular, often have to emphasize their agency, their sense of conscious choice. Willa Cather's great 1915 novel about a classical singer, *The Song of the Lark*, follows the fictional Thea Kronborg from her childhood in the Great Plains hamlet of Moonstone, Colorado, to success in Chicago, Europe, and New York. On the way there she has to find the right teachers, and to avoid romantic entanglements that would hold her back (when she does marry, it's an anticlimax, tacked on at the end). Thea also has to learn how she can reinvent, remake, refashion, her embodied self. Even her kindest teacher, Mr. Harsanyi, calls her talent a force of nature: "All the intelligence and talent in the world can't make a singer," he remarks. "The voice is a wild thing. It can't be bred in captivity."[20]

He's not wrong. And yet Thea has to leave the Midwest, and leave

1989

Harsanyi, in order to become who she needs to be. She needs to claim her own adult self, as she does on a trip to Arizona, before she returns to civilization to emerge as an artist and an adult: "to find yourself, to emerge *as* yourself," as Cather puts it (emphasis in original). Thea tells one devoted suitor "that if one became an artist one had to be born again, and that one owed nothing to anybody." Cather—who had strong tastes in opera singers, and mixed feelings about popularity—might have spurned Taylor's hits. And yet Cather's Thea might have understood the reinvention, the break from the past, the sense of control over the remade self and the reborn voice, that these new concert versions of Taylor's old hits, along with "Style" and "Blank Space," represent.[21]

The launch of *1989* saw Taylor telling journalists, first, that she loved her new life in New York, and second, that she had taken a break from dating. "What does seem possible and easy and comfortable is having this entire league of incredible girlfriends," she said. "I can trust them." If dating feels bad, and touring feels good—if romance feels unpredictable and dangerous and sad, and friendship feels powerful and available—why date? It's the logical conclusion to the troubles that Taylor described on *Speak Now*, and on *Red*, and on parts of *1989*, where the most hopeful, happiest songs describe, instead, a carefree single life ("Shake It Off") or a healthy breakup ("Clean"). "I just stopped dating people," Swift told Scott Raab, "because it meant a lot to me to set the record straight—that I do not need some guy around in order to get inspiration, in order to make a great record, in order to live my life, in order to feel okay about myself. And I wanted to show my fans the same thing."[22]

It's a claim that the throbbing, cleansing, steady one-two-three-four bass of "Clean" supports, a life ("finally," as the song says) worth waiting to lead. And it's a life—according to Swift's own interviews—in which she does not even try to separate decisions about her heart and her story from her sense of how fans tell that story. She wants to be the person that she wants her fans to see, and that's more important—for the creator of *1989*—than what any boyfriend could possibly think. "Clean" means freedom, but also simplicity: no baggage, no complications, no escalators that you can't get off. It offers a chord progression simple even for *1989*, a loop including just four common chords (I, IV, V, and vi), with repetitive accidentals (notes not in the home key) in the vocal melody, and a pulse of reliable eighth notes in the bass. Again, it's an aspirational song because it's a model for post-breakup self-reinvention: It shows not how you *will* feel, once you extricate yourself from the wrong guy, but how you *could* feel. If you trust your friends. If you're willing to wait.[23]

More: *1989* registers Taylor Swift's self-remaking, her claim to adulthood, in musical, not just in narrative, terms, because it reaches back before the year of her birth for its sounds. Glenn McDonald, the former Spotify data guru, writes that Swift's generation could reach back to decades past and still fashion pop hits: "Plenty of people making music in ProTools in the 2020s," he quips, want "to make it sound like music from the 1980s. Whereas in 1982, when I was 15, a 37-year-old song would have been from 1945." Swift's retro-pop album about moving forward into adulthood, avoiding familiar, conclusive stories, also amounts to a new mode for looking back.[24]

Swift does not only quote 1980s style and praise "style" over substance in general. She also names a stylish music and fashion subculture from the 1980s, the British New Romantics, who favored synthesizers, drum machines, fancy dress, elaborate makeup, and androgyny. The song "New Romantics" boasts (as "Long Live" had) about friendship and solidarity. But it also boasts (as "Long Live" had not) about an ecstatic, ephemeral artificiality: Swift and her friends and her fans feel "so young we're on the road to ruin." The video for "New Romantics" displays the stadium tour for *1989*, an enticing montage of crowds, aerial views, and lights. The song itself, though, imagines not joining a crowd, but resisting attack. "I could build a castle / Out of all the bricks they throw at me," Swift exults. She's learned to love clubs and streetlights and late-night crowds, becoming artificial as a joy and as a defense. If you accept Swift's invitation, joining her New Romantics, you get not a happily ever after, but an electronic liberation: from escalators, from old standards, from sexual shame.

Other tracks on *1989* may seem to work against this view of the album as aspiring to, speaking to, even recommending a life in the moment, off the escalator. Does "All You Had to Do Was Stay" torch the idea that *1989* opposes relationship escalators? Doesn't that song suggest that Swift wants to get on one of those escalators? Not really: The Swift of that up-and-down song, with its controversially chirpy backing vocals, wishes her guy had given her not a ring or a house, but a sense that she could trust him. What about "This Love"? The only song on *1989* (including the vault tracks) with no coauthor, it's one of the last songs Swift recorded with Nathan Chapman in Nashville, and it became the second single. Perhaps the ballad was a bone thrown to the label, a way to keep one foot in non-club, non–New York–based pop?

To say so would be to underrate "This Love," which poses a technical challenge to Swift as a singer: another way that she foregrounds her own ambition, her wish to do well, to pass tests, to show us how hard she tries. Anyone with performance experience will tell you that an unusually repetitive set of words gets unusually hard to sing, especially when there are syncopations involved. So here: "This love is good, this love is bad, this love is alive"; "You were just gone, and gone, and gone, and gone"; "I could go on and on and on and on." In the coda the title repeats twelve times. Compare Cather's Thea Kronborg again, this time as a child seen by her teacher: "She had a kind of seriousness that he had not met with in a pupil before. She hated difficult things, and yet she could never pass one by. They seemed to challenge her; she had no peace until she mastered them." "This Love," as a piece of pop music, sounds like something Swift wrote to show her mastery.[25]

The song also follows a challenge to a romance: In it, two partners split up and get back together and take other people to bed and run the experiment to see whether they belong, and when the results come in, they do. It's a cleaner, and more exciting, and overall better, way to test a relationship than the one in the vault track "Say Don't Go," Swift's only collaboration with the famous songwriter and tearjerker Diane Warren: No wonder Swift held that one back in 2014. "Say Don't Go" gives us a Swift held hostage to whatever a partner has chosen to say. It also presents a set of nested speakers, like talking Russian dolls: Swift says to her partner that *she* would stay forever if *he* would say, to her, "Don't go": She depends on his words. No thanks.

Among all the synthesizer-driven songs that made it onto *1989*, all the songs that look back to the chart pop of the 1980s, "You Are in Love" stands out for its optimism. It's also the slowest track on the album: Its soft rock texture and tempo could almost fit a 1980s act like Air Supply, though the lyrics supply the quirks that the backing tracks lack. In it Taylor has set herself the technical challenge of writing every line in units of exactly four syllables, except for the doublets (eight syllables) in the chorus: "You can hear it in the silence / You can feel it on the way home / You can see it with the lights out / You are in love." She's found some kind of balance; she's hit her mark, and she (or the figure she addresses) has come home.[26]

1989

The Swift of *1989* had entered a kind of stratosphere that no other working artist could touch: not just in her standard of living (worthy of RWPF), not just in her A-list fan group, but in her commercial clout—when she withheld her music from streaming services to protest inadequate royalties, the streaming services caved. No wonder she worked so hard, and so visibly, to remain relatable outside the songs themselves, as well as within the lyrics and arrangements. For example, Swift invited online superfans to her house, and brought others to secret sessions, where they got previews for songs on the way. You can watch, via YouTube, a so-called secret session on a rooftop in New York: It hardly looks like a slumber party, but it doesn't look like an arena show—fans get closer than they otherwise would. "I want to meet as many of you as possible," she told those fans, the lights of the Empire State Building behind her. Covering Swift for the *Guardian* in 2014, Hermione Hoby wrote that "her stadium shows have the confessional good feeling of mass sleepovers." Her bond with her fans would survive the change in genres, as well as her growing distance from their lives, because her need for them, and their need for her, had not changed.[27]

It's a need almost no other pop stars display as she does. Professional pop songwriters such as Diane Warren (or Liz Rose) often advise that lyrics should stay open-ended, so that many, many listeners can see themselves in them. "Songs should be universal," advises one best-selling how-to-write-songs book. Swift goes instead for trust through giving specifics, opening herself up. Chuck Klosterman's 2015 profile of her explained the paradox of her self-portraiture: A listener has "to think about her persona in order to appreciate [some of] what she's doing creatively. This is her greatest power: an ability to combine her art and her life so profoundly that both spheres become more interesting to everyone." If it's a newish phenomenon in pop music, it's familiar to readers of poetry. Alexander Pope ("Epistle to Dr. Arbuthnot"), and William Wordsworth ("Lines Composed a Few Miles Above Tintern Abbey"), and Robert Lowell (*Life Studies*), among others, all insisted that we could best enter into their art once we knew stacks of details from their real lives.[28]

Of course, we might decide—hearing *1989*—that Taylor Swift doesn't really share our feelings. It's all artifice, not real. All style, no substance. No wonder, then, that *1989* includes one more song in defense of art, and artfulness, and escape, and pretending, as well as one more attack on the idea that the best romances must lead somewhere permanent. That song is "Wonderland." Compared to most pop hits, this one displays a lot of moving parts, including a two-note repeated ringing bell, along with a stack of false stops and starts. Wonderland represents the purpose-built place where you live if you're a celebrity conducting your romance in the public eye, but it also represents the artificial place where you can get lost in a romance, where you can lose, or regain, your mind. Taylor calls this kind of love "mad," in the British sense of the word, as in the Cheshire Cat's "We're all mad here": "In the end we both went mad." Alice cannot stay there all year. It's a rabbit hole. But at least it's not an escalator.

William Butler Yeats rewrote and remade his earlier poems often (though he never called the revisions "William's Versions"). When readers objected, he wrote a quatrain for them: "The friends that have it I do wrong / Whenever I remake a song," he protested, "Should know what issue is at stake: / It is myself that I remake." The synth-pop Taylor Swift remade herself too, even before the advent of Taylor's Versions. She did it in a way that showcases getaways, wonderlands, self-parodies, self-conscious artifice, and synthetic style. And in doing so—that is, in framing so many frustrations, anxieties, distractions, and romantic

1989

escarpments while doing so—she has shown us the challenges that reinventions pose. We don't know that our new self will improve on our old self; we don't know if we can make it in New York. We might find that every day feels like a battle, that heartbreak is our national anthem, that we need help to keep from driving off the road. That's why the album ends in the way that it does. The Taylor who begins by showing us her particular circumstances has ended up inviting us to join her: "Please take my hand!" She may feel newly welcome in New York, but she's still our hermeneutic friend.[29]

After the COVID-19 quarantine months of 2020–2021, when everybody stayed in, attempts to bring young adults and new adults and older adults out dancing became big business. Some of those attempts relied on Swifties. In the wake of the Eras Tour, the entrepreneurs Courtney Gibson and Caitie Phillips opened a series of "Taylor Swift Inspired Dance Parties" at clubs throughout America: Toad's Place in New Haven, Connecticut; the Bell House in Brooklyn, New York; the Harrisburg, Pennsylvania, Midtown Arts Center. Gibson lives in Orlando, Florida, where hundreds of people showed up for her first Taylor night: The bar next door to the club holding the event had to start playing Swift's songs to accommodate the overflow. The clubgoers wanted, specifically, Swift, and not just her dance numbers: "People really love hearing . . . a lot of Taylor's slow songs too," Gibson told *Newsweek*.[30]

The photos of these Taylor Parties, posted online from Atlanta and Chicago and Philadelphia, show sweaty kids, in groups of four or five, with cowboy hats or braids or making hand-hearts. They remind me (I'm Jewish) of nothing so much as a happy, well-executed bat mitzvah. The faces are overwhelmingly women's, or girls', and they are not all white; few look elderly, but some look old enough to order expensive cocktails. Others look like they just had their own bat mitzvah, or quinceañera. I've considered attending a Taylor Swift Inspired Dance Party, but it doesn't seem like a good idea unless I can bring my own friends. Instead I watch the videos and I see the connection that these particular parties, these collective escapes, keep up, not just with Taylor's music broadly, but with *1989*: I think about these temporary wonderlands, these rabbit holes, these places for new romantics (if not retro New Romantics) to follow Swift's lead and feel remade.

The remade, synthesized Swift of *1989*, projecting her newly urbane confidence, inspired younger artists too. Consider Chappell Roan, who sings about remaking herself, backed by purposefully tinny synthesized keyboards, at the Pink Pony Club; who promised, adagio, achingly, to keep things "Casual" on the song of that name; who offered up not a blank space for using up men, but a pansexual "Femininomenon" so she could ignore them. Could Chappell have happened pre-*1989*? Would her song "My Kink Is Karma" have happened without Swift's "Karma"? Chappell Roan rose up in a pop world that Swift helped to build, but she is not one of the dozen-odd young female artists whom Swift helped to elevate, starting in the early 2010s, with public praise and tour support. Most of those artists came (like Taylor herself) from genres defined by guitars. But there's an exception. Griff (born Sarah Faith Griffiths, in Hertfordshire in 2001) opened for Taylor on the Eras Tour in London, night two, less than a year after Swift commented on Griff's song "Vertigo" on Instagram: "Damn Griff I love this one."[31]

Griff has said that her earliest musical memory involves *Fearless*: She's been a Swiftie since almost before she could read. And yet her music has little to do with *Fearless*. She works in a synth-pop tradition, from the Human League through *1989*, FKA Twigs, and CHVRCHES.

1989

It's hard to imagine the throbs, the passion, and the syncopation of Griff's "Vertigo" without "Style" and "New Romantics" and the four-word clusters from "You Are in Love." "Vertigo," too, offers words up in four-word lines. It learns from Swift as it invites us to share its dejection: "I'm scared of love," the singer confesses. "Well aren't we all." Her hit then swerves from one kind of synthetic pulse to another, nodding toward the builds and drops of modern club music, then resolving into the kind of hushed repetition Taylor gives in "Out of the Woods."[32]

You can hear *1989* in other Griff hits too. "Tears for Fun" learns from what Taylor learned from Max Martin: Start with the chorus, keep the vocals clear, whack the kettledrums every so often, build up to a climax, isolate the vocals, get the listener singing a short phrase over and over. "Tears for Fun" also looks back at Taylor's self-conscious angst: "Will I always be collecting my tears?" You can watch Griff's rehearsal for her Eras Tour gig on YouTube, where Griff sounds like a New Romantic, like someone ready for shiny self-reinvention, even though (or because) she used to take orders from guys. "I would have done anything you wanted," Griff tells her imagined ex in "Anything." The implication is: not anymore. She's off his escalator. She's looking, below her big indoor glasses, at us. She's synthesizing her new self, choosing her new sound over her own ex-lover. We can see ourselves in Griff, as Griff once saw herself in Taylor: Like her, we can follow Taylor's lead.

7

REPUTATION

Most white Taylor Swift fans—at least the ones I know—prefer not to talk about Taylor and race. Her detractors sometimes focus on it. "If you like Taylor Swift we have nothing in common," the celebrated essayist Vanessa Angélica Villarreal wrote in 2024. "She's a billionaire racist," a "Nazi Barbie." During the *1989* era, actual Nazis admired her whiteness: National Public Radio reported that white supremacists had adopted her as their "Aryan goddess." And if the 2009 VMA Awards controversy had a subtext—often thought but rarely said outright—that subtext was race: A pretty young white girl had "stolen" something a Black adult woman deserved.[1]

Too many writers and listeners in America treat race as important only for artists of color, making whiteness—what it enables and what it conceals—seem invisible or unremarkable. Those treatments aren't fair, and they're not fair to Swift, whose sixth album, *Reputation*—the sharpest break in her career to that date—almost demands that we think about Blackness and whiteness, even if some of us find the result hard to take. Her first non-rock, non-country album, *1989*, favored the Anglo-Swedish sounds of 1980s synth-pop and 2000s chart pop. *Reputation* more often chooses the musical idioms of 2010s Black pop and R&B, with elements of hip-hop, and with rappers as collaborators.

With these elements in her own songs for the first time, Swift could accomplish kinds of writing she had rarely attempted before: satire and polemic; songs about "adult" behavior in bedrooms and mansions; answer songs that go beyond isolated teenage retribution into extended visions of righteous revenge. Emotional goals in *Reputation* point outside music too: to earlier feminist clapbacks, to popular television drama, and to poems from the English eighteenth century. To think about how *Reputation* sounds, though, and about how it fits into Swift's art, we need to think about Black and white in America, and about racial undertones and overtones in Swift's earlier career.

We also need to think about Kanye West. Half the standout songs on *Reputation* address Swift's reignited feud with Kanye and his then-wife Kim Kardashian. Most of the rest of those songs show her distance from the good girl, the ingenue, and the people-pleasing persona she assumed on her first three albums and much of her fourth, as well as her distance from the optimistic party girl, the new romantic guide to wonderland, we met on *1989*. Swift gets that distance by embracing the powers of Black pop, by letting alert listeners notice her whiteness, and trying to reject, musically and lyrically, the powers and limits, the blamelessness and childlikeness, that American white girlhood has long implied. Swift's rejections of white-coded musical styles, and her embrace of R&B, give the album much of its power, both aspirational (what if we wanted to be like her?) and relatable (what if we already are?).

They make it disquieting—once we notice them—too. Has Swift reinforced harmful stereotypes about Black music, or Black culture, or Black people, in trying to ditch the limits of her own whiteness? Is the whole album an act of appropriation? Is anything here okay? However you answer that question—and there's room for conflicting answers—the songs of *Reputation* ask their listeners, especially white girls, to try on feelings less sweet, and less acceptable, than the emotions that dominated *Fearless*, *Red*, and *1989*. They might prompt white people to think about whiteness, and to think about race, that omnipresent force in American life that so many white people (myself included) grew up attempting to avoid or ignore. Some songs on *Reputation* show us how socially acceptable characters might learn from, or see ourselves in, stigmatized revengers, glamorous lawbreakers, and other characters who reject taboos. Those songs may show us, too, how to get past shame: how to own our feelings, how to come back once we've been put down.

Everything about *Reputation*, when it came out, suggested controversy and counterattack. The album cover appears to reference Prince's *Controversy* (1981): Both show close-up photos of the artist over collages of newspaper headlines. And the album itself arrived ready to fight. Swift's eloquent prologue attacked "baseless gossip" and internet rumormongers: "We are mosaics of our worst selves and our best selves," Swift insisted, and if we're lucky, our lovers and friends "will still choose us even when they see all of the sides of the story."

That story felt rough, to her, despite her obvious privilege. The *Lover* diaries record a steady emotional (and commercial) ascent all the way to 2014. "I'm grateful for being happy right this moment," says one entry from 2011. From 2012: "I love writing so much, it's the only thing that makes sense to me." From 2014: "We wrote this chanty cheerleader bridge that I absolutely LOVE." The excerpt from 2016, though, ends on a nearly blank page: "Aug. 29, 2016. Nashville. This summer is the apocalypse."

What happened? Her romantic life got messy. She and the A-list DJ Calvin Harris, known for his work with Rihanna, started dating in early 2015, then split up in 2016. "The aftermath of that relationship," Harris remarked, "was way more heavily publicized than the relationship." Internet gossip seized on the breakup, especially since Swift immediately began dating the actor Tom Hiddleston, who played Loki in the Marvel movies. The two flew to England, Italy, and Australia that summer while he was making *Thor: Ragnarok*. Then they broke up. Daily life in New York—despite the 2014 giddiness of "Welcome to New York"—by 2016 offered little comfort. Taylor had grown so famous that paparazzi clogged up her every move. The singer Lorde quipped that making plans with Swift felt like "having a friend with an autoimmune disease. . . . There are certain places you can't go. Certain things you can't do."[2]

That summer, too, Swift began preparing for her legal case against the Colorado radio DJ who had groped her in 2013. According to court proceedings, the DJ, David Mueller, had grabbed Swift from behind and reached up her skirt during an industry meet-and-greet. Taylor and her mother, Andrea, let his employer know. The station fired the DJ, and the DJ then sued Taylor and Andrea over his lost career. Swift countersued for $1, alleging assault and battery. After months of legal preparation, a federal jury in April 2017 ruled in favor of Swift.[3]

REPUTATION

August 29, 2016—the date in the diary—also saw Swift skip the 2016 VMA Awards. Entertainment watchers speculated that she was avoiding Kanye West. In fact, she had jury duty in Nashville that day, though the judge excused her on the grounds that the Denver lawsuit would keep her from being impartial in a rape trial. A juror named Tracey Bates tweeted that Swift had been nice to everyone in the jury pool, had allowed Bates to take photographs for private use, and had signed Bates's copy of *The New Jim Crow*, Michelle Alexander's book about Black people in America's jails and prisons.[4]

Whatever Swift may have learned from the book, if she read it, she did not speak out about race, nor about electoral politics, at the time. As the 2016 presidential election approached—despite the outrageously racist and sexist comments of then-candidate Donald Trump, and despite his reputation as a sexual harasser—Swift declined to endorse a candidate, telling her followers on Election Day only to "go out and VOTE." Fans and journalists roasted her for the decision, calling her cowardly or selfish: "Sorry, fans: Taylor Swift is never, ever, ever going to tell you who she is voting for," concluded Caroline Framke of Vox Media, "because speaking up is never, ever, ever going to benefit Taylor Swift." As Swift herself explained later on, in *Miss Americana*, she had been told—having come up through country music—never to say anything about politics that might alienate any fans. In 2016 she wasn't ready—or didn't think it would do any good—to defy her elders' advice.[5]

None of these controversies would have hit as hard—some might not have hit at all—without the return of Swift's feud with Kanye West. In the *1989* era the beef seemed over. West and Taylor appeared together onstage at two 2015 awards shows, declaring a public friendship. West claimed that the pair might collaborate; he also sent her a bouquet of white flowers the size of a St. Bernard. Then, in February 2016, Ye released "Famous," a Rihanna collaboration, with the lines "I feel like me and Taylor might still have sex / Why? I made that bitch famous." The video for "Famous" showed West cavorting with naked sculptures of celebrities, including Donald Trump, Caitlyn Jenner, Rihanna, and Swift. West claimed that Swift had given him permission, over the phone, to record those lyrics; Swift denied it. In July, Ye's then-wife Kim Kardashian released a recorded phone call that seemed to support West's version. Kim then called Taylor a snake on social media, spreading hashtags such as #TaylorSwiftIsOverParty. And as Kirsty Thatcher of *Elle* put it, "The Internet sided with Kim."[6]

The internet got it wrong. Someone in Camp Kanye had edited the recording, and in 2020 the whole original leaked. Taylor was telling the truth. She knew about "might still have sex"—she had talked him out of the lyric "Taylor still owes me sex"—but she never consented to "that bitch." On the unedited recording, she asks Kanye to reconsider the song ("sounds crazy") before advising him to follow his heart. He then delivers disjointed monologues about his debts, and West Coast venture capital, and his own musical prowess. In the 2016 edit, Taylor calls Kanye's call "a really good show of friendship" and says "We're fine. . . . It's fine." In the real, complete call, she says those things, and tells him "I'll always respect you," but she also seems to be trying to get him off the phone. He tells off a camera operator—part of his secret recording team—after Swift hangs up.[7]

By the time the unedited recording leaked, the damage had long been done. Bridie Jabour of the *Guardian* wrote, on Swift's late 2016 cancellation, "Many hundreds of thousands of people seem to have been waiting for this moment for years." Twitter filled up with hashtags about the backlash: "Finally someone exposed Taylor," a representative comment ran. Swift said years later that the phone call, and "Famous," and #TaylorSwiftIsOverParty, and their aftermath "took me down psychologically to a place I've never been before. I moved to a foreign country" (that is, England). "I didn't leave a rental house for a year. I was afraid to get on phone calls. I pushed away most people in my life because I didn't trust anyone anymore." She explained in *Miss Americana* that during that period—the fall of 2016 to the fall of 2017—"nobody physically saw me for a year. That's what I thought they wanted."[8]

Nobody likes getting canceled or shamed. But for Taylor—given what her music and her interviews reveal about her reasons for performing—the experience must have felt especially crushing. For one thing, she had worked hard to alienate no one, to be (as she sang) a careful daughter, to avoid giving offense, to welcome everyone into the public parts of her life, and—when injured—to shake it off. She had just constructed, with *1989*, a new adult persona, setting a cosmopolitan example of resilience, ebullience, and positivity. West and Kardashian were lying, and many people seemed to believe them. Moreover, Kanye brought his own reputation, not just as an artist whose albums sold in the millions but as a musical innovator, a genius pushing forward what pop—and rap and Black music—could do. Was Taylor not so much the aggrieved innocent as the pasty voice of the past, the privileged white girl from the suburbs who couldn't recognize genius or take a joke? Was she, in fact, the symbol for white supremacy, and for an airbrushed past, that her Aryan admirers took her to be?

Reputation shows how Taylor stopped being that girl. "Borrowing styles and approaches from black music," the *New York Times*'s Jon Caramanica wrote admiringly, Swift had made an album where "her target is herself—her innocence, her naivete," her previous "striving to be flawless" (not fearless but flawless). That target practice meant recognizing the wages of whiteness. It also meant an effort to grow up.[9]

The historian and cultural critic Robin Bernstein argues that American culture conflates whiteness with childhood, as well as childhood with guiltless joy, coding Black kids as adult-like, and white teens as children. Nineteenth-century novels, twentieth-century dolls and toys, and twenty-first-century studies by psychologists all support this upsetting finding: "Childhood innocence—itself raced white," Bernstein writes, can "retain racial meanings but hide them." Leah Donnella of National Public Radio's *Code Switch* podcast summed it up: "Girlhood is kind of classically imagined in our society as this time of real purity and goodness and innocence," which means that the archetype puts forward, imagines as the best, most ideal girls, "upper middle class, thin, pretty, white girls." Like Taylor Swift. White girls may feel that adults expect them to stretch their own childhood out indefinitely. Black girls, by contrast, get treated like adults too soon.[10]

Swift at least tried to acknowledge her whiteness earlier in her career. When Country Music Television (CMT) tapped Swift to make the introductory video for an awards show, she chose to create a self-parody rap persona, T-Swizzle, alongside the real pop-rapper and Auto-Tune aficionado T-Pain. The result looks ridiculous, purposely so. A "producer" bleeps Swift out at the end even though she never swears; when T-Pain objects, his regular speech still sounds Auto-Tuned. But Swift's love for the pop side of rap, even then, was no joke: "I'm really into rap at the moment, Nicki Minaj, Diddy, Dirty Money, T-Pain, Tupac," she told a reporter. But there wasn't much Nicki, let alone Tupac, in evidence on Swift's albums at that time.[11]

The cringey "T-Swizzle" video played on the contrasts between Black adulthood and white-blonde innocence that Bernstein describes, the contrast that led Charli XCX, ten years later, to complain that opening for Taylor Swift felt "like waving to five-year-olds." No wonder the grown-up Swift wanted to make an album about adulthood, complete with sex and alcohol and figurative drugs ("my drug is my baby"). No wonder she learned from the sound of Black pop, as well as from international dance-floor style, how to do it. "There's anger in the album," Swift explained. "There's defiance, there's humor, finally being able to laugh at something that hurts you. But there's also a side to that, you close the door and you let yourself feel all of the feelings.... And when you start to let yourself actually process all the complex emotions about having a bad reputation, that's when things can get pretty ... Delicate."[12]

That's the spoken intro that Swift uses, on the *Reputation* tour, to introduce "Delicate." She then slides into that song, with a vocoder, a rainbow dress, and the Balearic beat of the subgenre tropical house, reverberating in its adult invitation to someone (perhaps Joe Alwyn) to make her a drink, and to "like me for me." It's not—nor is "End Game"—a song about being a villain. Rather, it's a song about being your whole embodied self, rather than the restricted, sanitized version that earlier incarnations of Taylor—versions that could not "feel all the feelings"—put forth.

There's obviously something odious about the association of Blackness with villainy and taboo, especially when it's taken up by white artists. A more just society than the one we have would make it far easier for Black children to be children, and it would give white girls more space to grow. That's a point that the redeployed stereotypes and sounds on *Reputation* can—I hope—help white listeners discover, but it's secondary, in the course of the album, to Taylor's sense of what she wants her newest music to do. "Nicey-nice Taylor pop Taylor is dead," Kitty Empire concluded, reviewing *Reputation* in Britain's *Observer*. "In her place is a colder pop-R&B player." Yet R&B connotes, on this album, not becoming a chilly antagonist so much as presenting your whole self, with—as Swift later put it—"all that defiance, that longing to be understood," "that shame-born snarl and mischief." Listening to and working with confident Black adults on new Black-coded music, Swift repudiated—at least for a time—her inner, insistently harmless, agreeable, all-too-white child.[13]

The run-up to *Reputation* featured a gambit that few stars could pull off: On Friday, August 18, 2017, Swift's social media went dark, all posts gone or hidden. The following Monday, Tuesday, and Wednesday, her official Instagram added one, two, three videos of a cobra, followed by the first single, "Look What You Made Me Do." Then came the album announcement: "Reputation: The new album from Taylor Swift. November 10." More snakes popped up in the album's rollout: As Sarah Chapelle has noticed, the Gucci sweatshirt Swift wore that year on *Saturday Night Live* replicated "the crisp red, black and white stripes of a scarlet kingsnake." The *Reputation* tour kept the ophiology going, bringing on stage a sixty-three-foot inflatable cobra named Karyn.[14]

What makes that kind of snaky behavior relatable? Few among us have faced the level of tabloid opprobrium that comes with the life that Taylor, after *1989*, led. Many of us, though, have seen cancellation online; have faced libel or slander on social media, as well as within a friend group; have felt pursued by unchosen drama; have felt enmeshed in gossip that singles us out. "This is how the world works," Taylor muses, almost under her breath, in "I Did Something Bad"; and, in "End Game," "I don't love the drama, it loves me." If going after her once looked like stepping on a puppy (as Katy Perry put it back in 2009), now it meant waking a snake. Everything that hurt or cramped

REPUTATION

or pained her about her celebrity persona, all the allegations and the blame, would become her new material.

Reputation became in that way a fifty-five-minute, forty-five-second course in inspirational reputation management. It also showed Taylor, for the first time (unless you count the sarcastic persona of "Blank Space"), portraying a grown-up menace, acting like someone you might not want your kid to know. She wrote songs about lust, intoxication, and parties, "whiskey on ice" and "Sunset and Vine," in the ancient genre that lit-crit types call Anacreontic (after the Greek poet Anacreon, who wrote drinking songs), a genre represented best these days in Black pop and R&B. The Taylor of *Reputation* also adopted another classical genre, the apologia, in which someone defends their life and their actions—not a way to say, "I'm sorry," but a way to explain why they did what they did.

That's one reason *Reputation* embraces, as *1989* had not, the textures, timbres, and building blocks of modern hip-hop, as well as 2010s R&B. The album includes, also for the first time, phone calls, found sounds, and other nonmelodic interludes: normal on rap and R&B albums, rare in rock and country. The old Taylor can't come to the phone right now (because she's dead). The new Taylor might be thinking (for example) of the phone call at the end of Brandy's "Full Moon" (2001), or of Drake's "U With Me?" (2016). *Reputation* relies almost throughout on the track-and-hook songwriting that Taylor introduced, sparingly, on *Red*, where one creator makes beats and another makes lyrics and melodies. Unusual in rock and country, that method has become standard in R&B, in rap, and in dance pop, like the kind that Calvin Harris and Rihanna made. Swift and Harris even cowrote Rihanna's "This Is What You Came For," whose stretched-out version of "you" (up to ten syllables at the end of the chorus!) matches its dance-all-night vibe, while its cleverly minimal lyrics describe their own function: "We say nothing more than we need." Swift appeared in the songwriting credits as "Nils Sjöberg," apparently so as not to upstage Harris.[15]

The bounty of Sweden notwithstanding, the method points back to Black America. Making an R&B album, Swift not only chose "the coolest, most creative" genre around as of 2016 (as Kelefa Sanneh put it in his book on genre); she chose a genre that (in Sanneh's words) "can never quite decide whether it wants to be the universal sound of young (and not-so-young) America, or Black people's best-kept secret, or—somehow—both at once." Of course, it cannot manifest both at once, and yet that's the antinomy Swift wants to invoke. If she can't make the two things into one thing, maybe she can make, at the least, the sound of escape from a white-coded hypocrisy, the supposed white innocence of the alleged Aryan sweetheart, the paleness of Taylor Swift's past.[16]

That rejection began with track one. Caroline Sullivan calls ". . . Ready for It?" the first track in Swift's career where she presents herself as a "sexual aggressor." That track layers processed vocals over trap beats and a whomping subwoofer: Similar hi-hat effects crop up throughout the album, as Taylor creates some distance between her present-day, dauntlessly embodied, unhindered self and the girl she no longer wants to be. Other love songs on *Reputation* let Taylor sound naughty, openly seductive, no longer chasing a teenage dream of forever and always, but instead inviting her partner into a risky situationship, with bedroom eyes. Swift paints herself as the thief in the "getaway car," as the larcenous betrayer, as the captive who can escape ("Dancing with Our Hands Tied"). "End Game," with Future and Ed Sheeran, nearly suggests that she's dating two people at once, "drinking on the beach" with at least one of them, as she puts it, "all over me." It's a classic seduction song, living in the moment, with its booming electronic drum hits and trap beats, as if to say that she doesn't regret what the world made her do.[17]

That pattern lasts through every love song on the album, even through the midnights of "New Year's Day." "Gorgeous" begins by asking us to "take it as a compliment / That I get drunk and make fun of the way you talk," and then suggests that she'll cheat on her boyfriend for you, its four-note blocks building suspense. "Dress" invites us to imagine Swift naked: "I . . . Only bought this dress so you could take it off." The shimmering nighttime artifice, the slithering beats, in a song like "Don't Blame Me" take us as far away from valentines, rings, and fairy-tale good girls as a pop composition, in 2017, can go. But the song also promises warmth, and sex, and devotion: "Love made me crazy" (a nod to Beyoncé's "Crazy in Love"). "End Game" ends up, after all, as a love song too: Its volatile red-lipsticked version of Taylor, for all her big repetitions and big conversations, invites her man to choose her and settle down. "Delicate" opens new frontiers in tenderness, self-doubt, and vulnerability even as it invites its man—corresponding to Taylor's then-new real-life partner Joe Alwyn—to make her a drink.

"Dress" might count as a love song too, though it's mostly a sex song, promising literally to lead her man into a bedroom, to make a mark on her bedpost. The woman portrayed in the song now drinks to excess, and—by contrast with other songs on the same album—she does not want this man as her best friend. She wants him in bed, without clothes, and she'll pull out a whole menu of songwriters' and producers' devices to get him there, among them the false ending ("Say my name and everything just stops") and the serial ah's and ooh's that, at least since Donna Summer and Giorgio Moroder's "Love to Love You Baby"

(1975), have strongly suggested sex. "Dress" also points toward R&B in its harmonies, a series of sevenths and ninths; the vocals stay dissonant, straining against the instrumentation (in, for example, "don't *want* you like a *best* friend," with D's sung over the chords C and C7.

On tour, Swift dedicated "Dress" to the legacy of the modern dancer Loie Fuller. Swift's own dancers in that number moved amid colored silks, unfolding and rotating massive, fluttering wings in prismatic lights, a kind of dance Fuller invented. Behind them, text read: "In honor of Loie Fuller (1862–1928) / pioneer in the arts, dance and design / And who fought for artists to own their work." Fuller also became her own choreographer. And she took exceptional steps to maintain control of her art, suing a performer who copied her famous "Serpentine" routine. Swift's homages do not just pay tribute to Fuller as someone who stood up for artists' rights; they also remind us that dancers and choreographers, and singers and songwriters, are creators, that they have worked hard and long to do what seems flawless or effortless once it takes the stage.[18]

The Swift who saw herself in Loie Fuller defended herself as a professional, as a creator, as someone who had been wronged, and might strike back (or sue). At the same time the Swift of *Reputation* wanted to change, to expand her range, to distance herself from the blameless kitten she could no longer be. Adulthood, for her and for listeners who grew up with her, meant more than just staying out late at parties—it meant taking responsibility (as in "New Year's Day"). It also meant fighting back, and that's what happens in the tracks clearly aimed at Kim and Kanye. "This Is Why We Can't Have Nice Things" becomes a de facto narration of the Swift-Kanye-Kim timeline: "Therein lies the issue, friends don't try to trick you / Get you on the phone and mind-twist you / . . . Did you think I wouldn't hear all the things you said about me?" "Look What You Made Me Do" steps away from the literalities of music-world gossip to establish that the new Taylor Swift—the one who could come to the microphone—no longer needs to play the innocent. She speeds up her vocals as she launches into her mildly syncopated pre-chorus, placing the "I" on the second, not the first, beat: "but I got smarter, I got harder in the nick of time / . . . I got a list of names and yours is in red, underlined." This singer knows how to come back from apparent death, or from temporary silence.

Songs on *Reputation* not especially engaged with hip-hop, or R&B, or sonic reinvention still pay attention to Swift's new, damaged, sometimes sarcastic persona. "Getaway Car" brings back the driving beat Swift used for *Red* and *1989* (for example, in "Style"). Lyrically, though, the song casts Swift herself as a villain, in cahoots with another villain. She joins a crime, steals the loot, and disappears: The character she creates for herself gets away but accepts the blame (Swift-watchers believe the song refers to her months-long romance with Hiddleston). "Getaway Car" also takes up the notorious trucker gearshift, last seen in "Love Story," where the song modulates upward for a sense of lift and release (*re* becomes the new *do*). Maybe Taylor got away after all—but she left her partner in crime behind.

The album's center of gravity remains in contemporary Black pop. "King of My Heart," with its clicking, buzzing, booming sequence of rhythm tracks, picks up on what Swift learned from modern hip-hop. Early in the song she half-speaks, half-sings over finger-snaps. By the time she sings the title in the chorus, she's multitracked and Auto-Tuned. Post-chorus segments bring in, of all things, a drum line. This version of Swift may have tired of fancy cars—Range Rovers and Jaguars (pronounced "Jag-you-wars")—but she's willing to put the textures of her new romance up front, asking that we see ourselves in this newly infatuated, somewhat jaded adult.

Making an album in the modes of Black pop isn't the same as making public statements about racism and race. Swift wasn't ready to do that in 2016 or 2017, though she did it in 2019–2020, along with so many other white celebrities, telling Laura Snapes of the *Guardian* that she had learned "a lot about how my privilege allowed me to not have to learn about white privilege. I didn't know about it as a kid, and that is privilege itself, you know?" I do not mean to call her a civil rights leader. Nor do I mean that any of her songs functioned as explicit lyrical claims about white privilege and white supremacy. If that's what you want from white singers' pop music, go elsewhere (try Adeem the Artist's "Heritage of Arrogance," or Jason Isbell's "White Man's World"). But if what you want is an album showing how whiteness flattens and distorts white people's experience, what whiteness tells white people not to mention, what white people can learn about their own assumptions from listening to Black music, *Reputation* makes a decent choice. It's also catchy as hell.[19]

My point—in case it does not go without saying—is not that white women are genuinely more innocent, or Black women more aggressive, but that white Americans grow up, like it or not, surrounded by those awful stereotypes, and you can't fight them if you never acknowledge them. Nor do I mean that country and rock make representations of adulthood impossible: Both genres are full of adult men and women, presented as such (Bruce Springsteen, Jason Isbell, Loretta Lynn). Instead I mean that given Swift's need to change, given her history, given her felt need to reject her old self, those genres made sounding like an adult, standing up for herself, representing defiance, and owning her whole body seem impossible *for Taylor Swift in 2017*, unless she could find a new, and less white-coded, sound.

Swift's choices—in lyrics, in music, in self-presentation—throughout *Reputation*, as they invoke her whiteness, and other musicians' Blackness, leave her open to serious moral objections. One objection could occur to anyone who knows the history of white Americans making popular music, from Stephen Foster to Elvis Presley to the present day, using techniques developed by Black musicians. "In nodding to R&B cadences," as Kitty Empire put it at the time, "is Swift guilty of cultural appropriation," like Miley Cyrus on *Bangerz*, or Ariana Grande in "7 Rings"? Should Swift have stayed in her lane?[20]

The question has no good answer. Should Elvis have stayed in his lane? Maybe. Or maybe sounds, once invented, belong to whoever can use them well, though they carry their histories with them. Maybe white musicians need to earn the moral right to appropriate Black sounds by working to elevate the Black artists who created them, and by speaking up about race explicitly. It's a high bar to set. Few white pop stars would clear it (Eminem might). An ideally ethical, ideally self-aware, alternate-universe Taylor Swift could have courted further controversy, before *Reputation* came out, by speaking out against white supremacy, describing the history of the sounds she used, and singling out, for attention and sales, even more, and older, and less well-known Black artists, in addition to those who appear on *Reputation*. We can wish Taylor had done more in that vein, while listening to the Taylor Swift we have.

Another claim about—or against—*Reputation* seems more specific, if not more alarming. If the way out of white innocence and racialized, helpless, desexualized girlhood involves learning from (or appropriating) Black sounds, what does that choice say about Blackness? Has the Swift of *Reputation*, of "Dress" and "End Game," played into stereotypes she hoped to escape by reinforcing other stereotypes, namely the racist idea that Black people, even young ones, are hypersexual, dangerous, prematurely adult? If whiteness means innocence and vulnerability, what does it say, what stereotypes get reinforced, when the way to hit back is to start sounding Black?

Reputation looks, from this point of view, like one more example of the centuries-old phenomenon that Toni Morrison's *Playing in the Dark*—and many later critics—have described. Swift becomes one more of the many white artists relying on Blackness, Black sounds and Black people, to represent something scary, repressed, or hard to name in our white selves. Certainly there's something alarming about an album, or a person, or a culture—American culture—that associates whiteness with harmlessness, and Blackness with confrontation. That association, put in practice by law enforcement, gets Black people killed. At the same time it feels like a stretch to blame Taylor Swift's choice of drum-machine patch for those killings.

A defense of the racial politics in the sounds of *Reputation*—a defense I find as plausible as (though no more so than) the critique—might say that hiving off certain kinds of fears, fantasies, threats, and "adult" ideas from others, and then projecting them onto Black people, onto Black characters, is exactly what *Reputation* does not do. Instead, the enticing textures of R&B, the collaborative (and still confrontational) ethos of modern rap, turn out to fit not some invented, ventriloquized, or appropriated Black character, but Taylor Swift herself. Like every other product of white America, she must learn to listen to Black culture and Black-coded art forms so that she can recognize, and honor, the rejected, ignored, suppressed, bracketed parts of herself. White people, white artists, should stop—as soon as possible, and almost however possible—assuming we're the heroes, the innocents: We need to get off our white horse.

REPUTATION

And, a defender would say, that's what the musical resources of *Reputation* at least attempt to do. Disclaiming and refusing the musical fantasies of whiteness bound up with the styles that her earlier records deployed, Swift, and her coauthors and collaborators, from Max Martin to Future, went to the music they saw as powerful, helpful, and less constrained. They worked to learn. They showed (knowingly or not) how white-coded musical styles and resources can render invisible, or fail to register, white people's emotions. And Swift did these things, from ". . . Ready for It?" to "This Is Why We Can't Have Nice Things," without attempting to speak for, or from, Black life. In this sense she did try to stay in her lane.

With *Reputation* Swift also became a figure of no-holds-barred, long-delayed feminist revenge. In doing so she invites us to join her as what feminist critics used to call a "Resisting Reader," celebrating a woman—such as William Thackeray's Becky Sharp, or the X-Men's Jean Grey—who resists sexist hierarchy and upsets a patriarchal order, no matter how often "they say she's gone too far this time." When Taylor sings "I can feel the flames on my skin" ("I Did Something Bad"), she might be complaining about being burned as a witch, but she might also revel in her new place in hell, alongside John Milton's devils. The same song begins self-referentially with pizzicato violin while Taylor sings "I play 'em like a violin"—Swift does nothing by accident. If *1989* was her Phoenix saga, her triumphant and flamboyant self-reinvention as a cosmopolitan creature of fire and life itself, *Reputation* would be her Dark Phoenix: There's even a death and resurrection. We might wish we could see ourselves in that kind of comeback.

TAYLOR'S VERSION

Beyond this panoply of parallels, *Reputation* has an acknowledged source, one with its own disturbing politics. Megan Friedman of *Cosmopolitan* spitballed, after hearing the album, "Maybe Taylor is a huge *Game of Thrones* fan"; Rebecca Skane, writing in *Portsmouth Review*, called it "a perfect theme song for our beloved Arya [Stark]." Years later, Swift said these writers were righter than they could have known: She spent her months in seclusion binge-watching the series, whose sanguinary, revenge-themed stories inspired half the album. "'Look What You Made Me Do' is literally Arya Stark's kill list," she told *Entertainment Weekly* in 2019. "'I Did Something Bad' I wrote after Arya and Sansa conspired to kill Littlefinger." Moreover, "'King of My Heart' was influenced by Khal Drogo and Daenerys. It's even got this post-hook of drums—I wanted them to sound like Dothraki drums."[21]

Arya Stark seems especially important. In perhaps the series' most famous episode, "The Rains of Castamere," the aristocrat Walder Frey throws a party designed to entrap and slaughter the whole Stark family. The teenaged Arya, late to the party, gets locked out and survives. Arya later recites a list of enemies—her kill list—before going to sleep every night. She goes on to kill some of them through swordplay and subterfuge, feeding Walder his own sons' thumbs, baked into pies, before she slits his throat. (For what it's worth, the "barbarous" Dothraki are one of the series' quasi-African, quasi-Asian racial others; the Starks, and the Freys, all played by white actors, present as white.) That thumbs-in-pies killing goes down in Season 6, episode 10, "The Winds of Winter," first aired in June 2016. Arya and her sister Sansa kill Littlefinger, however, in Season 7, episode 7, "The Dragon and the Wolf," which aired in late August 2017, just three months before *Reputation* dropped. Swift must have written, and recorded, fast.

REPUTATION

"I Did Something Bad" builds not a confession so much as a series of warnings, addressed to other women who date men as much as to the men she's supposedly wronged. "Leave before you get left," and don't drop Taylor's name, or she'll drop you. It's a song about gleeful self-defense that also introduces a gendered solidarity, like Arya's with Sansa. When Sansa finds Arya's masks, or Faces—disguises she's made from the people she's killed, such as Walder—Arya explains, "We both wanted to be other people when we were younger. You wanted to be a queen . . . I wanted to be a knight." But neither happened: "The world doesn't just let girls decide what they're going to be. But I can now. With the Faces. I can choose. I can become someone else. Speak in their voice. Live in their skin. I can even become you." Of course she can: She'll be the actress starring in her enemies' bad dreams. The video for "I Did Something Bad" cycles through actors who play Taylor's previous selves, as if they were Faces, and as if she meant to reject them, or kill them off, too.

Every big thing in Swift's catalog has not just a musical precursor but an older literary parallel. The Swift of *Reputation* refers explicitly to *Game of Thrones*, and learns from Future, but she also shares goals and tactics with the great eighteenth-century poet Alexander Pope. Raised Catholic in England (thus legally barred from most professions), visibly disabled—four and a half feet tall, hunched over, in constant pain—Pope had few potential career paths other than the poetry that eventually made him rich. He, too, came to be recognized while still in his teens, for pastoral works of great beauty (compare Swift's own country pastorals, from her debut). Pope then published satirical poems attacking (as he saw it) corrupt politicians, bad poets, empty-headed nobles, and venal businesspeople. Some targets wrote back. Swift retreated to a house in Westerly, then to a rental in England; Pope built a retreat, of sorts, in his famous artificial grotto at Twickenham. At one point he had to carry a pistol, fearing ambush by his literary enemies. Pope's friend and physician Dr. John Arbuthnot asked him why he insisted on writing satire: Why call people out?

Pope's poem "Epistle to Dr. Arbuthnot"—his version of *Reputation*—amounts to an eloquently defensive response. Everyone either hates him or wants a piece of him, and nobody ever leaves him alone: "What walls can guard me, or what shades can hide? / They pierce my thickets, through my grot they glide" ("grot" means grotto). Parents blame Pope for children's misbehavior, and jilted husbands blame him for their errant wives:

> Arthur, whose giddy son neglects the laws,
> Imputes to me and my damn'd works the cause:
> Poor Cornus sees his frantic wife elope,
> And curses wit, and poetry, and Pope. . . .
> What drop or nostrum can this plague remove?
> Or which must end me, a fool's wrath or love?
> A dire dilemma! either way I'm sped,
> If foes, they write, if friends, they read me dead.

("Sped" means "sped off to hell," cooked, destroyed, done for.) Pope once tried to rise above the fray, to ignore his foes, to shake it off: "Were others angry? I excus'd them too; / Well might they rage; I gave them but their due." At this point, though, he can't help but respond, though he'll only call out people who deserve it: "A lash like mine no honest man shall dread, / But all such babbling blockheads in his stead." Look what they made him do.[22]

REPUTATION

Pope identifies his foes, in the poem's final version, through pseudonyms: code names and Easter eggs, if you will. Some of those foes get respect as great writers (Joseph Addison, or "Atticus"), unfortunately driven by jealousy to dishonor Pope so hard that Pope has to respond. Other foes get no mercy. One aristocratic writer, Lord Hervey, attacked Pope for being lowborn, disabled, and ugly, so Pope calls him effeminate, and a snake: "a cherub's face, a reptile all the rest," hardly worth the time it takes to insult him:

> "Satire or sense, alas! can Sporus feel?
> Who breaks a butterfly upon a wheel?"
> Yet let me flap this bug with gilded wings,
> This painted child of dirt that stinks and stings;
> Whose buzz the witty and the fair annoys,
> Yet wit ne'er tastes, and beauty ne'r enjoys.

The eighteenth century's most successful English poet ends his poem of self-defense by retelling his life story, an apologia of sorts: Raised by unpretentious, loving parents, Pope grew up neither "fortune's worshipper nor fashion's fool, / Not lucre's madman, nor ambition's tool," hoping for nothing more than the kind of love and stability as an adult that he knew in his youth. Celebrating real allies, repudiating false friends, the epistle is Pope's attempt to stay relatable after his fame had made him a target. There's no better model in earlier literature for the kind of creation that *Reputation* tries to be.[23]

Reputation does not just react to gossip and malice and revenge in New York and Los Angeles and Westeros, as Pope reacts to the slanders in his England. Swift also reacts to gossip and malice online, which could follow her anywhere: Her album about the limits of whiteness, about rejecting her good-girl image, is also an album about the new reach of social media. "My reputation's never been worse," she announces, through thick vocal processing, on "Delicate." A master of social media since her MySpace days, Swift reacts on *Reputation* to what she's seen—or withstood—on Instagram and Twitter.

How do reputations work, for a new generation, on these new platforms? The sociologist danah boyd's 2013 study of teens online, *It's Complicated*, found that youth who grew up with social media hung out, and gossiped, and planned, and split up online very much as prior generations might have done in person at a 1950s malt shop, or a 1750s coffeehouse. Some things, though, as of 2013, had changed. Anything 2010s teens put online could potentially stay online indefinitely, where friends, acquaintances, and strangers could find them (boyd named these phenomena "persistence" and "visibility"). As a result, parts of teens' lives that teens might prefer to separate from each other—say, a Dungeons and Dragons friend group and a cheer squad—could easily collide. Your boyfriend might find out on Instagram about your fifth-level warlock. Or about your girlfriend.

Boyd called this networked phenomenon "context collapse." It can lead people (not only teens) to shut down their social media, or to shut down psychologically. And it's one more way to think about *Reputation*: as not just an album about Black pop and white privilege, and not just a way to think about professional writing, and resentment and revenge, but also as the sound of context collapse. How does an international pop star who's also an all-American country star who's also a self-conscious role model for teens who's also on the town in New York City who's also a constant target for paparazzi who's also on tour (and not used to dancing in skimpy, shiny outfits) sort it all out?[24]

She doesn't, and she can't. Not even before she got—thanks to Kim and Kanye and online snakes—canceled. ("Millions of people were telling me to disappear," she later told *Vogue*. "So I disappeared.") No wonder Swift felt that dating anyone, in secret or in public, would be "dancing with our hands tied." The song of that title emphasizes its starts and stops, its hesitations and silences in between beats, along with its "bad feeling": It's sexy but awkward, full of the feeling that "the world would divide us," confessing almost too rapidly that "I'm the mess that you wanted," painted in contrasting colors on contrasting platforms, villain and victim, star, sexpot, and good girl all at once.[25]

The last entry in the *Lover* diaries bears the date January 3, 2017—the time when Swift would have been writing, or recording, *Reputation*: "Now I'm essentially based in London," Swift wrote, in a thick and unfamiliar black pen, "trying to protect us from the nasty world that just wants to ruin things." By "us," she meant herself and Joe Alwyn: "We have been together and no one has found out for 3 months now. I want it to stay that way because I don't want anything about this to change." That privacy seems valuable not just because it protected Alwyn from reputational damage, but because it gave Swift room to change. Kathleen Hanna of Bikini Kill, whose Riot Grrrl powers we saw in Chapter 4, wrote that her first post-college boyfriend gave her "a certain privacy, permission to not be entirely consumed by my love for him. To keep writing and making things as a way for us to share our interests with each other rather than evaporate ourselves." That's the kind of romance that Swift, by the end of *Reputation*, tells us she's found: not because he owns her, but because he really knows her, and therefore gives her (sonic, emotional, social, and creative) space.[26]

We learn as much in another head-spinningly multigeneric love song, "Call It What You Want." Again, non-rock and non-contemporary sounds come together for a postapocalyptic reconstruction. The bass line climbs down and then back up, step by step, to match her confidence as Swift intones, in one of her strongest bridges, "I want to wear his initial / On a chain 'round my neck, chain 'round my neck / Not because he owns me / But 'cause he really knows me." She's not looking for white knights or white horses either: "You don't need to save me / But would you run away with me?" The answer turns out to be no, because the new couple expect responsibilities: to their remaining friends, and to the future they expect to build.

That's the choice behind "New Year's Day," a song that contemplates—for the first time since *Speak Now*—settling down. Swift performs the song nearly solo, mostly on electric piano, a kind of contrast both with Swift's track-and-hook material and with the guitar-led numbers in her prior work. It echoes other work and foreshadows future albums: "Polaroids on the hardwood floor," like the Polaroid on the *1989* album cover; Gatsbyesque parties, from "This Is Why We Can't Have Nice Things"; "I want your midnights," as in *Midnights*; "You and me, forevermore," as in *Evermore*. The song imagines romance not only as risky, sexy, resilient adulthood, but also as mutual care, not a red romance nor a damn-the-torpedoes fling but a long-term relationship. Almost every memorable line in "New Year's Day" begins a half beat or a whole beat (an eighth or a quarter rest) after the start of the measure, as if to show how persistence and patience sound.

The lessons of *Reputation*, of Swift's apocalypse, of her experiments, of Black music and white privilege, by that quiet last track, have come through. The kind of venomous avenging figure she portrayed on half of these songs would not return to her work until

REPUTATION

Midnights. But the lessons she took from R&B and rap, from contemporary dance beats and club charts, would percolate through her later songs. So would her interest in worldly power, and in justice and injustice. She would emerge from this nest of snakes wiser and readier and—at least sometimes—calmer, ready to clean up after the party, or the battle, ended.

Up through *1989*, every Swift album came with coded messages, spelled out by capital letters in the lyric sheets. *Reputation*, which lacked them, came instead with two poems by Swift that were meant to be read, not sung. These poems also marked my first—and worst—attempt to write about Swift's artistry, when *Cosmopolitan* magazine asked me to evaluate them as stand-alone poems. I didn't like them; I'd rather not quote what I said. And now, coming back to the poems as guides to the songs, I'm finding more to say. Swift's poem "Why She Disappeared" explains—without collaborators, and without music—not just her social media blackout, but her decision to defy the haters, and then return. She imagines a near-drowning that becomes a kind of baptism, and a rebirth, like a happy ending for Kate Chopin's "The Awakening" (another story about a supposedly ruined woman). And she describes her emotional volatility not as a flaw but as a resource for her future: "May your heart remain breakable," she tells herself, "but never by the same hand twice." She's literally wishing that we as listeners can keep seeing ourselves in her.

The other poem gets less attention, because it's not so much about Taylor's particular struggles in 2017. Instead, it's about her fans: how we see ourselves in her, and why we would want to. Each stanza begins "If you're anything like me." If you're not, are you sure you'd be reading these poems? If you are, Swift continues, "you bite your nails / And laugh when you're nervous / You promise people the world." You're a people pleaser. You want everyone to love you, and you want to believe that the world operates according to some system of karmic balance, though your own yearnings (for respect, for retribution, for love) end up confining you "in your own little golden prison cell." You might see Swift aspirationally. You might want to resemble her more than you do. But Swift knows enough not to want such a thing for you: "If you're anything like me / I'm sorry." And then, less persuasively, she tries for reassurance: "Darling, it's going to be okay." How does she know? She would have to learn from experience—the experience of support, of affirmation, of feeling safe far from home and far from New York. She would find it on *Lover* and sing about it there.

8

LOVER

LOVER ANNOUNCED ITSELF (THAT IS, SWIFT announced it) as a return to joy and optimism, bright colors and bright expectations, symbolized by a butterfly and the colors of dawn, a tribute to love itself. She almost called it *Daylight*. Made and released during Donald Trump's first term in office, it's also her first album with overtly political songs, the first released after she endorsed a candidate, the first to state opinions about how public figures behave. And it's the first one she made after her well-publicized split from her previous label, Big Machine. Taylor's new deal with Universal Music gave her the rights to her future masters, along with a commercial independence that almost no other pop artist enjoyed. *Lover* tries to celebrate that independence, and to show her devotion to her then-steady partner, and to call out what's wrong with the wider world.

No wonder it's a mess. It's certainly full of aspirational moments, as well as relatable ones, but it does not feel like a whole. If *Red* and

Reputation worked like journeys, *Lover* works more like a map, perhaps a London Tube map, with multiple points of interest, multiple obstacles, and multiple ways of getting from place to place. If you imagine the last part of *Lover*, from "You Need to Calm Down" to "Me!," as if they were a set of bonus tracks, then you can hear the first part as a beautifully failed attempt to make a case for romance with happy endings, all the way from "I Forgot That You Existed" (clearing the obstacles out of the way) through "Lover" to "False God," where Taylor (backed by saxophones) promises to devote herself to love even if it requires blind faith.

Maybe that's the best a lover can do. The songs that establish her confidence and her control include some of the weakest, most strained, or most gimmicky. The strongest tracks—about public life, about romantic love, and in one case about both—emphasize her doubts: They undermine the joy that other parts of *Lover* project. And the album makes sense—when it does—only if we can break it up into those parts, thinking first about its public statements toward the end of the first Trump term, second about its joy in romantic love, and third about the way it plays (or flirts, or toys) with childhood and gender.

To hear what *Lover* does, or tries to do, you might need to know what came before it in Taylor's own life, starting with the *Reputation* tour. She visited seven countries for fifty-three concerts during the spring, summer, and fall of 2018. Along with her band, her crew, her parents, and Karyn, the giant inflatable cobra, Swift traveled with the filmmaker Lana Wilson, whose authorized documentary *Miss Americana* premiered on Netflix in early 2020. Much of what fans know about Swift's life in 2018–2019 comes from Wilson's film.

Swift had a lot going on. In June 2019 her former manager and label boss Scott Borchetta announced that he was selling that label, Big Machine, and also selling the rights to her masters (the original recordings of her first six albums). Borchetta offered Swift the rights to her recordings, but on unreasonable terms: She would have to sign with Big Machine again and would get one old recording back for every new album she made. The label, and hence the masters, ended up in the hands of Scooter Braun, an entertainment mogul closely associated with Kanye West and the Kardashians. Swift called the sale, on Tumblr, "my worst-case scenario." "I knew he would sell my music, but I couldn't believe who he would sell it to," she told CBS. Swift went public about her sense of betrayal. Then—perhaps following Kelly Clarkson's tweeted suggestion ("U should go in & re-record all the songs")—Swift resolved to do just that: She would re-record and release all six of her previous albums, so that she could own their music—in Taylor's versions. She did it for albums two through five—*Fearless* through *1989*—before, in May 2025, acquiring rights to all her older originals: as of that date *Taylor Swift* (her debut) has been re-recorded, but not released.[1]

Miss Americana depicts (among its many other clips from Swift's life) a 2018 argument between Taylor and her father and management over her decision to endorse political candidates for the first time. The midterm elections were coming up; Trump had won the 2016 election. Fearing for her safety, her father and manager advise her not to; her mother acts as a mediator. Taylor, in the end—in tears—simply asks for their forgiveness, because she's decided to go ahead with the endorsements anyway, for Democratic candidates in her then–home state of Tennessee. Taylor announced her support for Jim Cooper, for reelection to his then-safe seat in the US Congress from Nashville, and for Phil Bredesen, a former governor of Tennessee, for the US Senate. Swift's statement, on Instagram, cited the Republican Senate candidate Marsha Blackburn for her opposition to queer rights, to reauthorization of the Violence Against Women Act, and to equal pay for women. The endorsement made international news, though it did not give Bredesen victory (no Democrat has won statewide in Tennessee since).[2]

Despite the political failure, in 2018–2019 Taylor seemed to be living her best life. She was settled in London with Joe Alwyn, seemingly recovered from the reversals of 2016–2017. She was back in the public eye, planning concerts for the fall. And she was not only writing *Lover* but also collaborating with the designer Stella McCartney on co-branded clothing and merchandise ("Stella x Taylor Swift"). Against that rosy backdrop came bad news: In March 2019, the Swifts learned that Andrea's cancer, diagnosed and treated in 2015, had returned. The album launch, over the summer of 2019, returned to the multimedia, multi-interview, spotlight-ready publicity that had accompanied *1989*—a break from the wary coyness of *Reputation*. Its rosy stage sets and limited-invite shows seemed designed to project Swift's new confidence, her delight in the life she had built for herself in London, and her willingness to speak out (from London) about the parlous state of American politics.

Commercially, everything worked: The album release set Swift's usual records for downloads and physical sales. Critically? Not so much. The first single, "Me!" threw the kitchen sink at its listeners, with a guest vocalist (Brendon Urie from Panic! at the Disco), a military snare drum, a vocoder, backing vocals full of soulful long *o*'s and *e*'s, and the forced positivity associated with Disney anthems. The whole thing feels like very expensively made children's music—the kind parents buy for their kids, not the kind kids make. And Swift seemed to know it. The initial version of "Me!," released as a single, had Swift proclaiming, "Spelling is fun!" and Urie explaining, "You can't spell awesome without me!" So many listeners hated it that Swift removed the exchange from the album version—the only such post-release edit Swift has ever made without obvious ethical reasons.

"You Need to Calm Down"—the second advance single—displays a similar confidence, even as it takes, or tries to take, political stands. The midtempo anthem urges fans to shun internet bullies, reject homophobia, and avoid joining online pile-ons. Social media junkies should stop "obsessin' about somebody else," and nobody ought to get angry over the mere existence of queer people: "Why are you mad when you could be GLAAD? / . . . Shade never made anybody less gay!" The song surely turned some Swifties on to the existence of GLAAD, formerly the Gay and Lesbian Alliance Against Defamation, a well-known advocacy group.

The whomping disco backbeat of "You Need to Calm Down" could have fit on *1989*; it's a logical extension of the queer-friendly vibe in "Welcome to New York." Unlike "Welcome to New York," it speaks to the haters, but like "Welcome to New York," it seems unaware of its privilege. It's perhaps the safest possible stand for Swift to take, standing up (as GLAAD does) for visibly queer—and successful—people in media, rather than, say, for incarcerated people, or undocumented immigrants. And it's a stand that would not make her many enemies. Cisgender, heterosexual people in the entertainment industry may not socialize knowingly with unhoused people, nor with undocumented immigrants, but they will certainly know plenty of queers. Public figures can, and do, stand up for queer and trans people without much questioning class, or racial, or institutional, or economic privilege. That's what, for example, the US Supreme Court did in *Obergefell v. Hodges*, the 2015 decision that greenlighted same-sex marriage, and in *Bostock v. Clayton County*, the 2020 case that established some antidiscrimination protections for gay and trans Americans.

When Taylor Swift writes about body image, and bullying, and public shaming, she's writing about what she knows. Tying those topics to anti-gay prejudice, though, Swift ended up reeling in something attractive but shallow, a shallowness only underlined by the candy-colored, guest-star-packed video for the song, with cameos from the influencer Todrick Hall and Tan France from TV's *Queer Eye*. "You Need to Calm Down" tells haters, homophobes, and online bullies that they just "need to calm down," as if a period of peace online would make all the prejudice simply fade away. The video portrays haters as deplorables, unwashed hicks from a literal trailer park, carrying poorly made protest signs outside a fabulous same-sex wedding. The wedding itself gives us spiffy cerulean suits, then a parade of drag queens, matching Swift's line "we all got crowns." Rich, colorful Hollywood types (the video implies) accept queer and trans people, while bigots are dirty hillbillies in trailers. Who would you rather be?

What if you live in a trailer? What if you're poor and rural and also gay? As politics, it's (at the least) unfortunate, in the same way as presidential candidate Hillary Clinton's 2016 remark about the "basket of deplorables" who supported her orange competitor. The song is an earworm, but it's not much of an argument. Nor does it invite us—as all Swift's best songs do—to see ourselves effectively in it. Swift defended "You Need to Calm Down" in an interview on the grounds that at least she made an effort. "I didn't realize until recently," Swift said after *Lover* came out, "that I could advocate for a community that I'm not a part of. It's hard to know how to do that without being so fearful of making a mistake that you just freeze."[3]

Her fear of making mistakes—her sense that everyone's watching—gave her the subjects for other, stronger songs, on *Lover* as on all her other albums. The problem with "You Need to Calm Down," and especially with its video, has less to do with appropriation than with social class. If all gays and trans people look glamorous, then if you're not glamorous, maybe you're not really trans (a suspicion that kept me from coming out for years). Portraying all the homophobes as hillbillies lets high-class, well-dressed bigots off the hook. It also creates a no-win situation for rural, poor, or scruffy queers. What can they do? Will Todrick and company care about you? In those clothes? It's not a problem Swift chose to solve. (The singer who's solved it best remains Adeem the Artist, a trans and nonbinary songwriter with a working-class background and a sharp sense of humor.) But it's a problem that a stronger song, or another video, might have noted. Instead, the song treats anti-queer prejudice as just another subcategory of online bullying, and the classism passes without comment in a video that seems both hurriedly scripted and expensively made.

Swift's strongest political songs speak to social problems she has personally experienced: online bullying, but not homophobia; social exclusion and body-shaming, but not class prejudice; casual contempt for successful women, especially from powerful men who assume that men are, or should be, in charge. That's why "The Man" works so well, on the record and as a video. Swift, in 2019, could not credibly claim that patriarchy had kept her from success. "The Man" claims instead that patriarchy prevents her from enjoying success, that its slings and arrows and double standards—which keep other women down—exasperate and exhaust her. "The Man" here means both white capital and power ("sticking it to the Man"), and an admirably suave individual ("You the man! No, you the man!"). It also means recognizing the double standard: Men are "playing the field" rather than refusing to commit; "complex" and "cool," not distant or hard to read; "fearless leaders," rather than pushy, bad listeners.

Above all, "the man," and manhood, mean security—social and emotional, not just financial—that America will not let women have. You can be Taylor Swift and succeed. But you can't be Taylor Swift and feel secure. And you shouldn't have to be Taylor Swift in order to succeed as a woman in a male-dominated world. That's what "The Man" says—and it's funny, even sarcastic: "When everyone believes ya," the song asks, "what's that like?" People keep doubting her wins, undermining her agency, shaming her for her obvious success. We might remember our own encounters with male chauvinism, at least if we know what it's like to be non-male. These protests—all offered in first person, as complaints from Swift herself, over the simple pulse of a disco beat—never mention the wider political climate of 2018–2019, but anyone who had read headlines would see the links. The most famous, most arrogant, rich man in the world, at the time, was President Donald Trump, who boasted in the infamous Access Hollywood tape that he could "grab 'em by the pussy . . . When you're a star, they let you do it." Was he a real man? Was he The Man?

Swift's most pointed political song came with what might be her strongest video. A bearded, suited-up, white bro ("Tyler Swift") strides confidently through Swift's New York. He gives orders at his office, manspreads, lights a cigar on the subway, and pees on a tile wall whose graffiti lists Swift's albums, including the mythical, never-released album *Karma*, alongside a sign banning scooters (i.e., Scooter Braun). "Tyler" then reappears on a yacht, with champagne, surrounded by women in yellow bikinis, "just like Leo in San-Tropez." He rages on court like John McEnroe, and no one minds. In old age, he marries a young woman, and the bridesmaids applaud. Tyler gets to act out his anger, to own his space, and to act adorable too. He's even the World's Greatest Dad, as a banner says, taking his little blonde daughter to Washington Square

Park while women ooh and ah (and he takes a cellphone call). Who wouldn't envy this kind of power? Who wouldn't feel connected to the other people—almost all of us—who've never experienced it?[4]

The people around this Man assume he's in charge. The same people—industry people, bigwigs, journalists, men—have not made that assumption about Taylor Swift. She told CBS News that even as late as *Lover*, she would "always have somebody saying 'Does she really write the songs?'" "A man does something, it's strategic," she continued. "A woman does something, it's calculated. A man can react; a woman can only overreact." When the song ends, the video continues, and the man playing Tyler comes up to Taylor in her director's chair, asking her whether he hit the marks she set. She asks him to play it sexier and "more likable."[5]

Then, over the credits, we see how makeup artist Bill Corso and his colleagues turned Taylor herself into Tyler. "Putting on the makeup . . . took five hours every morning," Taylor says in a behind-the-scenes video. "I've never thought about how men walk," she added, but to play the character, she had to learn, with the help of movement coaches. Trans people who want to pass (that is, who want nobody to notice we're trans) think about such things constantly. So do certain actors, and dancers, and movement coaches. Swift—and many cisgender fans—do not. And if the results of the video turn out comedic, they also make in reverse the point Simone de Beauvoir made in the 1950s: One is not born a woman, *or a man*. We learn, and make, our genders. But we do not make them just as we please. We can aspire to Swift's level of power, to her skill at assisted mimicry, in this video, in this song, and anywhere else. We might also see ourselves in her sense of how much easier men have it, how many contradictory rules about being likable, and sexy, and confident, and yet pliable, both men and women expect women to obey.[6]

"The Man" speaks to one aspect of American politics, one aspect of Taylor's life, albeit an aspect that tints everything: gender-based prejudice. "Miss Americana and the Heartbreak Prince," another song about politics, tries to do more. Cowritten with Joel Little (who worked frequently with Lorde), the song returns to Swift's early association with high school love and high school drama in order to envision the modern, adult Taylor as a "homecoming queen," "lost in the lights," afraid. Rather than projecting cheery confidence (like "You Need to Calm Down," like "Me!") or broadcasting sarcasm (like "Blank Space," like "The Man"), it's an echoey, slow-building song, one of Taylor's most vulnerable, about suspicion, and self-suspicion, and fear. The version of Taylor in the song, despite her acclaim, says that she's "feeling helpless" before her opponents' macho antics: "Boys will be boys then where are the wise men?"

They're nowhere, or at least nowhere near her allegorical school. Taylor's team, it seems, has lost a game, and the winners might come for her: "I saw the scoreboard / And ran for my life." Her spreading sadness threatens to "paint the town blue." She cannot (she says) trust anyone except her prince: "It's you and me, that's my whole world." Tired of high school, scared of America, this singer wants nothing more (she says through oscillating bells and bass swells) than to "run away with you." The song's allegory of high school as dangerous romance triples as an allegory of the United States under the first Trump administration. Taylor's blue team (and mine) lost the game (the election), and now her home turf, Tennessee, feels unfriendly (to her), if not perilous (to her queer and trans friends). Should she feel bad about running away (to England)? Should she have tried to stay home, or to stay in school?

The song works so well because it presents uncertainty, rather than promising victory (or a dance party). It feels real; it feels scared. That's what makes it relatable. The billionaire singer faces no physical danger from a Trump administration, then or now, but she could lose her audience, her reputation, her psychic equilibrium, and (as we know, or should know, seven albums in) she needs our approval so she can approve of herself. And those fears—not her confidence, not her fabulous friends, not her Stella line—link her to us: We might be afraid during Trump's terms in office too. It's hardly a fight song. Its arm-pumping moments ("Go! Fight! Win!") seem sad, like we've already lost. Yet the song proved quotable anyway. The online group Swifties for Harris in 2024 used "Paint the town blue" as a slogan, while multiple political commentators, among them the cartoonist Tom Tomorrow and the political action committee for the Congressional Black Caucus, have responded to Trumpian choices with "Play stupid games, win stupid prizes," quoting another line from the song.[7]

"Miss Americana and the Heartbreak Prince" hurts to hear now, just a little, and not just because its malevolent visiting team has taken over the White House again. Rather, its fight-song-gone-sour feel speaks to the frustration we might experience with even the most successful, even the most sincere electoral politics, since that part of life will never not be a contest, a zero-sum game: Someone will always win, and someone will lose. The game never ends, unless the democracy falls. Sadder still, the song suggests that it can find no better model for romantic love than a zero-sum game, a high school popularity contest, or (at best) exile together when you and your sweetie know you've lost the game. The song thus hints at explaining why Swift moved to England: She's the disappointed, disgraced, scared former homecoming queen of America, unwilling to stay in a place that feels so hostile because it once promised her so much. As Swift says on "Death by a Thousand Cuts," alas, "it was a lawless land." The musical structure in "Miss Americana" mimes disappointment, too: The song opens its verses on B minor, but the chorus resolves to G. In classical music terms, that's i-VII-VI: a deceptive cadence in a minor key, and an ending that doesn't feel like the end.

"Miss Americana," though it's not track five, feels like the centerpiece for the album, because it puts all the album's moving parts uneasily and unhappily together: Swift's new attempt to make political statements in the first Trump era; her interest in childhood and youth and its tropes (in this case, high school), now that she's no longer so young; and her attempt, unstable as it might be, to make a forward-looking album about the wonder of her British love. The song works so well because the combination works so poorly. Her go-for-broke tries at optimism about romance, on *Lover*, founder on the complexity of her own feelings, and of a hostile social world.

Nonetheless, the album insists on that optimism. Chirpy and upbeat, the album's leadoff track, "I Forgot That You Existed," manages to brush off an unnamed rival, or enemy, or frenemy, or even an ex-lover: It's the sonic equivalent of a big shrug, a way to clear the air and clear the ground. Most listeners saw it as a reference to the supposedly buried feud with Kim and Kanye, though a few also saw in its danceable beats a kiss-off to the DJ Calvin Harris. What does that cleared ground, that new start, enable?

For starters, "Cruel Summer," the track cowritten with Jack Antonoff and Annie Clark (St. Vincent) that topped pop charts (thanks to streaming trends) an improbable four years after its release. It's a giddy love song, whose chorus insists "It's new!" The pre-chorus, on the other hand, delivers a prescient warning: "I don't wanna keep secrets just to keep you!" That chorus may ask us to shout it together from the rooftops, but the shouts may not save the romance, founded as it is on a love that seems not red, but "blue": secret, exciting, confusing, immediate, dependent on its initial rush, not built to last. We might see ourselves in that up-and-down excitement, or else we might wish that we could.

What's cruel about this cruel summer? Maybe its sheer insistence on Taylor's happiness, a way of protesting too much. Maybe its second thoughts about the man Taylor loves too hard and too strong, who may not reciprocate: Can she count on him? Maybe the way that this summer, and this song, and the album's apotheoses of romantic love—pink and blue this time rather than red, adult or adult-ish rather than high-school-ish—present a nearly unlivable ideal. The late literary and social critic Lauren Berlant named such ideals "cruel optimism": the very American promise that love, or history, or willpower, or something, will save us and ensure a happy ending, as long as we keep our hopes up, do everything right, and want what we're supposed to want. The equally American corollary for that ideal, of course, says that if you don't get the happy ending—if your marriage ends, if you break up, if you lose an election, if you get sick—then you've done something wrong.[8]

That cruel optimism—weighed, considered, reinforced, sometimes rejected—runs through the album's attempts to celebrate love, from the grinning evanescence of "Cruel Summer" ("I love you, ain't that the worst thing you ever heard?"), to the fragile promises of "Paper Rings," to the princely ambivalence of "False God." An album that set out to celebrate love ends up describing the obstacles to that celebration, the doubts and clouds amid the daylight and sunshine. In the same way, an album that promises pride, politics, and self-assertion in its first singles ends up describing, with "Miss Americana," with "Cruel Summer" (and other songs, too), her recurrent anxieties. Swift is simply too good a songwriter, too insightful a judge of human character, to write a whole album about the happy endings and the special celebrations that her PR, and her first few singles, presaged.

Cruel optimism, the paradox behind the love songs, also links all those songs to "Soon You'll Get Better," Swift's song about the recurrence of Andrea's cancer. Its acoustic arrangement feels out of place in this otherwise glossy collection, as out of place as cancer in Andrea's life: She will get better, Swift and the Chicks insist, "'cause you have to." The alternative would defy cosmic order and justice: Surely such a result could not stand (though it could). True love will always find a way (will it?). I won't have to keep secrets just to keep you (or maybe I will). I don't mean to undercut the power in either "Cruel Summer" or "Soon You'll Get Better," two of the strongest songs on the album (and maybe in Swift's whole catalog). Instead I mean that they work, that they stay relatable, that they're not shallow, because they're ultimately sad. They recognize the paradox of cruel optimism that their lyrics contain; they acknowledge that things might not get better, tomorrow or ever, no matter how much we care about them today. Romantic love, like everything else important in life—so "Cruel Summer" insists, in the clusters of eighth notes that make up its pre-chorus—isn't a destiny. It's more like a crapshoot, fit for devilish games of chance, and it makes "angels roll their eyes."

The more *Lover* insists on the weird contingencies in its stories— the losses in its politics, the fragility in its hookups and its memories—the more the songs bring us along and let us in. Conversely, the more the songs tell us how good Swift has it, how everything will work out okay, how we just need to keep calm and carry on, the weaker, and less coherent, the album seems. That's what's wrong with the frankly ridiculous Anglophilia of "London Boy," where her infatuation with Joe Alwyn and his apparently upper-class background ("high tea, stories from uni, and the West End") now seems skin-deep. It's what's disturbing in "Daylight," the album closer, with chugging, invariant quarter notes that point back to the synth-pop of *1989*, and a pre-chorus that makes an impossible promise: "I don't wanna look at anything else now that I saw you / I don't wanna think of anything else now that I thought of you." Who wants to live that way?

It's what's wrong, too, inside the earnest, slow title track, whose waltz time Swift first used in (of all places) "Dear John." Verbally, "Lover" is a sequel to "New Year's Day"—leaving up the Christmas lights, telling her beau how she feels at home with him. Musically, it looks to doo-wop, to 1950s pop composition, even to Alex North and Hy Zaret's "Unchained Melody," the world-famous standard performed by the Righteous Brothers and later by Elvis Presley. Swift—who wrote "Lover" on a piano before arranging it for guitar—sings about how domestic contentment feels, except that she's not exactly content. "We make the rules," she purrs. "We make the call." And yet "I'm highly suspicious that everyone who sees you wants you." She does not seem to want to give her man a moment alone, at least not before the wedding. It's almost as if she knew that this wedding (to Alwyn) would never happen—or that the word "love," the generalized, undifferentiated idea of love, means too many things. That popular usage discourages us from deciding which kind of love, which implications for "love" and "lover," we mean.

Some tension between Swift's public and private selves, the one wholly confident, the other uncertain, holds *Lover* together far more than its stated commitment to joy. The video for "Lover" even placed Taylor in a fishbowl: To love her, you have to jump in and agree to be seen. When a Tumblr user interpreted it that way ("Everyone can watch how she's living her life . . . and her lover just dives right in . . . to be with her"), Swift herself replied, "THIS WAS THE POINT THANK YOU THANK YOU SINCERELY FOR GETTING IT." The exchange feels more meaningful alongside "Cruel Summer," and "Cornelia Street," and "False God," and—in retrospect—her later breakup songs about Alwyn, "So Long, London" and "You're Losing Me." The single line "I don't want to keep secrets just to keep you," in "Cruel Summer," feels closer to the heart of Swift's imagined listeners than "You're my, my, my, my / Lover" in "Lover" ever could.[9]

Swifties know that track five on every album says something especially fraught. Here track five is "The Archer," a restrained, angry, anxious song that keeps listeners waiting for the percussion to kick in (it never does) while directing most of Swift's anger at herself. What if (as she put it in a 2019 live performance) you "have to stop yourself from thinking that the worst is always going to happen" in each romance? What if you're drawn to conflict? What happens to people who can't stop seeing erotic love as a pursuit, as a contest, as a hunt? What happens once you bag your prey?[10]

What if you are that prey? The sense of romance as a hunt, or a pursuit, goes back much further than modern pop music. Consider Sir Thomas Wyatt's sixteenth-century sonnet "Whoso list to hunt, I know where is an hind" (that is, a deer). As long as we imagine love as a deer hunt, no long-term romance—and no healthy marriage—can last. But what if we can't *not* think about it that way? That skeptical sentiment now has a lengthy name: Cultural critics call it "heteropessimism," the idea that under current conditions of dating and mating, straight and straight-passing relationships doom themselves, and romantic love never works.[11]

Swift and coauthor Jack Antonoff build frustration—with love as pursuit, with love as a universal goal—into the music, deploying common pop chords in unusual ways. Normally a pop song in a major key (here, C) would end a verse or a chorus on the tonic chord (C) or the dominant (G). Both verse and chorus end instead on the subdominant (F). Or are we in A minor (same notes as C major), with deceptive cadences (ending on F)? Who knows? The song feels uncertain, unsatisfied, unready to end, and the drone note through the whole song—a C—makes that effect more intense. So does the word "stay." It's a kind of ode to impostor syndrome, as well as a plea: "Help me hold on to you."

Another standout song about romantic love, "Cornelia Street," gives us new ways to see ourselves in its fears, as well as ways to imagine ourselves in its bliss: Its lover no sooner moves into a Cornelia Street flat than she fears she'll have to move out. Like "The Archer," it's at once a romantic overture and an ode to constant anxiety. With its phased keyboards burbling through the verses, its chorus sung all at the very top of Swift's range, the song celebrates a new home with a beau at the same time it follows Swift's anticipatory stress: What if you leave me? What if it ends? What if I have to leave Cornelia Street, the West Village, New York City, America, and never return? Swift's line "Back when we were card sharks" makes love a game too, its outcome undeterminable. She can't stop thinking about the sad possibility of a "heartbreak time could never mend," even when she's with her guy right now. A clinical psychologist might call the line—or the song—a sign of anxiety, excessive or intrusive worrying about potential future harm. If that's how mature love feels, maybe the game's not worth the candle, or the cards.[12]

Maybe it's better to play children's games. The sunniest view of romantic love on *Lover*, and the best of its several songs that suggest children's music, "It's Nice to Have a Friend," puts forward a best-case scenario, a throwback at once to "Never Grow Up" and to "Mary's Song (Oh My My My)," with actual "9- to 18-year-old singers" from a Toronto music school in the back of the mix (thrown in by Toronto-based producer Frank Dukes). The firm friendship that starts at recess and concludes with thrown rice and a wedding dress stands apart from the ups and downs of romantic love as portrayed on the rest of the album (even in the title track). Together with the frivolity in "Paper Rings," these parts of *Lover* advance a claim that feels like the flip side of heteropessimism: It's better to act like a girl (with girls' forever-friendships) than to become a woman involved with the jealousies, anxieties, and archer-target relationships that accompany conventional heterosexual love.[13]

Could the love object in "It's Nice to Have a Friend" herself be a woman? Gaylors (mentioned in the chapter on *Speak Now*) think so. Like most conspiracy theories, Gaylorism admits no disproof: It flared up again, understandably, after "You Need to Calm Down." Nonetheless, Occam's razor—the principle that the simplest explanation is usually the most likely—suggests that Swift is as straight as she says she is. Her fierce loyalty to her girlfriends, and her songs about that kind of loyalty, testify to the overlap between intimate friendship, the kind of love that means you would do anything for someone, and erotic attraction, the kind of love that makes people want to take their clothes off together. "It's Nice to Have a Friend" shows how and why so many Sapphic listeners find this apparently straight woman so relatable, because the song traces both kinds of love at once.[14]

Nor do you have to take my word for it: At this point it's easy to go online and find conspiracy-free Sapphic fans addressing the difference that Taylor's music has made. In August 2024, for example, a commenter on Threads posted that "coming across Taylor Swift's discography through a queer lens in 2021 changed so much for me as a sapphic person married to a man. It gave me a portal to online queer community. It gave me space to feel and grieve my comphet indoctrination and process personal queer experiences that I didn't realize were so universal." "Comphet" here (and elsewhere online) stands for "compulsory heterosexuality," the social pressure to act (and even to consider oneself) straight. Swift's music becomes an antidote to compulsory heterosexuality. Her work brings women together in spaces where women's experience becomes the norm, and men—no matter how hot—feel like guests, or exceptions. Community around that music has let countless women figure out how they really feel about other women, whether they want to kiss other women or (as seems to be the case with Taylor) hang with our besties but date only men.[15]

Lover may be—as the saying goes—a mess, but for many Swifties it's *our* mess. I know people who say it's their favorite album. It's incoherent, manifesting, replicating, and critiquing the very American summery optimism of smiling faces and inevitable happy endings, mixing dance-floor-ready bops and blares with melancholy, drumless electro, and both with ukuleles, in a way that bespeaks not growth and striving so much as confusion. The album speaks out from a position of power against the Trumpian politics that hurt the vulnerable, the politics that also made even Swift feel undermined, insulted, and sad. And it looks back sweetly at friendships, and at sounds, from childhood, while promising wedding bells. On its weakest tracks ("Me!," "London Boy"), Swift sounds too close to perfect, too unlike us. Few of us can define ourselves solely (as Swift's prologue to the album told us to do) through what we love—we're defined, alas, by our anxieties, and our wounds, and our unkept promises, and our failures too.

Those definitions found their way into the messy and various sounds in the album's high points: "Miss Americana and the Heartbreak Kid," "Cruel Summer," "The Archer." And those high points kept Taylor visible as someone who could reach out even to listeners who outwardly weren't much like her: to people feeling trapped, as the expat Swift could never be, inside Marsha Blackburn's Tennessee or Donald Trump's America; to Sapphic fans; to working stiffs, stay-at-home moms, underemployed post-adolescents, and anyone else who could never even pretend to be The Man.

Swift's non-*Lover* projects of 2019 also set her up, anomalously, as unlike her listeners, distant from our concerns, even when they offered up clean fun. In other words, they're a mess too: Most of them ended up (at the least) critically unsatisfying, even while Swifties, as ever, admired and bought them. (We might see in them, and in Swift's *Lover* era generally, what the business writer and Swift expert Kevin Evers calls "premium-position captivity," when a brand, or a company, or an artist, becomes so dominant that they're not sure what to do next.) "Christmas Tree Farm," Swift's holiday single for 2019, alluded to the actual Christmas tree farm in Wyomissing where she grew up, where she once had to take moth cocoons down from the trees. But the song depicts no cocoons, no labor, and no difficulties on the way to Swift's imagined family: It's just an orchestrated, glossy, terribly catchy Christmas hit, closer to Mariah Carey than to Dolly Parton, or to the real-life Christmas that some of us dread.[16]

Swift's *Lover* era also included her last (as of 2025) appearance in a scripted Hollywood film: the CGI-filled movie version of Andrew Lloyd Webber and T. S. Eliot's *Cats*. This time, at least, she stood for idiosyncrasy: Swift's character, Bombalurina, descends from a high ceiling, rides a crescent moon, and sprays what appears to be aerosolized catnip over a crowd of fellow felines as she sings a tribute to Macavity, the master criminal who can steal anything—even, perhaps, his own masters. "I loved the weirdness of it," Swift said later. The number (if not the whole film) merits watching, if only to hear Swift assume a synthetic upper-class English accent for the first and maybe the last time in her career—another element, perhaps, in her temporary adaptation to London joy with her London boy.[17]

Lover holds more songs than any previous standard edition of a Swift album: nineteen, to the fifteen on *Red*, fourteen on *Speak Now*. It arguably has more emotional range, because it's sillier ("Me!") and just as deep ("The Archer"); just as high-energy ("Paper Rings") and at least as sad ("False God"); extremely electronic ("Cruel Summer") and old-school acoustic ("Soon You'll Get Better"). Bonus tracks on the deluxe edition held no new compositions, just piano demos of "Lover" and "I Forgot That You Existed." It does not tell a story, and it does not hold together around a style, any more than the concept of happy endings, romantic love, and pair-bonded bliss hold together unquestioned and unexamined for those of us who want to pursue real-life love.

The album as a whole, though, does tell us where Swift preferred to stay: in London, with her sweetheart; visibly proud, after hiding before *Reputation*; in clear control of her future, and her work, and willing to speak up about it. That kind of self-mastery—who wouldn't aspire to it?—shows up in one more Swift rarity from this period. After leaving and denouncing Borchetta and Big Machine, but before she began her re-recordings, Swift refused requests to use her music on TV, in films, or in advertisements, lest Big Machine benefit. She would be complex, and cool, and in total control, just like The Man.

When Swift did license her own rendition of "Look What You Made Me Do," for the television show *Killing Eve*, she made available a re-recording under the band name "Jack Leopards and the Dolphin Club," with vocals by Taylor's younger brother, Austin. "Why would Swift start a fake band to release versions of her old music?" quipped the journalist Jael Goldfine. "So she could get the song on TV without Braun earning a cent." The fetching and haunting result also adopts another genre Swift never attempted before: It points back to the early 1990s, when gravelly, mopey artists like Codeine and Red House Painters ruled a gloomy, as-slow-as-possible corner of the indie kingdom. The Dolphin Club version also works as a rebuke to Ryan Adams's indier-than-thou 2015 remake of *1989* (showing that Swift knows her own songs better than he does), and as one last so-there to that indie snob Jake Gyllenhaal.[18]

Swift performed at one-off events (including a concert in Paris) in 2019, but *Lover* never generated a tour, despite a planned event called Loverfest. COVID intervened. Instead, Netflix viewers could see *Miss Americana*, released at the end of January 2020. The documentary follows Swift through the writing and touring of *Reputation*, the decision to endorse Democratic candidates in 2018, the writing and the premiere of *Lover*, the making of its first two music videos ("Me!" and "You Need to Calm Down"), and the writing of her 2020 political anthem, "Only the Young." The Taylor of *Miss Americana* struggles against the older men around her for the control she craves over her life. She cares, helplessly and to excess, what everyone thinks about her: She's been a good girl, a striver, a performer, a "work person" (as she put it), for so long. She can't stop working: Why would she? She also keeps Alwyn almost invisible.[19]

Instead we see plenty of Taylor's cats, beginning with Olivia (named after Mariska Hargitay's *Law and Order: Special Victims Unit* character) walking over Swift's piano keyboard. Cats, uniquely indifferent to their public image, have played an outsized role in Swift's adult life: The cat's oblivious cuteness contrasts with Swift's drive to be good, to look good, maybe to do good. "My entire moral code, as a kid and now, is a need to be thought of as good," she tells director Lana Wilson in *Miss Americana*, conflating (as many of us do) being a good person, being good at something (like singing or songwriting), and being seen as good (keeping a good reputation). "The main thing I tried to be was, like, a good girl. . . . That pat on the head was all I lived for." No wonder she "became the person who everyone wanted me to be," "living for the approval of strangers."[20]

Miss Americana seems to tell the story of how Swift learned to make her own decisions (even when her father objected), and to love herself. It certainly tells the story of the trough she experienced after 2016: "I just wanted to disappear. Nobody physically saw me for a year." It shows the effect of her countersuit, resolved in her favor in the summer of 2018, against the DJ who sexually assaulted her in Denver. "Something is different in my life, unchangeably different," after Denver, she tells Wilson. "No man . . . will ever understand what that's like." The film then shows how she reacted by crafting her own narrative about her reemergence: The documentary, once released, and the decision to enter political life—as shown in the film—in fact brought her approval, and praise.

None of those phenomena mean that her decisions were staged, or contrived, or fake. Indeed, the documentary—like the song that shares its title, and like "The Man," and like the video for "The Man"—explains Swift's no-win situation. Once people start alleging that you're fake, or constructed, or calculating, or artificial, there's no way to prove otherwise. Anything you do to show that you're real, that you make decisions against your own interest, that you're vulnerable or messy, can look to hostile observers like just another calculation. At some point, if you can (a big if), you have to stop caring what they think.

Those attempts don't work. She still cares! But the attempts let *Miss Americana* hold together as a film, in the way *Lover* never does as an album. They make *Miss Americana* more clearly relatable, and more clearly aspirational, too: Imagining, and seeing, how it feels to be this touring superstar, we might also liken her fear of exposure, her fear of disapproval, her wish to be everything to everyone, to our own. It's hard to imagine watching the film without gaining sympathy for Swift's dilemmas, even as it depicts her privilege: Who else gets to take her cat on a private plane? Who else has survived and thrived under so much constant pressure to look good, to sound good, to be good, and brought that sense to so many listeners who welcomed her as a role model, as an articulate example? And who else has demonstrated so well—almost despite herself—the divide between public professional and private romantic life, able to triumph, in bright colors, to fall and rise again, in the former, while the latter remained such a tough row to hoe, a source of light still half-hidden behind morning clouds?

Miss Americana concludes with the writing of "Only the Young," another explicitly political song; the finished composition plays over the credits. Swift never released it on an album, and no wonder: It wouldn't have fit at all on the folky, angsty, mostly acoustic pandemic albums, or amid the angsty personal electronics of *Midnights*, or, four years later, on *The Tortured Poets Department*. The song belongs to the *Lover* era because it doesn't fit anywhere at all (nor does the song seem aware of "Only the Young," the effortlessly hollow 1988 arena rock hit by Steve Perry from Journey).

At best, Swift's "Only the Young" becomes a kind of pendant to "Miss Americana," set in a troubled school, but addressed to the students, who "brace for the news" and "go to class scared wondering where the best hiding spot would be." Swift tells her audience, with a hope she may not quite believe, that "only the young can save us," implicitly because the Democratic candidates and causes of 2020 need the youth vote. Then the song says, over a resonant, trebly held tone like an orchestral celesta, that "only the young . . . can run." Where would they run? Would they, instead, run for office? Maybe they should: The admirable organization Run for Something, founded in 2017 and still active in 2025, encourages hopeful progressives to run in local elections, and has amassed quite a record of helping them win. But that's not what Swift's chorus comes out and says. She sounded more believable, more sympathetic, and closer to her listeners in "Miss Americana and the Heartbreak Prince," in another line from the new song: "Darling, I'm scared."

9

FOLKLORE

What did Taylor Swift's biggest fans have in common with Taylor herself in 2008? The answers seem clear: They were teens and tweens, concerned with self-image, friendships, dating, and the personality-crushing drive for success and approval that shapes so many modern girls' lives. What did her fans share with her in 2012 and 2014? They were, or wanted to be, or wanted to learn about, young people stepping out into the world, navigating romance without being consumed by it, trying to live in the moment, to imagine being twenty-two (even if they were twelve, or twenty-eight, or seventeen). What did fans share with Taylor in 2019, as of *Lover*? Less than before, or so the album implied: Avowedly optimistic, in fact all over the place, at once a document of expatriate privilege, gleeful shouting out loud, and look-over-your-shoulder fears, *Lover* made Swift's direction hard to see.

Maybe her stardom had made her, at last, inaccessible; maybe, now that she'd recovered her reputation, we would have trouble relating to her.

COVID-19 took care of that problem, and fast. Swift started writing *Folklore*, and finished writing its sequel, *Evermore*, while she—like almost everyone else in the developed world—spent month after month stuck at home or else alone in the great outdoors, prevented from touring, or clubbing, or undertaking anything but the most meticulously planned travel. With limited access to sophisticated studios, and no in-person collaborators except for Joe Alwyn (credited on the albums as "William Bowery"), Swift had to reset her songwriting process to something like the acoustic guitar and piano she used as a teen (along with Jack Antonoff's and Aaron Dessner's electronic backing tracks). Swift had become, suddenly, much more like us.

"The pandemic and lockdown runs through this album like a thread," Swift says in the 2020 documentary about *Folklore*, *The Long Pond Studio Sessions*. "It's a product of isolation." Her tour dates got canceled: She had no public appearances to plan, and nowhere to go, and nothing to do besides write songs. And like so many of us, she wanted to think about something besides her own life, something besides quarantine, and stay-at-home orders, and tests for COVID-19, something that would get her imagination, if not her body, out of the house. That's what she did on *Folklore*, and again on *Evermore*, making up characters, allegorizing her own life, and giving her listeners ways to look back, and other scenes to consider.[1]

Along with the shift to characters and storytelling came a shift in textures and arrangements. *Folklore* and *Evermore* fall into three related modern genres: folk, with traditional song structures and acoustic instruments (think Joan Baez, or Lori McKenna); indie-folk, with the same instruments but odder structures (think Elliott Smith or the Mountain Goats); and folktronica, which mixes folk with electronic accompaniment (think Sufjan Stevens). The albums thus incorporate instruments and textures that Swift's earlier models James Taylor or Joni Mitchell would recognize. They offer music for listening, not for dancing; music for thinking, not for celebration; music that comes off as adult, rather than teenage (even when it portrays teenagers); backward-looking or pastoral, rather than futuristic; meditative and deliberate even when its tempo picks up. Rather than bounding across the ocean to the West End for her London boy or taking to an arena stage with her cobra, the Taylor Swift of *Folklore*, and then of *Evermore*, could join us in our lonely living rooms. It was a radical change, in some ways a step back to Nashville. It brought Swift's persona, and Swift's voice, closer to us than anybody would have predicted in 2019.

It also made for an album almost unrelievedly sad: Almost every character Swift portrayed on *Folklore* either felt rejected, or faced down waves of anxiety, or wanted to run away. The same album, released in a "normal" year, might have come across as a downer. In the time of quarantine, though, when everyone felt stripped-down, isolated, and already glum, it worked as uplift, taking us away from our locked-in, indoor lives. This melancholy collection of home recordings and long-distance collaborations, characters, reminiscences, and made-up scenes generated some of Swift's most thoughtful moments and most loved hits. Reviewers threw all the stars they could find at the album. As Dave Fawbert, founder of a club event called Swiftogeddon, told the *Guardian*, "All those 50-year-old men who dismissed her were forced to admit how good she was." She wasn't, especially, making music for them. But she was making music, for the first time, in alliance with their favorite artists, including not only Dessner, from the band the National, but also another sad indie-folk titan, Justin Vernon, from the band Bon Iver.[2]

That music might have portrayed her own life, but it also let her bracket that life. "This was the first album [where] I've ever let go of that need to be 100 percent autobiographical," Swift says in the film *The Long Pond Studio Sessions*. "I was watching movies every day. I was reading books every day. I was thinking about other people every day. I was kind of outside of my own personal stuff." In March and April 2020, very few people wanted to stay inside their personal stuff, and even fewer had brand-new, exciting personal stuff to relate. The streets looked empty. So did the bars and the schools. There was no place to go out dancing, and no one could dance with you, unless you had Dance Dance Revolution at home. "Picking up a pen was my way of escaping," Swift herself told fans, in the letter that came with physical CDs. The Swift of *Folklore* might have endorsed Willa Cather's rhetorical question from 1936: "What has art ever been but escape?"[3]

So why—if that's the goal—would folklore, or folk instrumentation, suit? Of course, they fit the circumstances of Taylor's—of everybody's—isolation: It's easier to write, or make demos, or even record, at home if all you need is a piano and a guitar. Folk conventions also fit the sense of security, consolation, and pastoral that the album tried to project. The scholar Mark Slobin writes that folk music's "handmade, homespun sounds" let fans imagine an old-fashioned "face-to-face community," one that doesn't need big cities, or high technology, or fancy gathering places, in order to find support in hard times. That's what Swift's *Folklore*, with its mandolins, ukuleles, and quiet open spaces, lets us imagine too.[4]

Sometimes that's also what the lyrics say. The first five songs on the album all evoke some sort of nostalgia, some kind of history. Almost all the others look back, as she sang, on "what could have been." In "The 1," Taylor remembers tossing pennies in a pool, and "the Sunday matinee" (who, in the quarantine months, could go to the movies?), before she speculates: "The greatest loves of all time are over now." In "Exile," the character sung by Justin Vernon wants to go back to his town, but he's been kicked out. Poor guy. Poor everyone. The underrated, understated track "Peace" has Swift imagining herself as the hearth fire to her man's earthy shelter and blue soothing water. Quoting, of all songwriters, Randy Newman ("You've got a friend in me"), she proposes to start a family in the home they make together, and then asks whether their version of safety for the next generation "could be enough." She welcomes the home he makes, but she'll stay worried, just as the synthetic one-note drone at the start of the song worries itself raw throughout the otherwise guitar-oriented, campfire-ready piece. The next track, "Hoax," looks back to a place and a time when Swift, or her character, felt at home. She would prefer to stay blue, and sink into those memories, alongside the almost lullaby-like piano, rather than venture out to find something new.

Folklore presented another version of pastoral: a simpler, more rural space and time than the present, one that both the creator and the listeners recognize as a fiction. The props and settings of Nashville-based country itself, with its pickup trucks and its moonlit lakes, worked that way on *Taylor Swift*, but these settings look different, more English than Appalachian. Critics labeled *Folklore*'s genre "cottagecore," a term introduced in the late 2010s (probably on Tumblr) for an aesthetic of cozy escape, often with a farm or forest retreat. The Eras Tour even made the cottage literal, building a wooden "cabin" (Swift's term) onstage with a moss-green roof.

For all its sense of pastoral retro security—and for all its distance from rock, and dance pop, and R&B, and Nashville country—*Folklore* does not quite follow the rules that folk music purists would apply. None of the songs are traditional standards. None follow traditional ballad forms, which use only verses and choruses. Everything on *Folklore* has (at the least) a bridge. And many songs—starting with the first track on the album—depend on that bourgeois, indoor, nineteenth-century instrument, the piano. The people of *Folklore* yearn to return—and to bring us, their listeners—not to the preindustrial past, but to the life they might have lived in previous years, either as characters or as listeners. The lucky ones do return, as in "Cardigan": "You'd come back to me." The unlucky ones live in isolation, as in "Exile," where Justin Vernon's startlingly low male voice—at the bottom of his own range—makes Taylor's alto seem even farther away.

If anything Swift wrote before the pandemic anticipates the goals she set on *Folklore*, it's not a song on an album; instead, it's "Safe and Sound," from the soundtrack to the first *Hunger Games* movie (2012). "Just close your eyes and you'll be safe and sound," Swift and Joy Williams croon over acoustic guitars and, jarringly, cymbals, while military drum sounds grow in the background. If you know the story of the *Hunger Games* trilogy you know that this safety won't last. You also know that the tenderest moments in the first *Hunger Games* book, and the movie, show the teenage Katniss Everdeen taking care of vulnerable younger girls. Fan-made videos, easily found online, layer Swift's song (which never appears in the film) over the scene where Katniss comforts the dying Rue. "Safe and Sound," in other words, speaks to vulnerability and care, and especially to the way that girls can care for one another when men, and women, and the entire outside world, cannot.

In this way, too, it looks forward to the pastoral care, the retreat and the safety, of *Folklore* in a family (as in "Peace"), or in a couple (in "Cardigan"), or between girls (in "Seven"). "Seven"—much discussed, especially among the Gaylors—looks back to the times when Taylor (or her character) felt strongest, the days when "I used to scream ferociously," as the song puts it, before she learned to control herself for adults. In those days when two girls, taking refuge in nature, on swings above creeks, could protect each other for good. "Seven" also looks back to the earliest homosocial bonds that girls (including Sapphic girls) remember, the feelings you have before you can give them names: You just want to sail away and be pirates. The piano doubles the vocals at the beginning, as if to say, Please let these two friends stay together (just as the piano stays with the words). Please let them both get away. The other girl had to hide, from her dad, in the closet.

Maybe she later came out of that closet. You don't have to be a Gaylor to find queer subtexts here. In "Seven"—as in "Safe and Sound," as in "It's Nice to Have a Friend," but more so—Swift's music represents, for teens and for grown-up women, the kind of solidarity that we get told to give up as we mature into compulsory heterosexuality, i.e., learn to date men. The song implies not just love between girls, but also youth and safety and shelter, as from an abusive household. The British television show *Heartstopper*, whose plots consist entirely of queer teen romance, picked up on the vibes in that *Folklore* song: "Seven" plays in the background during the finale of Season 2 as the character Darcy flees her homophobic, bullying household and moves in with her girlfriend Tara, who happens to keep a *Folklore* poster on her bedroom wall.[5]

Most of *Folklore* envisions made-up characters, or characters who might well be made up (no one knows if the girl in "Seven" is real). Most of *Folklore* tells melancholy stories. And most of *Folklore* works, one way or another, as pastoral escape. That does not mean all its songs celebrate solidarity among women and girls. "Illicit Affairs" looks back on a high-energy romance that required marital infidelity. It speaks to Swift's earlier, and later, songs about love that turns red, about self-destructive passion: "For you, I would ruin myself / A million little times." Mostly, though, the song invites us to imagine the entire arc of a romance now ended, as if we saw a 1950s weepie at 10x speed. We might feel seen, if we've wanted to ruin ourselves that way for a guy; we might also aspire to the frisson involved.

For the real heartstopper here, though, we might pick "Betty," a song that stands out both because it's so musically conventional and because it's so damn catchy. The verses add, to the very common chord progression I-vi-IV-V, the equally common descending walking bass found all over classic rock: Compare the opening of "Betty" to the beginning of Procol Harum's "A Whiter Shade of Pale," the Kinks' "The Village Green Preservation Society," or the first verse of "Stairway to Heaven." Taylor and her acoustic guitar return to this rock cliché in ways that supercharge its nostalgia. James wants to go back to the moment before he ran away with Augustine, while Betty—in the companion song "Cardigan"—wants him to keep on coming back to her.

What's aspirational about the dumb seventeen-year-old boy in "Betty"? Why do his troubles amount, for pandemic-era listeners, to an imagined shelter, a sort of escape? For one thing, Taylor frames the song so that it seems to have both high (for James) and low (compared to adult life) stakes. The worst thing James has ever done (according to James) was getting into a car with Augustine when he should have stuck with Betty. Unwise, but not exactly a global disaster (especially not if you're listening during a literal global disaster). The party, the sidewalk, the porch, the steps in "Betty" try to turn back time. The song even tries to reverse the story of Eden: James would like Betty to let him back into her garden, as if he were Eve, and Augustine with her car were the tempting serpent.

That reversal seems to work out well, and its success comes with another rock cliché repurposed to good effect, that trucker gearshift, last seen in "Getaway Car": The last chorus to "Betty" modulates a whole step up. The album also implies that "Cardigan" and "Betty" describe the same couple at different times, from different perspectives, which means that both songs point to a happy ending, for them if not for the odd woman out in "August." Taylor in *The Long Pond Studio Sessions* even confirmed it: "Betty and James ended up together." Otherwise she might not have named these characters after the children of her friends Blake Lively and Ryan Reynolds. "The names are the names of our kids," Reynolds told an interviewer in 2021, adding, "We trust [Swift] implicitly."[6]

Other songs envision other escapes. "Invisible String," another song built on a walking bass, invokes literal travel, from Nashville's Centennial Park to the English Lake District to the Spanish settings of Ernest Hemingway's *The Sun Also Rises*. Swift sets Hemingway's famous last line, "Isn't it pretty to think so?" alongside the figure of invisible string tying lovers together from Charlotte Brontë's *Jane Eyre*. Her lyrics play on our word-by-word expectations: not a chain around her neck, but around her demons; one single thread, not of wool as in the previous line, but of gold. The Dessner/Swift composition also relies on guitar strings plucked one by one, so that they sound less like the big chords of conventional folk-pop, as in "Betty," than like other instruments with other, harder strings: a banjo, or a pizzicato viola.

The pastoral feel of Swift's folk music, and the refuge we might take in even her saddest stories, amount to nostalgic escapes from a grinding present, akin to earlier writers' own choice of refuge: All these parts of *Folklore* look back not only to folk music's own traditions, but also to the English Romantic poets named at the end of the album, on the bonus track "The Lakes." William Wordsworth (who grew up around there) and Samuel Taylor Coleridge (who did not) moved to the northern mountainous district of Cumberland, England—the Lake District—in the late 1790s, fleeing the crowds, the hurry, and the political persecutions of London in the years after the French Revolution. The song also remembers Swift's own holidays, with Harry Styles and then with Alwyn, in Cumberland. As she explains in *The Long Pond Studio Sessions*, "When we first went [to the Lake District] I said, 'Man, I could see this! You live in a cottage and . . . of course they escaped like that!' . . . The Lakes is really talking about people who hundreds of years ago had the same exit plan."

The song offers shelter from all sorts of modernity: cities, crowds, packed schedules, and paparazzi, "hunters with cell phones." Wordsworth wanted to flee similar scourges. His preface to *Lyrical Ballads*—written in 1800, revised in 1802—can sound like a modern curmudgeon attacking social media: "A multitude of causes, unknown to former times, are now acting with a combined force to blunt the discriminating powers of the mind and, unfitting it for all voluntary exertion, to reduce it to a state of almost savage torpor." Life in cities, with boring jobs, Wordsworth believed, "produces a craving for extraordinary incident which the rapid communication of intelligence hourly gratifies," along with a "degrading thirst after outrageous stimulation," made worse by new (printing) technology, newspapers and pamphlets: the 1790s version of Twitter.[7]

"The Lakes" looks back acoustically too. The opening figure, likely a Mellotron, evokes schmaltzy pre-rock pop of the sort that Taylor's grandmothers (and mine) might have enjoyed; so do the strings in the outro, both pizzicato and bowed. The first finished version, released in 2021, used even more strings, and more electronics. Swift and Jack Antonoff assembled this many-layered version, choosing retro sweetness over simplicity, then stripped it down to bring out a folk feel. Swift's Instagram post, on releasing the sweetened version of the song, looked back at the lockdown months with a kind of nostalgia: "It's been one year since we escaped the real world together and imagined ourselves someplace simpler," where "it's just you and your imaginary cabin and the stories you make up to pass the time"—stories, in her case, about "Rebekah, Betty, Inez, James, Augustine, and the lives we all created around them."[8]

It's hard to overstate how welcome the pastoral atmospheres, the nostalgic instrumentation, the faraway stories, of *Folklore* felt in mid-2020, when so few other stories—besides the pandemic—seemed to change most listeners' daily lives, when so many of us felt stuck in the house. It's easy, though, to overstate—Swift herself, in interviews, has done it—the distance between the characters Swift created for *Folklore* and the concerns of Swift's own life. "This Is Me Trying" records a collapsing relationship, but it also grows out of a wish that all good girls share: If only the world would reward us for our effort, our diligence, our earnest attempts to please. The song radiates solidarity between Taylor and other lonely would-be overachievers: I worked so hard to build this romance. Why won't my partner give me an A? That same sense of futility, an immense effort wasted, animates the church organ, processed vocals (à la Imogen Heap), and funereal imagery in "My Tears Ricochet," the first song Swift wrote for *Folklore*, and one of the roughest. This version of Swift can never go home, no matter how she tries.

Other versions of Swift, and stand-ins for Swift, on *Folklore* look back to their own escapes. By the end of the 2010s she kept up several residences, in Nashville, in England, in New York City, in Los Angeles, and one on the Rhode Island seacoast, called Holiday House, the site for the Fourth of July parties she threw from 2013 through 2016. "The Last Great American Dynasty" tells the story of the mansion's previous occupant, the heiress Rebekah Harkness, one among several racy, rule-breaking, high society women who have found their way into Swift's songs. Harkness's second husband, "heir to the Standard Oil name and money," married her in 1947; he moved with her from St. Louis to Rhode Island and then, in 1954, dropped dead. Rebekah responded by turning Holiday House into the performance space, decadent party site, and fairyland that she had always wanted. It's true that she "filled the pool with champagne," adopted and then abandoned whole ballet companies, dyed a rival's pet green, and spent down almost all her fortune by the end of her life.

"All the sensible things I've tried to do have turned out to be a mess," Harkness told a journalist in 1965. "So I decided, 'Why not do what I want?'" And she did. Craig Unger's 1988 biography of Rebekah Harkness, *Blue Blood*, makes her life look horrifying and cruel. She neglected her children, formed life-wrecking prescription drug habits, and indulged her pointlessly wasteful whims. One of her children took her own life; another went to prison for murder. A severely disabled grandchild, rejected by Harkness's young lover, seems to have been left to die. But "The Last Great American Dynasty" makes Harkness seem more admirable than sordid. In Swift's version, Harkness "had a marvelous time," and ruined only things (such as her reputation), not people or lives. It was the kind of time, and the kind of party, that those of us listening to *Folklore* during the lockdown months could only imagine.[9]

The idea of escape means more when you know what you want to escape from; pastoral means more when you know what kind of modern life you mean to keep out. And characters created to be unlike you,

FOLKLORE

to pursue lives unlike your own, work best when you can also describe your own life: what you have, what's missing, what you think you need. That's what happens in one song from *Folklore* that's clearly and obviously about its real-life singer, Taylor Swift, and about the real-life sadness of staying home.

That song is "Mirrorball," and it's one of her finest. Mirrorballs suggest, for most of us, nights out in discos, the *Saturday Night Fever* movie from 1977, or the Bee Gees' "Stayin' Alive." They're sparkling globes that represent the world, and we learn to dance in their shiny lights. That's what they mean, for example, in an earlier autobiographical song called "Mirrorball," by Everything but the Girl, in which Tracey Thorn remembers going out dancing as a teen, trying to live up to boys' observations, endlessly scrutinizing herself. Taylor, though, sees herself not among the dancers, but as the ball itself. Then she sees the mirrorball in pieces: dozens or hundreds of tiny mirrors, showing you "every version of yourself" even if you gaze at them alone. Swift says in *The Long Pond Studio Sessions* that the bridge to "Mirrorball"—"They called off the circus / Burned the disco down, . . . [T]hey sent home the horses / And the rodeo clowns"—represents "one of the only times that the time that we're living through is actually lyrically addressed." She adds, "I wrote this song right after I found out all my shows were canceled."

"Mirrorball" knows what it fears, what it wants to get away from, what it's afraid to lose. The song spends a lot of time in the relative minor (on the vi chord), as if it can't know if it's going to be okay. This version of Taylor shares not just our pain but our eagerness to please, our ability to work ourselves half to death just so you'll like us, so you'll see us. It's one of her most self-conscious songs, and it offers the opposite of the advice—be yourself, be authentic, take time to reflect—that we might expect folksingers to give. Who is this character when she's not performing? She's still on that tightrope—a musical pun, since she sings about a tightrope while crossing the bridge. Can she sound natural? Or ignore her audience, even in lockdown? Not without contradiction: "All I do is try, try, try." This is her trying.

If pandemic-era Swift becomes our mirrorball, she's chosen to be whatever we want her to be, in order to show us our own best lives, keeping her own unsightly troubles hidden. Again, the parallel here lies not with earlier pop songs so much as with modern poets; again, we can look to James Merrill, another child of privilege with unimpeachable technical skill. Merrill even wrote a poem called "Mirror." The mirror speaks the poem, which begins:

> I grow old under an intensity
> Of questioning looks. *Nonsense,*
> I try to say, *I cannot teach you children*
> *How to live.—If not you, who will?*
> Cries one of them aloud, grasping my gilded
> Frame till the world sways. *If not you, who will?*

Rhyming penultimate with ultimate syllables (intensity-nonsense, children-will), Merrill's mirror wonders whether he, or she, holds any lesson, or truth, or self, inside: whether a mirror that ceases to show the viewer every version of themselves, in real time, would have anything left to do.[10]

Taylor, stranded, wonders the same thing: What can she show us? What escape can she give? Songs that would otherwise be mundane or sad or melancholy become, on *Folklore*, hopeful and nostalgic and uplifting, because they allow us to go back in time and relive what things used to be like, when you could go riding past someone's house on a skateboard and they might invite you in, when it was possible to show up at your party, when people held parties. If the album no longer feels quite as glossy, because the lockdown (though not the pandemic) has ended, the songs stick around as slices of life, pieces of realistic fiction, pieces of the broken mirrorball, and versions of partly successful escape.

On my last trip to Nashville, Bryan West from *The Tennessean* and *USA Today*—still the world's only full-time dedicated Taylor Swift beat reporter—picked me up at the airport and showed me around. The sun set before my plane came to rest on the tarmac; by the time we hit downtown Nashville, most of the restaurants and all the non-convenience stores had closed. Bryan took me to the locally owned, locally famous Baked Bear for ice cream sandwiches, then to Centennial Park, in order to show me the smooth public green space and the lit-up Parthenon, a replica of the Athenian original that looks (not coincidentally) like the Lincoln Memorial. He wanted to show how downtown Nashville was not just a party town but a city with peace in its heart.

He also wanted me to see the bench in Centennial Park that the city dedicated to Taylor in 2023, after the lyrics for "Invisible String": "Green was the color of the grass / Where I used to read in Centennial Park..." It's a lovely bench, lit indirectly by streetlamps in the calm and temperate dark, set in a thick arbor, really a bower, like something out of faerie stories, all vines and curling leaves and curving softwoods. As we approached, we saw two people, both in deep shadow, curled up, silent, seated on that bench, one leaning on the other, reclining under a cloak or parka or blanket. Perhaps lovers; perhaps unhoused and asleep, and likely to spend the night. Behind us someone else—almost certainly homeless—slept on a long playground swing.

Facing that bower with Bryan, I thought about Swift's music as traditional, as parklike, as pastoral. I thought about Bryan's cool job: As he has explained on several podcasts, he left journalism years ago so he could stop chasing down crimes and fires, quit seeking to fill the "cravings for extraordinary incident" (as Wordsworth put it) that feed local news. He came back for, and only for, Taylor. I thought about the escapist ambitions—musically realized—on *Folklore*. And then I thought of a famous painting by Nicolas Poussin: In it three wandering shepherds, like something out of Italian folklore, confront a huge, carved, rectangular stone in a place that looks green and floral and heavenly, an idealized park centuries older than Nashville. The stone bears a Latin inscription: *Et In Arcadia Ego*. Generations of viewers thought the phrase escapist or congratulatory—"I, too, have been in Arcadia; I, too, have known Paradise." Then the art historian and polymath Erwin Panofsky, in 1936, corrected and reinterpreted the Latin: "Even in Arcadia, I am." Death speaks the phrase, from a tombstone; Death isn't kidding. Death and tragedy and disappointment come even for people who live in walled gardens, and teenage trilogies, and lakeside retreats. Not even Taylor can keep us away from it all.[11]

10

EVERMORE

GOOD SEQUELS DON'T HAVE TO REPUDIATE the original—they need not even be (whatever that means) just as good. They do, however, need to do something different: They can't just come off as more of the same. Released with only a few days' notice in December 2020, *Evermore* got received at first as more of the same: *Folklore 2: More Lore*. If you didn't pay much attention to lyrics or rhythms, only to instrumentation and melodies, you might mistake it for vault tracks from that melancholy, escapist, pastoral, fall-themed summer release. It's another folk, indie-folk, and folktronica album, to be sure, with the same cast of mostly long-distance collaborators: Jack Antonoff, Aaron Dessner, "William Bowery" (Joe Alwyn).

And yet it's not just more of the same: In rhythms, in character creation, in what kinds of stories it tells, *Evermore* is something new. It's not just a sequel: It's *about* sequels, about coming afterward, grieving and moving on. The songs on *Evermore*, and the stories within them, by contrast with *Folklore*, cannot or will not return to the past. Instead they try (more or less successfully) to close doors and say their goodbyes. They settle for partial wins while walking away. They mourn the dead (who cannot come back). And, in one case, they get away with a killing.

Like *Folklore*, this album arose from remote compositions: "Willow," and then *Evermore* as a project, started when Aaron Dessner sent Taylor an instrumental track called "Westerly," after her adopted town in Rhode Island. Taylor wrote lyrics to it the next day. Those lyrics emphasize endurance, bending, surviving duress. And they apply that figure to troubled romance: I am a willow, I can handle this kind of relationship, Swift's character warbles, because I don't get all my self-worth from it. If you're going to date someone entertaining, energetic, and unreliable, someone who can wreck your plans and make you miss your train, you better know that you can board the next train without him. The song also makes jokes: Can Swift, the mastermind of *1989*, come back like a nineties' trend?[1]

Of course she can. She already has. *Evermore* testified as well to Swift's inexhaustible energy: She said that she wrote it using the inner resources she otherwise would have given her stage show. "When you plan a live show, at least when I do it, I'm writing interstitial music, I'm planning this set piece goes off while this goes on while we distract them over here and this song calls for this and this song calls for that and that's all creating," she explained to the journalist Zane Lowe. "And if you take all of that away what happens? I learned that it's very possible to write more music with that bandwidth in your brain." Not all musicians design their own tours that way, as Swift has since *Fearless*. Not all musicians schedule, as Swift does, "surprise" guests, or think about how the guests interact with the fans. And that kind of planning shows how much Swift gets, how much she sometimes says she needs, from fans: Lowe asks if those needs amount to "a kind of dysfunction," and she answers "yes and no."[2]

Released at Christmastime, the album also includes Swift's best and most thoughtful Christmas song, "'Tis the Damn Season"—quite the contrast with her saccharine 2019 release "Christmas Tree Farm," as well as with her 2007 Christmas EP. The people in "'Tis the Damn Season," stuck with matching "aches," grew up together. Now they're long-distance friends with benefits that extend through the difficult holidays, but no further: "You could call me babe for the weekend." The song's protagonist, Dorothea (the girl from the song of that name) seems at home neither in this town nor in Los Angeles. Her reflections speak to anyone who has come home from college, from the big city, from far away, to high school friends who never left. The insistent 3-3-2 organization in Dessner's measures, with their one dominant note, adds to the unease; so do the rough drums (like truck tires?) in the chorus. We might see ourselves, growing up or already grown, in the song's unease around romance and family: What if our lives don't fit into their boxes? What if we only want a babe for the weekend?

What if we don't quite belong, either in our hometowns, or in LA? The uneasy, unconventional, not-quite-romance relationship the song depicts feels like an answer to the all-too-conventional family-oriented Christmastime that Swift, along with tens of millions of other Americans, envisioned growing up. The queer theory titan Eve Sedgwick wrote about the tyranny of heterosexual family life around the Christmas holidays: As December 25 approaches, "families constitute themselves according to the schedule, and in the endlessly iterated image, of the holiday itself constituted in the image of 'the' family." Christmas rituals assume that many aspects of family—"the bonds of blood, of law, of habitation, of privacy, of companionship and succor," as well as the bonds of sex within marriage and child care—go together. But they need not. You can hook up with your ex-boyfriend for Christmas, this year or every year, without trying to run your life backward, or trying to relive your past, or moving back home.[3]

As in the teenage trilogy from *Folklore*, songs with the same plots and characters deploy multiple points of view. Dorothea comes back to Tupelo for the holidays to sing "'Tis the Damn Season." Take me for the weekend, she tells her ex-boyfriend, or ex–best friend. Enjoy me for who I am. And then I'll go home. But her ex wants her back to stay. He's her road not taken, as she says over the unease of seventh and ninth chords. Writers who notice Swift's literary citations all seem to note how "Dorothea" quotes Robert Frost: "The road not taken looks real good now." But those writers only get halfway there. Taylor does not so much quote Robert Frost as quote an entire culture's previous quotations of Robert Frost, since Frost's own "The Road Not Taken" comes with an ironic, even a cynical, context: The two roads are just the same, and the choice—perhaps all choice, everywhere in human life—is illusion. The critic and poet David Orr wrote an entire book on "The Road Not Taken," calling it "the most misread poem in America," a "wolf in sheep's clothing." Dorothea is no wolf, but she has no wish to remain in her hometown's fold.[4]

Songs on *Evermore* tend to come in pairs. "'Tis the Damn Season" and "Dorothea" make a pair, as Swift's liner notes for *Evermore* confirm. She added (on YouTube) that "Dorothea went to the same school as Betty, James, and Inez" from *Folklore*. "Willow" and "Gold Rush" make another pair. With its witchy, spooky, beautiful video—the closest Taylor has ever come, visually, to her friend Stevie Nicks—"Willow" invokes sea journeys, train tracks, tree climbing, hiding, and a man who will "wreck my plans." It's a declaration of love that doubles as a declaration of resilience. Her man will come back to her, and she'll come back to him, not because she feels compelled but because she's strong enough to want to make that choice. Showing that strength, she doubles the Swift of "Gold Rush," who speaks to a much less worthy man: Nobody else can resist him, but she can. She's walking away. "My mind turns your life into folklore," she sings there. And folklore, like *Folklore*, belongs to the past.[5]

Looking back, looking forward, trying to make a break and move on, "Gold Rush" bears psychological as well as musical resemblances to Lorde's "Green Light," a 2017 song about wanting to leave an unsuitable, exciting partner, with the same backbeat and the same tempo. Jack Antonoff produced and cowrote both, and you can sing the words to one over the other, as shown in several YouTube mashups. The songs appear to use the same chord progressions, along with the same shift to a flatted seventh (a Mixolydian mode) at the chorus. And both songs marshal excitement, not in the service of a red love, but to signify a decision to leave a bad lover behind. It's a red shift away from a gold rush, if you like, or a green light for a blue streak, going away.[6]

Surviving, and mourning, a beloved elder represents another kind of going away, and there's nothing not sad about it. That's "Marjorie," Swift's elegy for her maternal grandmother Marjorie Finlay, the opera singer and TV host who became her childhood role model. "Marjorie" also becomes a kind of musical sequel, because Swift wrote it over an unused segment of the Dessner track that became the *Folklore* song "Peace." The song even samples—reuses, casts itself as a sequel to—Finlay's own vocals: "My mom found a bunch of old records, old vinyls, of her singing opera," Swift told Lowe, and Dessner mixed the vinyl into Taylor's song. Swift remembered that Marjorie "would have these wonderful parties at her house, and she would get up and sing. She always wanted to be on stage. . . . And when she would walk into a room, everyone would look at her, no matter what. She had this thing, this it-factor." The song casts Taylor herself not just as a mourner but as a kind of sequel or remake for the grandmother she remembers: Can this twenty-first-century good girl, this "work person," hold up this worthy legacy?[7]

Here no one can sidestep the identification that comes with the homage. "My mom will look at me so many times a year," Swift said, "and say, 'You're just like her,'" locating Marjorie's spirit in "some mannerism I don't even recognize." Eras Tour concertgoers in Nashville held up portraits of Marjorie en masse. The line "If I didn't know better / I'd think you were talking to me now" suits the chorus not just because the memories stay vivid but because the advice with which the song begins ("Never be so clever you forget to be kind," and vice versa) stays valid. Swift's elegy enacts the best kind of haunting (what died didn't stay dead), reinforced by the fluttering reverb: not a troubling ghost but support from the past, mixed with the sadness of knowing that she's gone.[8]

That song might even teach us a thing or two about healthy grief and mourning. Other parts of *Evermore* present themselves as lessons from Swift's reading. "Tolerate It" grows from Daphne du Maurier's modern Gothic novel *Rebecca* (1938). As Swift put it, "When I was reading *Rebecca* by Daphne du Maurier and I was thinking, wow, her husband just tolerates her, she's doing all these things to impress him and he's just tolerating her the whole time, there was a part of me that was relating to that because at some times in my life I felt that way." Du Maurier's naïve young bride (never named in the novel) follows her handsome, secretive, older husband Maxim de Winter home to his coastal estate of Manderley, where he broods, and ignores her, and seems obsessed with his dead first wife. Du Maurier's narrator wishes, early on, that she could have "bottled up a memory, like a scent. And it never faded, and it never got stale. And then, when one wanted it, the bottle could be uncorked and it would be like living the moment over again."⁹

In other words, du Maurier's narrator wishes only to relive the past. It's a bad idea, and the novel says so. "I wanted to go on sitting there, not talking, not listening to the others, keeping the moment precious for all time," du Maurier's narrator muses early on, "because we were peaceful." She wants to go back to that past because, for most of the novel's length, she tries without success to get Maxim to pay attention, to acknowledge her efforts, to reciprocate her affection. "I try every day, every time I go out or meet anyone new. I'm always making efforts. You don't understand," du Maurier's heroine tells her husband. After he spurns her openly, she thinks about their inequality: "I was too young for Maxim, too inexperienced. . . . The fact that I loved him in a sick, hurt, desperate way, like a child or a dog, did not matter."¹⁰

He could not see that she was too young to be messed with. And she remains devoted to him even after his past (spoiler alert) becomes clear: Maxim murdered Rebecca, his previous wife, jealous of her superior charisma, her (supposedly) manipulative personality, and her (apparently) many infidelities. The woman in "Tolerate It," like the narrator in *Rebecca*, displays unsettling, unending devotion, looking up to a supposedly "older and wiser" man who cannot love her back. Her insistent unease matches the irresolution in du Maurier's heroine, who flees England with Maxim hoping the truth will never emerge. The song, like the book, describes women caught in the trap of loving too much: a trap whose other name is patriarchal inheritance.

That's one way to read "Tolerate It," and to read *Rebecca*. But there is another: We may reread du Maurier's novel as what the feminist critics of the 1970s called a "Resisting Reader," celebrating the now-deceased title character. As Mrs. Danvers, the housekeeper in *Rebecca*, explains,

"No one got the better of her, never, never. . . . She did what she liked, she lived as she liked. She had the strength of a little lion, too." A tempestuous, sexually aggressive, impulsive female head of an estate, throwing great parties, maintaining a mansion, putting up with her conventional husband's opprobrium, Rebecca here echoes the "mad woman" whose claws come out in *Folklore* in the song of that name, who—in an echo of *Rebecca*'s denouement—can sink a yacht. She echoes the antiheroes and bad girls and party throwers of *Reputation*, of "I Did Something Bad" and "This Is Why We Can't Have Nice Things." And she echoes the real-life heiress Rebekah Harkness, from "The Last Great American Dynasty," though that Rebekah—unlike du Maurier's Rebecca—survived her more conventional husband and lived to do exactly as she liked.[11] That way to hear the song, and read the novel, makes it aspirational: We might want to do as Maxim's first wife did, even if we see ourselves in his second.

Hearing "Tolerate It" for the first time, you might have found the song uneasy, unsettling, unresolved, as well as sad, and not just because of its words. It deploys a 10/8 or 5/4 time signature, the first of two tracks on *Evermore* in that unusual (for Western pop music) meter. "Tolerate It" uses 5/4 all the way through, and it keeps us hanging, melodically, rhythmically, and harmonically, like waiting at a red light for so long that we start to think the signal has malfunctioned. The melodies in other 5/4 songs (Dave Brubeck's "Take Five," for example) make neat units: We can hum them and see where they end. The words and the melody in "Tolerate It" do not. The title phrase crosses a measure and ends off the beat, so that the "it" in "tolerate it," landing on *do* (the "right" note), occurs one eighth note into the measure (in the "wrong" place). And the meanings in the words prove equally disquieting. Swift's character has to "wait by the door like I'm just a kid," when the last thing she wants to be is a child (or a child bride). She maintains a fantasy of leaving, of walking away from this relationship, but she will never do it, any more than the song will resolve in conventional fashion.[12]

If *Rebecca* has another spiritual heir on *Evermore*, that song could be "Ivy," another piece of English Gothic, also about a husband and an affair. And yet the real sequel and partner for "Tolerate It" must be the other song in 5/4, another Dessner collaboration: "Closure." This version of 5/4 time finds a kind of emphasis on the beat—and a version of closure—that "Tolerate It" could not even imagine. Taylor does not need "your" closure because she's already found her own. The woman in this song tells us she's *done*, and ready for something new.

So is Swift, in musical terms. With the industrial noises and found, torqued percussion that Dessner, Swift, and new-to-Swift producers BJ Burton and James McAlister placed all over "Closure," they brought the song close to hyperpop, the self-consciously artificial, anxiety-generated, electronics-first music popularized by Charli XCX (another Burton collaborator) and promulgated—mostly by teenagers and trans people—during the quarantine (one commentator calls it, approvingly, "delusional gay screeching atop loud, sometimes unpleasant noises"). Hyperpop, at the time, sounded like moving on, like giving up on old dreams of authenticity (the kind that come with folk, and rock, and country, and hip-hop), like starting something bizarre, artificial, and new. And that kind of moving on, and walking away, and resolving to do something new, is what *Evermore* gives us: It's what sets *Evermore* apart from *Folklore*, what makes the second album, despite its folktronic overlap with the first, exciting, even aspirational, in ways of its own.[13]

That hyperpop element—below the surface in "Tolerate It" and "Long Story Short," in-your-face during "Closure"—works against the pastoral elements, the retro folk, in this second pandemic album. If folk music imagines ways to feel natural, to create face-to-face community, hyperpop imagines ways to move on and rebuild even without those things, ways to become a new person while recording, mixing, and mastering in your bedroom. Hyperpop's "heavy emphasis on glitchiness and vocal modulation gives artists room to alter their voice," as Nic Johnson wrote in 2020—the year of the genre's emergence—while the "futuristic atmosphere of the genre allows trans artists to present themselves however they want." What the genre implies, Taylor's writing comes out and states. It's about picking yourself up and moving on, remaking yourself even when it doesn't feel natural, and rebuilding even when it's hard: Don't treat me like a situation that needs to be handled, I can move on, it looks weird and awkward but I can make this happen, I don't need *your* closure, I've already had mine. Perhaps you (listener) can now imagine how it feels to get closure too.[14]

Closure need not happen so abruptly, and it does not always imply telling your ex to go away forever. Achingly paced, dominated by seventh chords, "Happiness" also harnesses feelings of coming back to something, getting past something, having done it twice. At the same time it promises its character (who has spent seven years in a now-dead romance) that joy will come again: "I haven't met the new me yet." But—the song promises, slow and stately and not quite sure of itself—that new me will arrive. Most of the vocal motifs go in tight circles: "There'll be happiness after me," for example (*mi, mi, mi, mi, do, re, do, mi*). Far sadder than "Back to December," the song stands beside that earlier hit in the kindness it shows toward a former flame.

In *Evermore*, the doublings back and imagined futures, the dyads and patient counsels, the ways of moving past and moving on, extend not just to the folktronic ventures of *Folklore* but also to Swift's Nashville past. With its brush drums and its loping up-and-down bassline, "Cowboy Like Me" could easily be, say, a Kelsea Ballerini single, or a kiss-off sequel to Swift's own "White Horse." Look closer and the song tells another story about second choices and walking away. The man and the woman in the song, hanging out in airports and on tennis courts, are not literal cowboys but gold diggers, seeking romance with wealthy hotel guests. Instead they fall for each other. Aspirational? Sure: Why not imagine falling in love at the Waldorf, and then skipping out on your bill at the Ritz? Relatable? Absolutely: These characters' uncertain situations, finances, and love affairs, during the uncertainties of the pandemic, could speak to us all. As if to emphasize its country heritage, Swift put the song in an Eras Tour mashup with "Tim McGraw" in Singapore on night six.

Evermore keeps the fictional characters coming: cowboy-fraudsters, Dorothea and her ex and his truck tires, the stealthy wife drinking her husband's wine. For a distracting, entertaining song that does not in any way fit Swift's own life, though—and for a story about getting back your own, addressing the past, and then walking away—the clear choice is "No Body, No Crime." The song, written by Swift alone, tells the story of four characters (three without names) and two unsolved killings. First, Este's husband kills her so he can move in with his mistress. Then, Este's best friend—with help from Este's sister—kills the husband and frames the mistress.

It's quite a way to move on. And it's quite an aspiration for most of us (if nobody aspired to kill an abuser, we would have, at the least, fewer true-crime shows). The story looks back to the Chicks' early hit "Goodbye Earl," whose team of women kill an abusive husband. Its sense of women's solidarity benefits from the team of vocalists: Swift and all three of the sisters from HAIM, Alana, Danielle, and Este (just like in the song). And the changing pronouns in the chorus ask how men's crimes and women's crimes show up differently in police blotters: What counts as a crime of passion? What counts as wrong? The critic Jamie Lynne Burgess has compared Swift's sense of feminine vengeance on *Midnights* to Susan Glaspell's often-staged 1916 one-act play *Trifles*. Women investigating a man's death find clues that point to his wife, but choose not to report them, because they believe he was abusing her. Glaspell's play about self-defense and domestic betrayal certainly speaks to "No Body, No Crime": Only the women understand, and they're not telling the men.[15]

Perhaps the most obvious pairing on *Evermore* comes with its bonus tracks, "Right Where You Left Me" and "It's Time to Go." The former revives a whole country kitchen of country sounds, complete with a mandolin, and its character complains about staying forever twenty-three—Swift's age when touring on *Red*. The latter, largely electronic, describes moving on. There, too, betrayal—a fake sister, a promise broken—need not be the end of a road: The green light will return. The sister albums' contrasts, their separation in terms of Swift's goals, could not end up clearer: *Folklore* presented, with characters and examples, pastoral, refuge, escape; *Evermore*, with more characters and more plots, shows how and why we need to move on.

Another kind of moving on—with a train ride—drives "Champagne Problems," a Swift/Alwyn cowrite that's light on musical innovation (a standard four-chord loop) and rich (in several senses of rich) with story. The song can look aspirational, and relatable, for the same reasons as "The Last Great American Dynasty": Almost everybody wants the champagne, but nobody wants the problems. Swift's repeated title phrase slips smoothly into the elegantly lengthy middle section, in which we learn that the bride called off the wedding. "I love a bridge where you tell the full story in the bridge," Swift told Lowe. "I'm so excited to be in front of a crowd that will one day sing 'She would have made such a lovely bride, such a shame she's fucked in the head.'" And for two years, on the Eras Tour, that's what she heard.

EVERMORE

Swift gives albums in progress code names, so that she can send informal communication about them without leaking titles. *Folklore*, as she told Jimmy Kimmel, was *Woodvale*; *Evermore* was *November*. Its sense of how to move on, to let dead things and dead people go, points back to Romantic poetry too. Consider John Keats's sonnet sometimes called "The Human Seasons" (Keats did not give it a title):

> Four seasons fill the measure of the year;
>   Four seasons are there in the mind of man.
> He hath his lusty spring, when fancy clear
>   Takes in all beauty with an easy span:
> He hath his summer, when luxuriously
>   He chews the honeyed cud of fair spring thoughts,
> Till, in his soul dissolv'd, they come to be
>   Part of himself. He hath his autumn ports
> And havens of repose, when his tired wings
>   Are folded up, and he content to look
> On mists in idleness: to let fair things
>   Pass by unheeded as a threshold brook.
> He hath his winter too of pale misfeature,
> Or else he would forget his mortal nature.

We can hope to find solace in winter, here, just as Keats did; just as the Swift of "Champagne Problems," of "Closure," offered solace in walking away.[16]

On an album about post-pastoral, closures and sequels, the title track—with its anomalous middle section, its drastic change in tempo—works as a kind of sequel to itself. "I wrote this song and these lyrics when we were coming up to the [2020] election," Swift explained to Zane Lowe, "and I didn't know what was going to happen. I was almost preparing for the worst." "Evermore" also, Swift added, remembers late 2016, when she last had trouble "finding a glimmer of hope." The song—like "Exile"—came together through collaboration: Alwyn writing the piano parts, and Swift shaping them into songs with words and then sending the results to Justin Vernon.[17]

We can hear, as the song goes on, Swift (or her character) learning to move on, and changing her mind. "Evermore" first says that Taylor's going to feel this pain forever. A low five-note descending riff almost overpowers the vocals. Then the song climbs into that sped-up bridge, with its ascending treble figure, apparently Alwyn's idea. The bridge literally changes how we, the listeners, experience time. Then, in the third verse, Swift says that she will not feel this pain forever after all. Maybe we, too, can go.

If *Evermore* says what happens after *Folklore*, what would fans expect—what could Swift have expected—after *Evermore*? Would the "normal" life of Betty and James and Inez and Dorothea and Swift herself ever return? How would it look, if it did? The songs on this album do not try to answer those questions. Instead they point to how tough the answers might be—for Dorothea, going back to LA to try (and perhaps fail) at being a star; for the bride in "Champagne Problems," heading off to who knows where; for the ex-girlfriend, who's already found her closure; and for Swift herself, who created or cocreated these songs.

That's why the saddest song on *Evermore* is not "Marjorie" (which tells us how much Swift has learned, how much stays with her), but "Coney Island." Swift's character in that duet sits on a bench alone, "lost again with no surprises," getting colder, because she's lonely, because the sun has set, because it's winter (when Coney Island crowds recede), and because Coney Island itself no longer represents a much-wanted social experience: It feels abandoned, lost in time, like the couple in the song, who used to be like "a mall before the internet." The four-chord, minor-key loop, with its two-note countermelody, props up the sense of futility. Can the people in this song, with its disused candy stands and merry-go-rounds, find a future that does not just relive the past? Can the song itself find a way to move on? Perhaps not: The variety in the vocal duet makes up for the lack of variety in that instrumental bed. As long as we stay here, nothing big will change.

Feeling stuck in the quarantines and the pandemic, stuck in adulthood, stuck in a dying relationship, stuck in the winter at Coney Island: All these things, in the song, feel like one another, and all of them feel like being stuck in a dead mall. Swift grew up in the final heyday of malls, after the internet but before the Great Recession. For her generation, "the mall is personal," often the site for "their first jobs, their first piercing, their first boyfriend, their first CD." I quote the architecture critic Alexandra Lange's 2022 study *Meet Me by the Fountain: An Inside History of the Mall*, which traces the enclosed shopping plaza from its 1950s origins, through its decades as a gathering place, to its internet-driven and pandemic-enforced decline. Lange's history of teenagers in malls cites a "popular parenting manual" by Anthony Wolf from the 1990s, *Get Out of My Life, but First Could You Drive Me and Cheryl to the Mall?* It's as if Wolf, or Lange, had heard "Never Grow Up"—or else as if Swift had read Lange.

Lange's 1980s malls figured as "an 'alternate world' in which good teens held the center—the atrium—and troublemakers held the edges: the underlit halls outside the video game arcade and the edges of the parking lot." By the time she wrote her pandemic albums, Swift's stories of teens depicted both parts of that world. Lange's good girls might meet you at the fountain, but Augustine, the bad girl in the good girl/bad girl duo of Swift's teenage triangle, would meet James semi-secretly "behind the mall." During the quarantine of 2020, of course, illicit couples like Augustine and James, or even could-be-forever teenage couples like James and Betty, had nowhere to meet at all.[18]

Swift never undertook a full-on, Britney Spears–style mall tour, but she did perform at the Mall of America in 2007: You can still find her, on YouTube, playing sped-up acoustic versions of "Santa Baby," "Our Song," and three other originals while the crowd sings along. With or without an actual mall as a backdrop, a Taylor Swift concert in 2007, or 2011, overlapped, in social terms, with a mall: a space for girls' solidarity, a third space (neither school nor home) for youth, a "practice city, training wheels for the real world" (Lange again). What if the grown-up versions of Taylor Swift and her music, made for a world without arena concerts, could no longer bring girls, or women, or people, together that way? What if this adult, folktronica, critically lauded version of Taylor, describing escapes for listeners stuck at home, has no more social force than a dead mall?[19]

Those questions predate the pandemic: They're questions we might ask, too, as we grow up, evacuating the age of high school gatherings where all teenagers, supposedly, share the same interests and concerns. We could hear questions about age and obsolescence in Swift's songs as early as "Castles Crumbling." But they got bigger, and changed her music, right around the time we all learned to mask up and flatten the curve. Staying home and writing, collaborating through backing tracks rather than live in a studio, living remotely, Swift layered the isolation that we too experienced (relatably enough) over her own fears of isolation, obsolescence, and purposelessness as a star. That's why "Coney Island," a spooky, echoey song about chills in an old relationship, about sitting next to someone and feeling far away, also refers to the mechanics of stardom: a lifetime achievement award, a podium where "I forgot to say your name."

The great folk guitarist and songwriter Richard Thompson has written that touring singer-songwriters' work requires backward looks. "A painter paints a picture, sells it to a collector . . . and never sees it again," Thompson explains in his 2022 memoir. "A singer-songwriter . . . has to take himself back every time he plays before an audience, to render parts of his catalogue. Not that this isn't a pleasure, but it is strange to have this constant reminder of where you come from." Taylor had that experience over and over during the years in which she toured, starting in 2006 and concluding in 2018. During the lockdown months, it went away: She didn't have to play "Love Story" or "Blank Space" for anyone.[20]

Instead she wrote songs, first about escape and pastoral and shelter, and then about trying to put the past in its place. She leaned into new-to-her genres—folktronica and even hyperpop—and she brought in new listeners, making contemplative music, writing for bedrooms, not for arenas or dance floors. She underlined her literary predecessors, from Wordsworth to du Maurier, commemorated family, and showed her range. You'd think—if you didn't know better—that the critical and commercial success of the pandemic albums would have left her feeling good about those months, thinking that she had little left to prove. To think so would be to misunderstand this artist, whose goals, like the ghost of her inspiring grandmother, stay alive in her head. No matter what she's done, she could always do more, show more, reach out to her audience again. And—beginning in 2021—she would.

11

MIDNIGHTS

THE FIRST ALBUM TAYLOR MADE AFTER the quarantines ended, *Midnights*, might have picked up where *Lover* left off: professedly sunny, excited about love and stardom. Instead it's all about anxieties. *Midnights*, Swift told a reporter, described "13 sleepless nights" throughout her life: thirteen worries that at some point had kept her up until dawn. Swift made from those worries a musically stark, sometimes jarring album loaded with self-diagnosis, brittle defiance, reasons to go out, and fears that could keep her home. Individual songs from earlier eras highlighted Taylor's limitless wish for approval, her need for control, her perfectionism, and her sense that success today could mean (unless she kept working at it) failure tomorrow. But with *Midnights*, the highlights became floodlights: She could almost have called it—by contrast with *Fearless—Fearful*. The theme comes with irony: How could the world's most successful pop star feel so insecure? But it's also a way to relate, a way for our anxious selves to connect to hers.[1]

Swift wrote the album during a time that looked, to the outside world, like domestic stability, settling down with her six-year partner and sometime coauthor Joe Alwyn (still credited as "William Bowery" on songs). In 2021 Swift purchased a mansion in the Primrose Hill part of London, meaning to stay there with Alwyn, who preferred London to New York, privacy to attention, staying in to going out. The electronics of *Midnights*—by contrast to the synth-based hits of *1989*, and the singles from *Lover*—seem meant for staying in too. Few of them ("Karma" excepted) seem intended for dance clubs. They're introspective, lyrics-first, bedroom listening, with models in younger artists, especially Lorde.

And that sound makes sense: An album so much about anxieties—defining hers, supporting us in ours—would of course solicit listeners who craved safe spaces, listeners who wanted to take risks but still felt unsure or alone. The life that *Midnights* records, the confidence that some of its tracks effortlessly project, and the fears that resonate around it now seem less like domestic bliss than like a holding pattern: the sounds of a self-aware star who knows her feelings can't stay under her control, a star who needs to go out and be seen, and to share her anxieties, but can't always see how to leave home.

Every sound and word in almost every Taylor song not only solicits attention but rewards it. Time that we spend on her work won't feel wasted or pointless, even if our conclusions turn out wrong. Everyday life, though, promises no such rewards. The more chaotic life seems, the more our interpretive tools get frustrated or blunted. We chalk up to malice what we should trace to incompetence, see patterns that don't exist outside our own minds, and gaslight ourselves to avoid seeing how somebody else has gaslit us, or, perhaps worse, to avoid knowing when the world is just one damned thing after another. No wonder we find relief in an artistic world, a popular and accessible one, where—as Swift puts it in "Mastermind"—"none of it was accidental." The Swiftie podcaster Vanessa Zoltan jokes—though she's not entirely kidding—that watching the end of the Eras Tour movie with her kids (who loved it; she loved it too) reminded her how carefully Swift works: "Even [in] the bloopers at the end of the movie, I was charmed and thought, I get it, you're not a perfectionist." But of course (and that's the point) she is.[2]

That perfectionism became clear, gradually, over her first nine albums, and on tour. When she wanted something to change in her music, she got it; when she toured, she designed or codesigned the shows. When she felt out of control or manipulated, she struck back, like a cobra; and when she made a public statement, a fashion statement, or a political statement, she wanted to get it just right. *Midnights* brought Taylor back to life in the studio, with as many other musicians and engineers as she chose. It also brought her back to writing songs that she could plan to perform on tour. She took that occasion to keep building intricate, structured, musically perfect pop-song worlds. But she also told us how exhausting that construction project felt—and how her detail-oriented, perfectionist models of art broke down in the unpredictability of real life.

Her first high-tech studio album since *Lover*, *Midnights* at times can feel like a palinode to it, a nightside to its intended daytime vibes (remember that *Lover* was almost called *Daylight*). *Midnights* may also salvage material from a partly abandoned album called *Karma*, supposedly started in 2016. Could "Karma," the song, have come from abandoned notes for *Karma*, the album? Swift implies otherwise, calling it "a last-minute Hail Mary," perhaps the last of the *Midnight* tracks she wrote. By far the happiest, goofiest one, too, and maybe the only cheerful one not tied specifically to Joe Alwyn, "Karma" had a delightful second life on the Eras Tour as a triumphant concert-closer. Its pop purity almost demanded dance moves, stage sets, and the occasional rewrite. When Travis Kelce entered a stadium, Swift changed the lyrics so she could sing "Karma is the guy on the Chiefs."[3]

But "Karma," with its joys (and its cat references), placed near the end of the album, seems designed as an exception, a wrap party, a special treat. Most of *Midnights* reaches toward its hearers and offers its hermeneutic friendship by sharing distresses, bafflements, scraps of insomnia. *Lover* came in soft pink and baby blue (trans flag colors, perhaps by coincidence). *Midnights* prefers stark blank-page or hospital white. Swift's essay, printed in gold in the booklet that came with CDs, wove together all her songs' titles and subjects into prose studded with rhetorical questions: "Why are you still up at this hour? . . . You've gotten lost in the labyrinth of your head, where the fear wraps its claws around the fragile throat of true love. Will you be able to save it in time? Save it from who? Well, it's obvious. From you." Can Taylor save herself from herself? Can she show us the way?

Though the young Swift never settled in Hollywood, the actor, poet, and essayist Amber Tamblyn's account of growing up there says something about the Taylor of *Midnights* looking back on her own sleepless fears. "The better an actress I was," Tamblyn remembers of her on-camera childhood, "the more I could get hired, and the more I could get hired, the more I would be praised and, ultimately, seen. This is how I learned how to be loved. Not by my parents, but by everyone." Tamblyn goes on to wonder if she damaged her "central nervous system by forcibly emoting for a living, especially during an age when the body is still growing."[4]

Swift made her resilience, her ability to evade child-star pitfalls, her executive function, part of her brand. But she, too, decided to emote on stage for a living, as well as emoting in recording studios. She chose that life over Wyomissing and normalcy. That's the point of the *Midnights* track called "Midnight Rain": "He wanted it comfortable," she sings, "I wanted that pain." Swift means the pain of always striving, never knowing whether your public success will last, and she underlines that challenge—which she chose—in musical terms, inserting coarse electronic sound effects that don't belong to the melody, and taking the vocals up sharply, a whole octave, on the word "pain."

Swift never says that she regrets the choice. Instead, she writes new songs about her ambitions, and need for attention, and her perfectionism, and their cost. Even in supposedly celebratory songs about love and romance, Swift's introspection, her perfectionism, and her sense that everyone's watching stick around as subtext. Swift said in a 2022 Instagram reel that she found the phrase "Lavender Haze" while watching the TV show *Mad Men*: It's a 1950s term for being in love, for "that all-encompassing love glow. . . . When you're in the lavender haze, you'll do anything to stay there and not let people bring you down off that cloud." She deleted the Instagram reel when she and Alwyn split. The love song announces, even insists, that Swift's attachment to her beau will survive third parties' nosy inquiries. But she can't ignore them when he's not around. "I'm damned if I do give a damn what people say," she sings in "Lavender Haze"; she just wants to "get it off [her] chest," and "get it off [her] desk," and lose herself in the haze of protracted limerence (the name for that crushed-out, early-in-a-romance feeling). But she can't lose herself, or else she won't, at least not for long.[5]

TAYLOR'S VERSION

Taylor's sense of herself as a good girl—"too good of a girl," as she sings in "Bejeweled"—would not surprise anyone who has seen *Miss Americana*. "When I was naughty as a kid, I used to send myself to my own room," she told the UK's *Daily Mail*. "My mum says that she was afraid to punish me sometimes because I was so hard on myself when I did something wrong. I haven't changed much since then." The strongest songs on *Midnights* speak most clearly to her sense of herself, her need for control, her wish to be good, and to be seen as good. They're also her most confessional. They unveil parts of her life that most stars would hide, parts that might make her seem not just vulnerable but unreliable, or self-destructive. They're parts that make her more relatable, too: Not even Taylor Swift, the world's most successful pop star, knows how to feel normal, or stay calm.[6]

Midnights also deploys, for the first time in Taylor's songbook, the professional and clinical vocabularies of mental health. A listener in 2022 might expect lines like "my depression works the graveyard shift" (in "Anti-Hero") from Halsey, or Billie Eilish, or girl in red—artists younger than Taylor, known for their confessional styles, who grew up hearing Taylor's early work. From Swift herself they feel new. The scholar Christopher Grobe has written about similar painful, shameful revelations offered by others, including poets, memoirists, and stand-up comedians. These "confessional performers," Grobe insists, "dramatize the tension between their inchoate selves and the media they use to capture them.... They promised their public a self, and they never set out to make promises they couldn't keep." The Taylor who sings "Anti-Hero" and "Dear Reader," "Mastermind" and "Maroon," wants us to know that she tries to keep every promise: She knows we have already placed our trust in her. And now—after so many years onstage, deferring or pushing away some of her anxieties—she's ready to trust us.[7]

What does she trust us with? Her fears about herself. The album's lead single (and its only pop-chart number one), "Anti-Hero," offers up not just Taylor's midnight depression, not just "covert narcissism I disguise as altruism / Like some kind of congressman," but also her bad dreams. And it circles around one insecurity that comes with any public success: The bigger you get, the more people want something from you, and therefore the less you can trust their praise. No wonder Taylor feels like an awkward figure who fits in nowhere, because she's bigger than everyone around her. There's body dysphoria here, and a great heap of impostor syndrome, as well as a way to think about Taylor's success (she is, after all, the world's biggest pop star), and an allusion to Taylor's literal height (5'10"). She fears not only that she's too big (commercially) to find peers, but also that she's too big (too adult) to stay interesting to her young fans, and too big (literally) for Western standards of beauty.

Many of us have worried, as Swift does here, that our drive to success comes from culpable narcissism. Some of us—once we acquire cultural or economic power—wonder whether we can still trust other people's judgments, or merit their love. And yet a lot of us want to be like Tay anyway. Maybe the more so because she's so good at relatability, at vulnerability, at showing us how she struggles with anxieties that must even predate her fame. "We all hate things about ourselves," she told fans, describing "Anti-Hero" on Instagram, "and it's all those aspects of the things that we dislike and like about ourselves that we have to come to terms with if we're going to, like, be this person." But how?[8]

Her answer involves crafting (with Jack Antonoff) a song with aural contours that match the discomfort she says she feels, so that we can take this journey with her, feel her coming to terms with her lowest points. The song's highest notes occur in the verses. The chorus then goes all the way down a tenth, from *mi* ("me," "tea") to *do* (the "ro" in "hero"), from the G-sharp above middle C to the E below it. Displaying her whole vocal range, along with her notable psychiatric vocabulary, Swift ends up at one of her all-time lows.

Swift wrote and directed the "Anti-Hero" video, which shows her waking at midnight, eating a smiley-face made of bacon and eggs, and running, like the girl in a horror movie, from ghosts in the home. She's saved, or rescued, or defended, by a more cheerful, more put together, more outgoing version of herself, in Spandex, who comes to the door and invites herself in. This Other Swift teaches the First Swift the blackboard lesson "EVERYONE WILL BETRAY YOU," like a manipulative best friend who tells you to trust nobody else. Oversized, a giantess, she disrupts a family dinner like a normal-sized human reaching inside a dollhouse: She's too big, in every way, to have peers or friends, let alone loving partners. It's like a bad dream. Maybe it just is a bad dream.

If the song called attention to Taylor's tendency to overwork herself, her fear of being cast as the villain, the video instead highlighted anxieties about her height and weight. The first released cut of the video for "Anti-Hero" had Taylor panicking after she stepped on a scale and saw a sign that called her "FAT." Swift removed the image after real-life people of size objected. Writing for *Teen Vogue*, Catherine Mhloyi explained the problem: "We are being pushed aside to make room for thin cis white women, some who've struggled with eating disorders but have not struggled with being denied a diagnosis or treatment the way that fat people do because disordered eating is actually *prescribed* or encouraged for us. . . . Having an eating disorder is not an excuse for perpetuating fatphobia" (emphasis in original). The edited video removes the triggering image while still framing Swift's own body shame. Like the social-media-dependent protagonist in the Swiftie Zan Romanoff's 2020 novel *LOOK*, she knows that "technically, she's not fat.

That's just a numbers thing. But that's the word she knows to express that she's unhappy with her body, that she's always been unhappy with it. . . . What would it even be like to live in your body and not worry about its size?"[9]

The video then breaks for comic relief, turning her funeral into a murder mystery skit. When the music returns, Swift sits on a roof with her double, as if finally reconciled, or resigned, to the public-private split in her life. At least they can drink together, along with a third, giant Taylor who offers them a bottle the size of her pinky nail. It's a psychodrama, and a delight, and a mess, as well as a trope—good/bad, casual/sexy, fearful/daring—that goes back to Dr. Jekyll and Mr. Hyde, or at least to the original series of *Star Trek*, where a transporter accident split Captain Kirk into good (scrupulous, ineffectual, nebbishy) and bad (decisive, bullying, amoral) captains. The *Enterprise* needs both, in one body. So does the enterprise of Taylor's music, not to mention her then-planned worldwide tour.[10]

We can imagine two Taylors—one flummoxed by anxieties, one forceful but callous—looking back over her earlier career, wondering whether we've seen them both. We can find, in some songs, Good Taylor and Bad Taylor, Anxious Taylor and Confident Taylor, a Taylor in Love and a Taylor Out for Revenge. We can also find songs dominated by one of the two. "Vigilante Shit" has no coauthor, and it feels tonally, lyrically, like an outtake from *Reputation*. Perhaps it recalls a sleepless night from late 2016. Determined to "get even," "dressing for revenge," this version of Taylor casts herself as a private detective, retrieving "cold hard proof" for a friend's divorce case, with the familiar motto "Don't get sad, get even," jarringly emphasizing the "ven" in "even" (the "ven" in "vengeance," the "ven" in "revenge"). Here she sounds confident—but she's also the bad guy, the agent of someone else's pain, the bringer of hurtful news. It's not a role the sunnier Taylor of *Fearless*, or *1989*, or *Lover*, would choose to play—but (the song asks, harshly enough) could it be the role that suits her adult self best? The song itself concludes with no firm answer.

Each change in Taylor's sound, each one of her eras—except for the self-reliance-focused *Speak Now*—comes with a new set of musical models. On *Midnights* the influences are bedroom pop and next-generation electronica, and for the first time her models are younger than she is. Sonically though not lyrically, "Vigilante Shit" recalls Lorde (play it next to Lorde's "Tennis Court"). Two *Pitchfork* reviewers, Quinn Moreland and Vrinda Jagota, independently compared the whole album to the work of that Auckland-based singer, a friend of Swift's who had also worked with Jack Antonoff.[11]

The Swift of *Midnights* learned even more—about how to dramatize fears and mixed feelings, how to make music for sleepless nights, how to meet fans from their darkest places, and her own—from Lana Del Rey. When Swift accepted the *Billboard* award for Woman of the Decade in 2019, she devoted a paragraph to Lana's journey. Once "ruthlessly criticized," Lana had become, Swift said, "the most influential artist in pop. Her vocal stylings, her lyrics, her aesthetics, they've been echoed and repurposed in every corner of music." Lana's a model for Taylor on this first post-quarantine, post-lockdown album not just because she persisted, but because she makes such full, inviting pop songs out of her own rawest insecurities, and then rereads those insecurities as ways to bond with her fans.[12]

No wonder Taylor invited Lana onto *Midnights* for a duet. If you're looking for obviously aspirational aspects to this album—moments when listeners wish we could be Taylor—the duet with Lana Del Rey makes one. "Snow on the Beach" uses plucked strings, layered orchestra textures, and heavy reverb on the vocals, all Del Rey mainstays. It also introduces its love scene in a way that puts the romance in the background, and everything that vexes Swift in the foreground. Snow on the beach looks like lights in the sky look like the sparkles she gets from her beloved, especially welcome because "life is emotionally abusive." The verse and chorus together take us down a fourth, then down a whole step (a reverse T-drop!), then down by degrees until we land on the next lowest A. The layers of Christmastime bells, and the pulsing bass, stop long enough for Taylor to say she's "all for you like Janet [Jackson]" in her song "All for You" (2001). "My smile is like I won a contest," Swift reflects, "and it's fine to fake it 'til you make it," no matter how long it takes, how unlikely the promised shore.

Allied with Lana, exposing her insecurities, Swift works both to own the tools of slick pop and to make them fit her particular anxieties. The threat she saw on earlier albums coming from individuals, from haters and liars and vengeful rivals, now comes from inside the house, from the tools of modern pop stardom, which encourage her to make herself perfect and (therefore) to disappear. Writing on modern producer-confected pop like the Spice Girls or the Backstreet Boys, the rock critic Paul Morley warned against such disappearances, "disposable pop stars carefully stripped of all human texture and edginess," "an ultimate formula masterminded by the ultimate control freak," taking the heart of the human pop singer away.[13]

If there's an "ultimate control freak" behind Taylor Swift's music, it's Taylor herself. Nonetheless, some of the fears that keep her up nights, the anxieties that ally her to Lana and spark the lyrics for "Mastermind," speak both to her smooth electronics-led production and to her reputation for rationality, for self-control. What if she's tried too hard, what if she's focused so much on making herself too perfect, what if she's squeezed her creative self so tightly that there's nothing left inside? "Mastermind" looks like a song about orchestrating a hookup, then turning it into a long-term romance (the twist in the lyrics: The guy she's been manipulating knows he's been manipulated, and likes it). But "Mastermind" doubles as a song about career management. She's been telling us since at least *Speak Now* that she's the one in charge. What does she lose by scoring, planning, and writing out every move? Has she canceled out some authentic, spontaneous, loving part of herself?

Or has she become her true self, since that's the way she lives, and chooses, and loves? Against detractors who find her artificial, constructed, deliberate, Taylor insists that her artifice—her status as a mastermind—does not cut against her authenticity. That's who she is: the girl who can't help planning everything (almost as Vulcans from *Star Trek* can't help being logical). More generally, Taylor's work at this point says, art—style, making, deliberateness—does not conceal the real self: It *is* that self. "Mastermind," like "Bejeweled," like *1989*, looks back to 1980s synth-pop, but here the precedent feels more specific: Compare either song to "Only You," or to "Mr. Blue," by the electropop duo Vince Clarke and Alison Moyet of Yaz. These songs, too, reveal insecurities, obsessions, and depressions. They're bedroom pop, not dance club numbers, more confessional than New Romantic. And they depend on one electronic musician (Clarke) who programmed everything, as if he were chronicling his private insecurities, even though he relied on Moyet in Yaz (and then, in Erasure, on Andy Bell) to sing.

Once again, *Midnights* does not just chase Taylor's anxieties, now that she's on top of the world, bigger than everyone, ready to take the stage. It makes those anxieties into new bonds with her audience, new ways to relate, nowhere more so than in "You're on Your Own, Kid," this album's track five. On its surface the song describes hoping, expecting, preparing to date a man who will not return Swift's affection: "I wait patiently, he's gonna notice me / . . . I waited ages to see you there / I search the party of better bodies / Just to learn that you never cared." The song also looks back at the hypersocial, gossip-column-worthy life she's led since becoming a star, and at the disordered eating that she acknowledged in *Miss Americana*: "I hosted parties and starved my body / Like I'd be saved by a perfect kiss."

And then, as Swift turns to address herself ("You're on your own, kid"), the song tells us that we're more like her than we think: Her privilege, and her control, and her success, have taught her that she is, as we are, existentially alone, and that no romantic partner will fix us, even if that partner returns our love. So, the song advises, make the friendship bracelets (she must have known we would take that one literally). Rely on a group, a girl squad, or else on yourself. Don't put all your eggs in one boyfriend. That's been her regular advice since *Fearless*, but here she can look back on how long she's been giving it: We hear, in her bedroom pop, the flutters and fears that make her seem more like us. The verses' rhythms in "You're on Your Own, Kid" comprise almost nothing but eighth notes and quarter notes, as if insisting on self-regulation, choosing to follow premade rules. Then we get the chorus, and the title: sixteenth notes and dotted sixteenths. It's a lot more uplifting than "Anti-Hero," because it reaches out to us, and it's musically more conventional for that reason—designed for us to sing, or mumble, along.

Zan Romanoff's narrator in *LOOK* tries to learn to control her emotions by shaping her social media presence. She hopes that by paying attention to social media, she can "adjust the optics and control a scene instead of just starring in it." And yet—like Swift—she's still hung up on how people see her: "What does she want to wear? Can she separate it from what she thinks she's supposed to wear?" It's the flip side of the pride Swift describes in "Bejeweled": Who wouldn't want to make the whole place shimmer? Who wouldn't want to polish up real nice? The Swift who sings "Bejeweled," with "diamonds in my eyes," may feel all shiny and new, ready to meet the band and make the rounds at the party, but she still cries "sapphire tears." ("I think there are tiny inflections of me hyping myself up to return to pop music," Swift remarked of the song, after "years writing folk songs and being in this metaphorical forest.") Sparkly bells ladder up and down the song, but they may not, after all, lead up to "the penthouse of your heart": Public perfection feels like a consolation prize. *Midnights* opens up and leans into that scary feeling: the feeling that tells you that no matter how much you go out and have fun in groups, you're still on your own.[14]

Sleepless nights mean facing your anxieties; they also mean recapitulating your past, hearing long-ago bells you can't unring. Those bells ring loudest in "Would've, Could've, Should've," which Swift described onstage (Nashville, night three) as a "song about looking back at your life." More specifically, it looks back to John Mayer, and to "Dear John": the online Swiftie Ally Sheehan points out that Mayer, while he was dating Swift, lived in a repurposed church in Nashville, whose windows ("stained glass windows in my mind") incorporated stained glass. The song reaches out to girls and young women who have been in Swift's position: You made me feel important (Swift says to the older man who treated her badly). It felt like heaven at the time. Now it feels like a mistake, one that he made, in taking advantage of her, and it still hurts: "Give me back my girlhood, it was mine first." The surprise song version from Nashville dials up the anger beside the regret, as both Swift and Dessner work their acoustic guitar chords in speedy, repeated downstrokes.[15]

The fears and regrets on *Midnight* get sadder still. Even amid all these sleepless nights, "Bigger Than the Whole Sky" stands out for its unrelieved tragedy, its lack of consolation: Perfectionism may or may not solve your own domestic, romantic problems, but it can never bring the dead back to life. Backed by almost nothing except an organ for the first verse, with vocal reverb at cathedral levels, the song feels funereal. Something or someone has ended, or died, moving Taylor's character to say, or pray, "words I don't believe." Swift has understandably never explained the song: Many fans heard it as a reaction to miscarriage, so many that NBC's *Today* show ran a feature about it. At Rio de Janeiro, night two, Swift chose it as a surprise song, and as a memorial. The live performance there became plaintive and fragile in the vocal lines, almost angry in the emphatic piano solo between them. Her choice, and her delivery, reflected on the loss of Ana Clara Benevides Machado, who died of heat exhaustion after the Rio promoter failed to make enough water and ventilation available.[16]

A less mortal anxiety animates "High Infidelity." The song has no apparent connection to the number-one-selling album of 1981, REO Speedwagon's *Hi Infidelity*, but it begins—like the classic rock album—with stereo effects: a single test tone bouncing between the left and right speakers. "Put on your headphones and burn my city," Swift's character invites her listener. It's a song about angst, about feeling unloved and neglected, as the second pre-chorus says, and it presents a woman who feels lost both in the world of "picket fences" and in the faster-moving world of subterfuge and adultery, having given up on one and sought the other.

This version of Swift is still a would-be good girl, not a man-eater so much as a man-regretter, and it's not clear where she—"rain-soaking," "blind hoping"—wants to go next. Intrepid reporters at *Vox* (Rebecca Jennings, Gabriela Fernandez, and Shira Tarlo) filed an explainer for every song on *Midnights*, and they did sterling work for "High Infidelity," with its puzzling date of April 29: Back on April 29, 2016, Rihanna's single "This Is What You Came For" had dropped. Swift secretly co-wrote the song with then-beau Calvin Harris, who denied ever having cowritten with her, apparently afraid of being upstaged. Swift would soon leave Harris for Tom Hiddleston (Loki). The *Vox* team connects this song's intrigues to that real-life messy affair.[17]

"Mastermind" and "You're on Your Own, Kid" and "Anti-Hero" together make up the emotional and sonic center for this introspective electropop album: Its sounds and feelings orbit Swift's confessions about her own anxieties, her own perfectionism, her own fears that everyone will stop loving her, and that she depends too much on a boyfriend's—or, worse, a fandom's—love. Those fears fit the introspective, not-very-danceworthy electronics that govern the album's sounds, and those sounds in turn permit—for bonus tracks and late-album tracks and non-singles—effects that would seem out of place on Swift's earlier rock, folk, or club-oriented albums. The Dessner collaboration "The Great War" flaunts its snare-heavy, military beats: It's the first Swift track since *Reputation* (with its Dothraki drums) to emphasize percussion this heavily. It also advertises her long residence in the United Kingdom, with its military remembrances and its commemorative poppies.

MIDNIGHTS

Swift's sense of herself as wounded, as discouraged, like a soldier, comes back in the far less hopeful track "You're Losing Me," released after *Midnights* and before *The Tortured Poets Department*: in effect, a song, the only song, announcing that Swift and Alwyn had split. Shared military similes explain the two tracks' presence in one mashup (Liverpool, night two) from the Eras Tour, where she changed a line from "The Great War," "We survived," to "I survived." Relatable? Certainly, at least to anybody else who's dated someone clinically depressed, or watched a romantic relationship slowly dissolve. Aspirational? Maybe, if only for the almost gleeful artifice with which foreign matter, things alien to pop music (military snares or simulated medical recordings), work themselves so expertly into Swift's arrays of sound. The American Heart Association endorsed "You're Losing Me" as a way to restart a real heart: "The lyrics might be heartbreaking," an AHA Facebook post said, "but the beat could be heart-saving," with "the right tempo for performing Hands-Only CPR."[18]

The standouts on *Midnights*, and among its extra tracks, put Swift's fears first. She's up for romance and for parties and for performing, especially after a few years shut in. But she's anxious, too: anxious about depending on other people's approval; about needing too much from too many people; about becoming too big to trust, too big to love, too far away from us; about feeling lost, even when she thinks she's been found. All of the extra tracks on *Midnights*—with their found sounds, their unresolved frustrations, their oddities, even when they're also love songs—imply something else about Swift's (and perhaps our) anxieties, something that feels like an answer—or a palinode—not to the joys on *Lover* but to the synth-pop self-fashioning on *1989*. Even when you think you've found love and worldly success, real life—unlike the promised land of electronic pop composition—hits you with things you can't control.

TAYLOR'S VERSION

An album about the limits to perfectionism, made with modern electronic tools, *Midnights* also goes on (as her earlier albums had not) to harness the musical limits of electronic composition, its capacity to snarl or surprise or break or glitch. That's what the odd, nonmelodic, computer-made sounds and the clearly processed vocals spread across *Midnights* do. The presence of those effects in "Closure," on *Evermore*, seemed like a conscious experiment with a new genre (hyperpop), maybe a one-off. Their recurrence on *Midnights* commits to the bit. Production choices that once implied proud self-mastery now imply things going sideways, people getting lost, too-late second thoughts.

That's how the bleeps and swoops in "Labyrinth" speak to the lyrics: The almost atonal ascending keyboard figures that precede each verse feel like questions with no clear answers; at the same time, Taylor goes deep into her feelings, displaying her vulnerability, turning a love song into a show of fear, resenting, as she says, the way "everybody just expects me to bounce back." The song found a new place in Swiftie lore after the Eras Tour, on Buenos Aires, night three, when a passenger jet made its final controlled descent to a runway right behind the stage while Taylor sang the final couplet: "I thought the plane was going down / How'd you turn it right around?" Swift later tweeted a video clip with her caption: "Never beating the sorcery allegations."[19]

We hear the same anxieties—carried in the same electronic weirdness, connoting the same uncertainties—in "Glitch," which, as of November 2024, had the distinction of being the least streamed song on *Midnights*. It's neither an anthem nor an introspective ballad. Instead it's almost deliberately background-ish, a summertime slow jam, moving from the cat's-purr contralto register of the vocals to the very high—probably digitally treated—start of the chorus, to the almost spoken title line: "I think there's been a glitch."

That glitch, ironically enough, is the stable romance that the song discovers. The lovers hook up, almost accidentally, and "five seconds later, I'm fastening myself to you with a stitch." The crackle and hiss of an old vinyl record shows up all over the song, except for particular moments of clarity ("so sorry"): another glitchpop trick. The song leans, for unity, on the burble of its fretless bass. Maybe a life of glitches and counterfeits, digital remakes, versions and self-revisions, can turn out smoother, sexier, more fun, than a life where everything proceeds exactly as would-be good girls planned.

Maybe that unpredictability gives us hope too. The visual artist and curator Legacy Russell's "Glitch Feminist Manifesto" asks us to find hope in glitches, in everything digital that veers away from the offline, or primary, world. "For Glitch Feminism the digital arena becomes a regenerative site of creative and artistic experimentation wherein new selves can first be born via online performance, then borne beyond as the performing individual makes physical these online avatars." Electronic glitches and weirdnesses can show artists wrestling with their multiple selves, with the impossibility of total control, and with the persistence of their unwieldy past. And—on "Labyrinth," on "Glitch," in the interstitial synth runs of "Maroon," in the treated vocals and portamento (pitch-shifting effect) of "Midnight Rain"—that's what Taylor does.[20]

By the end of *Midnights*, after the end of the COVID quarantine, after the cancellations and un-cancellations and comebacks of Taylor's mid-2010s, this introspective, electronic, up-and-down album has made another point about anxieties and mastery (or masterminds) and control, too. It's not just that Taylor can't control her whole life, can't keep down all her fears, can't help thinking about how the dominoes might or might not fall. It's not just that some of us—especially the perfectionists, the performers, "all the wisest women . . . / Born to be the pawn / In every lover's game," as she sings—can't do it (which gives us a bright, clear way to relate to her). It's something else as well: If Taylor can't manage the kind of control she craves—over her feelings, over her love life, over how people see her or what they see in her—maybe nobody can. Maybe self-reliance of that kind just isn't a thing that human beings, even the hardest-working, richest, most fortunate, most cooperative Type A human beings, can keep. We need one another's hands, one another's friendship bracelets, and ways to avoid depending wholly either on ourselves or on finding the right, perfect guy.

That's how Taylor's ways of portraying herself as a survivor, repeatedly lost in a maze or a haze, meet up with her announcements about autonomy, about going out on her own: The first set of portraits undermine the second. Nobody, not even Taylor, can keep that kind of control. When you, and everybody around you, half-expect you to exercise it (after all, you're a billionaire, and a beautiful photogenic adult, and a pop genius!), it might look to you like you should be able to solve every problem, help all your friends out of tough spots, make romances, plans, and elections work as they should. Everybody might well expect you to bounce back: After all, they know you're a mastermind. If something goes wrong it's your fault. Everyone's watching. Why can't you make it right?

Swift spoke about that feeling as early as *Journey to Fearless*, where—still a teen—she observed that more than a hundred people depended on her voice to make their livings. Swift does not sing on *Midnights* about her musicians and crew, but she does sing about how she needs her fans, and how fans may need her, and about the frustration that comes with not being able to solve everything, even if she—and we—keep making the friendship bracelets, and singing to the crowd, and going around the world on tour. "Autonomy and independence," as the scholar and disability advocate Lennard J. Davis writes, are always—when you drill down far enough—unsustainable illusions. "Dependency and interdependence," accepting our flaws and our needs, make for better goals. With its confessional words, its introverted moments, and its glitches, much of *Midnights* reinforces that point.[21]

The Taylor Swift who shows her insecurities, who can't stop thinking about what she can't quite do on her own, also shares (as if revealing her greatest secret) how it feels to distrust herself. "Dear Reader" feels like advice both to us and to herself: Does she have to keep sharing everything? "The greatest of luxuries is your secrets." Should we even listen to her? "Never take advice from someone who's falling apart." She shares those feelings, too. Then she undercuts herself: Her first-verse advice to run away from everything, to "burn all the files," to become someone no one will recognize, feels like the same advice the chorus tells us not to take.

It's all very Lana. It's also the advice, or the set of tactics, that Arya Stark followed in *Game of Thrones*, becoming a Faceless Man to work her revenge. It matches the pitch-shifting, voice-disguising hyperpop mannerism that Swift uses, again, in the song's spacey outro ("You should find another"). If the song encapsulates her late-night anxieties, her self-accusations and sometimes self-hatred, better than anything else on the album, almost anything else in her catalog, it owes those powers to its arrangement, starting with piano and vocals alone before sliding, warily, into downtempo electronica, like a matching bookend to "Lavender Haze."

When Taylor sang "I think about jumping / Off of very tall somethings / Just to see you come running," she may have been recording *Midnights* at the same time, but she didn't put that lyric there: The lines come from "Is It Over Now?," a vault track from the remade *1989*. The sentiment, though—self-sabotage, self-dramatization, and the almost apologetic awareness that someone is always watching—runs throughout *Midnights*: People will think Taylor does everything with intention even if she's in a lavender haze; people will look at dried bloodstains that turn maroon and think they're part of her color scheme; people will look at her scars and see fashion statements. People want Taylor to exercise control over everything, and then they resent her for doing it. Taylor herself—who turned thirty in 2019—grew up trying to control everything, to please everyone, to depend on their approval, and now she has it: Can she keep it? Now what? She's better at planning and scheming and masterminding than anybody else whose art we consume—and yet she's at least as much of a mess as the rest of us.

The standard edition of *Midnights* ends on positivity, with "Sweet Nothing" (a relatively shallow love song, cowritten by Alwyn) and then "Mastermind." But the Till Dawn edition, released six months later, ends with two alternate versions of album tracks—and before those, "Hits Different," which emphasizes Taylor's angst. "You made a mess of me," Swift tells the man in "Hits Different," over electric guitars, almost the only ones highlighted on the album. It's a song of crushing, inconsolable heartbreak, where everything her friends tell her, including "Love is a lie," sounds wrong, because this particular lost love seemed so true. "I never don't cry at the bar," she croons in the pre-chorus, repeating his name "'til someone puts me in a car," adding three notes and three syllables to "car."

That guitar riff takes the song back to what used to get called "power pop." One of very few songs anywhere in Taylor's career that credit both Antonoff and Dessner, "Hits Different" resonates with the clean guitars of Antonoff's first successful band, Fun (usually stylized as fun., with its own period). "Hits Different" sounds like Fun, the band, but musically it also sounds like fun. The uplifting, aspirational part may lie in the guitar riff, because the vocals—like so much of *Midnights*—confess angst. An album that began with a lavender haze and segued into maroon ends with "catastrophic blues." An album that began with romantic love as a welcome distraction, then journeyed through warnings against loving too much, ends stuck once again on Swift's need for approval, from her public or from a man she's loved. Could the key in the door be that man who left, coming back? Could it? "Or," sings Swift, "have they come to take me away"?

It's one last pointer to the language of mental health that turns up all over the album, to the way it admits that not even Swift can keep down her worries, know what's coming next, or feel like she's always in control. But it also points to a solution: The Swift who came after *Midnights*, and after "You're Losing Me," and after Alwyn, would take herself out of London, away from New York, away from home, back to a life where she could at least control more of her time and motion, more of her days and nights. After so much introspection, so much studio time, so many moments of quiet vulnerability, Swift would get out of her own head in the same way she had done since 2007: taking herself, and her band, away from her private life, to plan her biggest tour yet.

12

THE TORTURED POETS DEPARTMENT
(THE ANTHOLOGY)

Taylor Swift isn't done making music. Nothing about *The Tortured Poets Department* suggests a farewell, or even a brief vacation: The album dropped not far from the middle of a two-year, five-continent, global phenomenon of a tour. It's an album about how she's managed to keep working, being herself through calms and storms, sharp peaks and precipitous lows, about how she's kept turning her emotional tumult, her need to be seen, and her sense of vocation into song. It's her longest album, by far, and her most ambitious in its lyrics, looking back constantly at her prior writings and at songs, books, and poems other writers have created. Those songs and those words, and the topics they share, make the album (whether or not Swift meant it that way) an occasion to see the powers she has exercised, and to see why a celebrity who has seemed to live on top of the world has remained emotionally available and emblematically vulnerable.

As with all of her albums, it means more if you know about her life when she wrote it. Sometime in early 2023, around the time the Eras Tour began, Swift split up with her boyfriend of six years, Joe Alwyn, a split that any listener could have seen coming in the slow heartbeats of "You're Losing Me" (written in late 2021, released in May 2023). At least one song on *TTPD*, "So Long, London," certainly speaks to the end of Taylor-and-Joe. Most of the rest of the songs on disc one, and several (it's hard to say how many) on disc two, speak to Swift's tumultuous romance with Matty Healy, the self-dramatizing, substance-abusing, absurdly charismatic frontman for the English indie synth-pop band the 1975. Swift and Healy first met in Los Angeles in 2014; he told an Australian radio show that he wouldn't mind dating her, then denied rumors that had them romantically linked. Healy and Swift worked together on at least one unreleased track recorded for *Midnights*. In January 2023 she premiered "Anti-Hero" at a 1975 concert. In May the couple themselves were photographed together. They took long flights to attend each other's concerts and declared their love, sotto voce, onstage. By July 2023 it was over. In April 2024 *The Tortured Poets Department* dropped.[1]

If the double album—all thirty-one songs—has a thesis, here it is: Taylor, like many of us, has long tried and hoped to be a good girl, to gain and keep our approval, to find success by working hard. That trying doesn't just come from outside. It's part of her nature; it's who she is. At the same time, she hopes and wants, and has long wanted, to fall head-over-heels for a rebel, a baddie, a hot, impulsive, energetic partner who can take her out of her own planned-out, deliberate life. Not for the first time, with Healy she did it. She found him. But she couldn't, shouldn't, wouldn't keep him. She can't have both hopes fulfilled, or not for long. Maybe nobody can. Maybe nobody should give up so much for a romantic partner, no matter how exciting, as Taylor once again felt tempted to do. Maybe we, too, have felt vexed, excited, pulled in both directions by the contradictory desires and angers that *The Tortured Poets Department* follows. And maybe we, too, can sort them out for ourselves.

Swift's ideals of hard work and deliberate craft—ideals that have helped her write so many songs—collide on *TTPD* with stereotypes about passionate, inspired, self-destructive artists or geniuses. Coming to terms with this meteoric romance means coming to terms with those stereotypes too. They're stereotypes, in particular, about poets. Thus the title, and thus the references, even the jokes, about poets and poetry throughout the album: Dylan Thomas and Patti Smith in the title track; Samuel Taylor Coleridge's "Rime of the Ancient Mariner," in "The Albatross"; Homer and Virgil in "Cassandra"; perhaps even Horace in "The Black Dog." (*The Anthology* refers to the double album, rather than to disc one on its own; it also suggests a collection of poems, though "anthology" normally means a collection with many authors, not just one.) From its first track to its last, as of mid-2025, the album, the supposed anthology, becomes not just Swift's last words so far about sweeping romance and vulnerability—words that connect her to so many of her listeners—but her last words so far about herself as a creator.

Showing that she writes the songs, and that she can work with collaborators, Swift remains a figure defined by her craft and her attention (like it or not) to the impressions her writing makes. The German philosopher-poet Friedrich Schiller sorted all poetry into "naïve" and "sentimental": The sentimental poet seeks lost nature (in the woods, or in love, or in childhood), while the naïve one must simply "be nature."

Taylor sees herself (rightly) as the former: She's never been a natural. She is, she's always been (this album says—*Speak Now* said it, too) a maker, a *makar*, to use the old Scottish term (a translation of the Greek word for "poet"), rather than a lawless, perhaps tortured figure who stands apart from ordinary mortals. The contrast the album invokes (and its implications for career shape) go back even further, to ancient Greece. Plato, in his dialogue *Ion*, depicted his stereotypical singer of poetry (also named Ion) as a helpless channel for divine inspiration, never in control of his own art, and knowing nothing for himself. That's the kind of poet, or artist, Taylor never wants to be. Instead, she's self-conscious about her craft, a "work person" also aware of her audience, a Type A, someone used to being in charge, even when she wants to be swept off her feet: Horace, not Ion; Carole King, not Dylan Thomas, or even Kurt Cobain.[2]

Dashingly irresponsible hotties, would-be go-down-in-flames artists, on *The Tortured Poets Department* as in real life, can make their poetic natures excuses for harmful, neglectful behavior. The novelist Jenny Offill nicknamed those hotties "art monsters," charismatic, amoral creators who care about nothing except their art: not their audience, not their bandmates, certainly not their boyfriends or girlfriends. In the presence of the right art monster, other artists get attracted, excited, sucked in, especially when those other artists are women or girls, no matter how strong their craft. And then those other artists listen to themselves, look back, hone their tools with conscious practice, and try to make songs or poems or novels from the truth.[3]

The Tortured Poets Department is not only Swift's longest album yet but also her saddest. Among its thirty-one tracks, only three address human connections that will not crumble or fail. One admires co-writer Aaron Dessner's young son Robin. The other two could address Swift's new (as of late 2023) boyfriend, the Kansas City Chiefs tight end and two-time Super Bowl champion Travis Kelce. "The Alchemy" piles up flirtatious football puns; "So High School" sets its enthusiastic, fluttery declarations over rapt shoegaze guitar: "I feel so high school every time I look at you / But look at you!" Swift repeats that last phrase while switching its meaning. Literary critics (like me) call that device *syllepsis*. Swifties (like me) call it fun. The rest of the album addresses pain and hurt. Men betray her, fame feels hollow. Obscurity beckons, spotlights demand escape, promises crumble like cities besieged, and Swift is Cassandra losing Troy, Wendy losing Peter, the girl who can barely save herself, much less fix doomed men. That's a big agenda, involving a lot of comparisons, and a big sheaf of claims for Swift's words to back up.

In order for those words to do their work, the music has to avoid getting in their way. For all its lyrical inventiveness, *TTPD* seemed at first like a retread, in musical terms. Some Aaron Dessner collaborations on disc two—especially "I Hate It Here"—resemble *Folklore*. "So Long, London," with its cathedral harmonics, looks back to *Midnights*. "Fortnight" recaps the 1980s synth-pop of *1989*, and "Down Bad," with its trap beats, echoes *Reputation*. Most of the album (though not "Clara Bow" or "So High School") resembles in texture and timbre some slice of Swift's earlier work.

As it must. For one thing, the album tries to look back. For another, if you're going to make big changes in one aspect of your practice, it's best to hold others constant, so that listeners (or readers or viewers) can notice what's new. It's a matter of figure and ground: for instance, holding the instrumental textures constant in order to highlight her voice. Swift reaches almost screechy soprano levels in "Who's Afraid of Little

Old Me?" and scrapes the bottom of her already low alto in "The Saddest Man Who Ever Lived."

More than testing her vocal range, though, the Swift of *The Tortured Poets Department* finds new heights as a writer, displaying her own poetic inventions, stretching her wings, demonstrating that you don't have to be an art monster, or a tortured poet, to make your words work. Swift expands her songwriting vocabulary, as well as her rhetorical arsenal: The people who like to list terms for figures of speech could have a week of field days with this double album. Besides syllepsis, there's adianoeta, hyperbole, epitrope, even zeugma, that is, one verb with two kinds of objects: "You crashed my party and your rental car." Sentences run on after the end of a measure, phrase, or line, altering meanings we thought we knew: "I'm so depressed I act like it's my birthday... every day." "All your life did you know / You'd be picked... like a rose?" I'd love to be picked—by a lover, by a prize committee, by fans. But I would not want to be picked like a rose.[4]

It's as if Swift looked at the tortured poets she'd dated, from the odious John Mayer to the drama king Matty Healy, and wanted to show that she could write better than they did. Swift's new lyrics also go all-out on vowel rhyme and other half-rhymes, as in "The Prophecy": "Let it once be *me* / Who do I have to *speak* to / About if they can *re*do the prophe*cy*? / ... A *grea*ter woman has *faith* / But even statues crumble if they're *made* to *wait* / I'm so *afraid* I sealed my *fate*." Other vowel rhymes play bait and switch, like the one that ends "Peter": "Please know that I tried / To hold on to the days / When you were mine / But the woman who sits by the window has turned out..." What would you expect to follow "turned out" and rhyme with "mine"? Maybe Wendy turned out just fine. But no: "The woman who sits by the window has turned out the light." She's not fine at all.

THE TORTURED POETS DEPARTMENT

Do these words and feelings make Swift a tortured poet? Certainly they place her in a lineage of writers injured by erotic love. Who was the first? Maybe the ancient Egyptian who wrote, sometime in the fifteenth century BCE, "My beloved stirs my heart with his voice. He causes illness to seize me. . . . My heart is smitten." Petrarch's sonnets, in fourteenth-century Italy, complained that love both scorched and chilled. But the trope of the tortured poet whose gifts would destroy him (less often, her) came about later, when European writers began to see poets as especially sensitive, anguished, or fragile. A genuine poet in nineteenth-century France might be a *poète maudit* (cursed poet), like Charles Baudelaire or Arthur Rimbaud, marked by fate, mental illness, or substance addiction. By the twentieth century, the type, or stereotype, could fit all manner of self-destructive and self-centered creators, most of them men.[5]

The Tortured Poets Department, and its title track, point back to this tradition, make fun of it, and reject it, as the prose that accompanies the album implies. "There is nothing to avenge, no scores to settle once wounds have healed," Swift wrote. "Our tears become holy in the form of ink on a page. Once we have spoken our saddest story, we can be free of it." Fans speculated that she appropriated the "tortured" mantle from a group chat co-run by Joe Alwyn, called "The Tortured Man Club." Those same fans expected an album devoted to Alwyn. But the fans were more than half wrong, as most of *The Tortured Poets Department*, when it points at any real person, takes on Healy. The title track certainly rebukes his pretensions: Healy really did, for example, write rock lyrics on typewriters, and though his resemblance to a golden retriever seems open to question, he boasts almost two dozen tattoos.[6]

Even as she records the seductive attractions of this *poète maudit*, the way he took her out of her good-girl life, she establishes that she's the better writer. Lines addressed to the art monster she has not yet left—"You're not Dylan Thomas, I'm not Patti Smith / This ain't the Chelsea Hotel, we're modern idiots"—refer to two well-known figures but could bring to mind others. Thomas (1914–1953), author of "Fern Hill" and "Do Not Go Gentle into That Good Night," brought evocative, lush figurative language back into poetry in the United Kingdom after two decades of modernist suspicion. He enjoyed transatlantic fame, and a strong reputation as a live reader, before collapsing and dying of alcohol poisoning. Smith's punk-era records contain passionate recitations of what we would now call "spoken word poetry," such as "Gloria" and "Horses"; she won literary awards for her memoir *Just Kids* (2010). Both Thomas and Smith lived for a time at the Chelsea Hotel, the long-famous venue on West Twenty-Third Street whose beautiful ironwork balcony, run-down interiors, and history of bohemia took in such other long-term residents as Bob Dylan and Andy Warhol.[7]

Swift doesn't want to be a tortured poet or an art monster. She wants—having loved men like him—to portray that kind of love, to show how much fun she's having while it lasts, and then to escape from its paradigm, and maybe to help us get out of it too. In other words, as much as it breaks new literary ground, *The Tortured Poets Department* returns to the drama and the advice that came with *Red*. We listeners can enjoy the vicarious drama, then take the advice. We don't have to date tortured poets. If we do, we don't have to stay with them. We don't have to be tortured poets in order to write well. And we don't have to become the people our drama-loving audiences expect: We can try telling those audiences to take a hike, even if (like Swift) we protest too much. "You wouldn't last an hour in the asylum where they raised me," Swift warns on "Who's Afraid of Little Old Me?" If she feels tortured, that's not because she's a poet; it's the logical consequence of a romance gone bad, and a life lived, from youth, in public. "I was tame, I was gentle till the circus life made me mean," she sings. "I am what I am 'cause you trained me."[8]

TTPD focuses on the art monster its title tells us to expect. But it does not exactly tell one story. It feels more like three braided together: one about ending a long-term romance with a sad Londoner, one about a head-spinning affair with a charismatic, substance-seeking performer, and one about Swift's relationship to her own fans. The first thread—the one that listeners expected, knowing about Swift's breakup with Alwyn—unravels a years-long romance with a boyfriend whose chronic sadness (according to the song) no girlfriend could assuage. "So Long, London" anchors this story, with its wary, twitchy 12/8 beat: "I stopped trying to make him laugh / Stopped trying to drill the safe / . . . It isn't right to be scared / Every day of a love affair." There's only so long you can stay with someone so depressed that you worry whenever you leave them alone, and only so long you can hold back what may become rage: "I'm pissed off you let me give you all that youth for free / For so long, London." The lines, sung slightly off the beat, evoke the continual wariness, and the weariness, in life as a de facto caregiver, life with someone so psychologically fragile that anything might set him off.[9]

The second, and dominant, story—the one supposedly about Healy—begins in the aftermath of that long romance. What do you do once you've fled a life so grimly and insistently domestic, with its "locks and ceilings," that it makes you think about prisons (in "Fresh Out the Slammer")? You look, if you can, for a symbol of freedom: an irrepressible performer, a ball of energy, even a Tortured Poet. That story encompasses head-over-heels devotion ("But Daddy I Love Him"), grinding desolation ("Down Bad"), and the harshest, most dismissive, most condemnatory song that Swift has ever written about anyone (more on that song in a moment).[10]

The leadoff track and the first single, "Fortnight," announces its connections to this Healy-like figure, outlining a brief (and British) romance. The track adheres more tightly than most of the album to older musical conventions: throbbing synth, one chord per measure, no prominent syncopations. It might almost have fit on *1989*, or on an album by the 1975. "I love you, it's ruining my life," Taylor intones, followed by her collaborator Post Malone. It speaks to somebody British, who might say "fortnight" (a period of two weeks), but it speaks to time on tour ("lost in America"). It covers a short, intense period, a time full of ups and downs, and painted, in retrospect, by regret. It tosses out red herrings to make the situation fictional: "Your wife waters flowers." And it thinks about substance addictions, which Healy has very publicly acknowledged; Taylor imagines herself as a "functioning alcoholic," sadly immune to the "move-on drug."[11]

As for the title track, Patti Smith and Dylan Thomas should come as no surprise. Nor, maybe, should the typewriter, a piece of technology that became romantic at exactly the moment when it became impractical. "Nostalgia for typewriting is everywhere," the Canadian poet Darren Wershler-Henry wrote in 2007. "Once typewriting symbolized all that was antithetical to poetry. . . . Now we believe that typewriting is poetry." If the first verse sets the scene for satire, or tragedy, the second dissolves into farce: Charlie Puth, the bland 2010s pop star and former YouTuber? A tattooed golden retriever, that proverbially unthreatening, welcoming pet? The munchies? The song should be funny. I think it's funny.[12]

But it's also a prelude to heartbreak. "I chose this cyclone with you," Swift sings, repeating the long *o*'s. It's hard to get over the impulse to choose a cyclone, when a cyclone makes itself available: It's hard, when you've tried to be a good girl for so long, not to seize the chance to get carried away, into an aerial danger even speedier and more powerful than a red car ride. The glittering, multiple, digital, arpeggiated backgrounds to each verse emphasize the glamour, and the rush, and the futility in the sexist myth of the poet who needs his muse. No wonder a woman who made herself passive, a caretaker, a patient first lieutenant on a ghost ship (all figures from "So Long, London"), would seek adventure, and risk, and the unknown, on the rebound.

The risks went badly, but the journey had its high points, and "But Daddy I Love Him" covers those. It's a masterpiece, exploding into a vibrant chorus that slaps a declaration (the title line) against a fourth wall-breaking joke: "I'm having his baby / No, I'm not, but you should see your faces." "Sarahs and Hannahs in their Sunday best," like busybodies and Karens from decades past, need to let Swift make her own, perhaps unwise, decisions about where to go and who to kiss and when—to let her make her own mistakes. Antonoff and Swift together do justice to the high-energy Swift who's pushing back against "judgmental creeps," her so-called allies as well as her surrogate parents, teachers, would-be supervisors. She's tired of being the good girl, tired of pleasing all of us, tired of being in charge.

The title for "But Daddy I Love Him" quotes *The Little Mermaid*, the 1992 Disney animated version. In a 2009 video interview for the *New York Times*, Swift tells Lynn Hirschberg that *The Little Mermaid* was the first movie she ever saw, and her parents wondered at her devotion as she sang them the songs from the film on the car ride home. Now she's the figure whose songs children learn to sing, and she's written a song against the stans and überfans who want to tell her—as the undersea adults told Ariel—how to live. Those stans have real-life counterparts too, as 2023 saw a wildly inappropriate online campaign—with its own hashtag,

#SpeakUpNow—demanding that Swift leave Healy on the grounds that he kept making offensive remarks.[13]

To some young listeners, Shaad D'Souza wrote in the *Guardian*, "the #SpeakUpNow letter probably seems like a totally normal interaction with a celebrity, despite it being exactly the kind of intrusive, judgmental behavior that so many fans purport to defend their favorite stars from." Swift's earlier albums, from *Fearless* on, and her Eras Tour stage banter and stage sets, and maybe even her choreography, suggested a kind of contract: She would help us live our lives and be nice to us, and we would be nice to her. Being a Swiftie felt like entering into a cosmic agreement: our devotion in return for her moral support (Mother would keep on mothering). *TTPD* asks us to look again at that contract, which she never exactly signed—she contemplates ripping it up. "Growing up precocious," Swift admits in "But Daddy I Love Him," "sometimes means not growing up at all." It might be the key to this album. Or to her whole career. Or to me.[14]

How does it feel to receive, from such a young age, such great rewards for doing what other people expect? How does it feel to become a public symbol of success, or bravery, or romantic distress? This question rises through songs set during romances and after they end. It's the question in "Who's Afraid of Little Old Me?" It's also the question in "I Hate It Here," a melancholy, self-accusing number whose flip, much-critiqued line about historical bigotry ("We would pick a decade / We wished we could live in . . . / I'd say the 1830s but without all the racists") obscures its real point: "Nostalgia is a mind's trick," and there's no time like the present for facing your demons. The same escapist anxiety animates "Florida!!!," a high-tension tune about swampy imagined escapes: "Your home's really only a town you're just a guest in." The phrase rhymes with Destin, the beach town near Pensacola. It also points to the rough parts of life on the road. And it shows why a public figure might prefer more touring over settling down where paparazzi, or ghosts, or old flames, might surround her.[15]

Swift's sense of herself as precocious, having grown up too fast, might have come from her own memory, or from other people's sense of her life. As early as 2011 the journalist Willa Paskin decried Swift's "precociousness problem." "Maybe 22 is the year Swift will stop seeming so precocious," Paskin mused, "and start seeming like an adult." Until she could do so, Paskin continued, she would keep coming off as insincere, a "good, smart stage kid" who "comes across as disingenuous in the very act of being herself," because she just seemed too darn nice. This version of Swift can't win for losing: Genuine adult authenticity, apparently, requires hostility, aggression, defiance, an unwillingness to do what mentors and collaborators expect. Better to laugh in their faces and run away with the man they all see as bad for you. Even if, a couple of months afterward, they turn out to be right.[16]

As much as fans and journalists try to chase down the real-life basis for so many songs, their power inheres not in Swift's biography but in the acoustic and verbal shapes that make that biography matter. "All that is personal soon rots," W. B. Yeats mused. "It must be packed in ice or salt." *TTPD* brings the salt. Again, she's flexing her writerly abilities, as well as making art from the shape of her life: inviting us in, and letting us look up to her, and showing us that you don't have to be a tortured art monster to write like a thoughtful poet—indeed, it helps if you're not. Characters on *TTPD*, like so many characters on the pandemic albums, sport details that set them apart from Swift herself: They date married men ("Fortnight"), chase Texans ("I Can Fix Him"), or heed professors ("The Manuscript"—Swift chose to skip college). And yet, even more than the pandemic albums, *TTPD* offers whole shelves full of self-references alongside its flaunted technique.[17]

This songwriter takes control over her material—her life—not just with Easter eggs and bits of biography, but also by showing and sharing her writerly prowess. "The Smallest Man Who Ever Lived," for example, tells its neglectful ex-lover, "You didn't measure up / In any measure of a man." The quip means he's short, or at least sensitive about it, and you can find the real-life Healy on TikTok getting upset when fans question his height. The quip also means that he did not measure up morally or emotionally: He behaved like a big baby, despite his "Jehovah's Witness suit" (another Healy trademark).[18]

Swift's music, too, reflects on his failure to "measure" by proceeding in an unsettling 7/4 time throughout each verse and chorus. Few pop songs use this time signature (one that does: the Beatles' "All You Need Is Love"). It's disorienting, like falling in love with the wrong guy, like dating someone you no longer trust. The song ramps up orchestration as it shifts into its 4/4 bridge ("Were you *sent* by someone"), or rather, into what could have been a bridge, a contrasting section after the second chorus. Instead—like the romance it outlines—it's a bridge to nowhere: There is no third verse.

Another piano song with minimal accompaniment is "loml," an acronym that could mean either "Love of my life" or "Loss of my life" (the typography on the album, like many other Swift titles, uses all lowercase, "loml"). Here the arc of a love affair has not so much hit a wall as plummeted into the depths of the sea. This Dessner collaboration keeps its six-note (sometimes seven) piano figure going for the entirety of the song, shifting its lowest note, but not its shape. It's what classical musicians call *ostinato* ("sustained" in Italian), and here it means that Swift's feelings for this man (whom Swifties will likely see as Healy, though some still think it's Alwyn) just keep on going, even as he proved subject to change. He "blew in with the winds of fate," lasted about as long as a "get-love-quick scheme," felt "legendary" but turned out "momentary" and "temporary." Again, Swift flaunts her verbal, even her poetic, talent: Her craft exceeds his, and her craftsman's sense of how to write exceeds his rule-free inspiration. Triple rhymes like "legendary," "cemetery," "momentary" can wind up comical, but here they remain as serious, as mournful, as the black and white snow on an open grave.

"Chloe or Sam or Sophia or Marcus" shows off its technical skill—as it repudiates its unreliable boy-man—in other ways. The song uses 12/8 triplets to create a rolling unevenness, holding its rhythm section back until the second verse. What gossip columnists might take as minor revelation—the ex in the song dates men (like Marcus) as well as women (like Chloe)—feels minor beside Swift's dejection. Its moody, disappointed arrangement builds up momentum, like the "wild horses" in the last verse, without ever telling us where Swift wants to go. Again, swept away for a while by this charismatic London hottie, Swift comes to her senses and shows who's the better writer, who knows her audience better, who's mastered her craft.

"The Black Dog" plays with Easter eggs and allusions too, to classic literature and to London life, even as it looks back on Swift's journey with another art monster of a man. A real pub named the Black Dog in central London became a pilgrimage site for Swifties: Healy and Swift might well have hung out there. Black dogs in literature and popular culture often represent depression: Consider *Taming the Black Dog: A Guide to Overcoming Depression* by Bev Aisbett, or *Killing the Black Dog: A Memoir of Depression* by the Australian poet Les Murray. Popularized by Winston Churchill, with help from a mistranslation of Horace, the phrase "black dog" for chronic depression persists in modern British English. But the man in the song seems less depressed than fickle and shallow: He put her through "hazing" for what she calls "a cruel fraternity," once admired her "rain-soaked body," smoked constantly, rejected her harshly, dates younger women now, and appreciates (though the younger women will not) a pop-punk band called the Starting Line, whose 2002 hit "The Best of Me" the 1975 had covered.[19]

In other words, the man in "The Black Dog" corresponds to the album's Healy-like figure, even though the song itself tracks the end of something that felt like it could be, should be, would be a long-term thing. If Swift has read Horace—or hangs out with people who have—she might know that the same poem, Satires II:7, that gave us the mistranslation "black dog" (for *atra*, properly a black companion or "black one") also excoriates a former friend's untreated compulsions: "You cannot spend an hour on your own: you flee your life's cares with wine, or sleep, but you fail: the black one follows you." Leaving her ex in the Black Dog, with his black dog, Swift's swelling conclusion shows how it feels to leave someone you once loved—someone who turned out monstrously selfish—behind.[20]

It's not all about an ex (or a pair of exes). But it is all about how to be Taylor Swift, and about how her need to work, to be seen, and her wish to be loved for herself have kept her vulnerable, and her art inventive, and her songs (still) both relatable and aspirational. An album about what makes a real poet, a real artist, need not stay so serious for so long, even as it keeps on looking back. Parts of *TTPD*, directed at art monsters or at other rivals, bring in not so much Easter eggs as outright jokes, demonstrating the range of her craft, and the way that she knows how (like any comedian) she needs an audience. "I Can Fix Him (No Really I Can)" brings in what seems to be a cowbell; a yawping, yawning

"Western" guitar; and the sounds of the open road as it follows Swift's failed, perhaps absurd, attempt to tame a chain-smoking, hard-riding Texan: It's practically a comedy song.

So is "Florida!!!," starting with its multiple exclamation points. "My friends all smell like weed or little babies," Swift sings, in a line that resonates with who knows how many thirtysomething women. Then she imagines becoming a Florida woman with no need for a Florida man, perhaps even a Florida woman who, like the HAIM sisters' persona in "No Body No Crime," did away with a bad guy: "I did my best to lay to rest / All of the bodies that have ever been on my body / And in my mind, they sink into the swamp / Is that a bad thing to say in a song?" Would an earlier version of Taylor break the fourth wall in that way? Maybe so (remember "Hey Stephen," or even "Our Song"). But here the fourth wall, broken, gives us a long look back at the tortured poets and stoners and would-be criminals that this version of Taylor (and her bestie Florence Welch) want to escape.

We get more self-consciousness about Taylor's craft, and about her success, and about her escape from humiliation, in "Thank You Aimee" (styled "thanK you aIMee"), a song about revenge on a high school bully that points straight back to "Mean." Here the breathy, intimate performance feels true to the resentment that bullies' victims nurse over the years. The hometown villain, always inflicting "the same searing pain," recalls the baddie in "Mean," except that now Swift's persona has already made it: She's looking back and still wants to hit back. The song's target, of course, appears to be KIM (note the capital letters in the typography)—perhaps Kardashian. Or is it? "I've changed your name and any real defining clues," Swift coos, perhaps sarcastically. Swift put the song in a mashup with "Mean" on London, night two, in what Bryan West called "a unique mashup for haters."[21]

Swift invites us to see ourselves in her, to admire her strength, to inhabit her story, not just because she's survived her swiftest, roughest, most over-the-top romance with a reckless hottie, but because she's come to terms with the way she needs—and sometimes needs to ignore and sometimes needs to go out and see—her audience. They're terms she's been pursuing throughout her career, and after the adult content of *Reputation*, the confessional bent of *Midnights*, the neglected mirrorball of *Folklore*, and the confidence of *Speak Now*, she's finally bringing those terms together. In "Who's Afraid of Little Old Me?" she's a ghost, a classic revenger, hiding where she knows she will be found. She's also showing her technical vocal range, going right up into that head voice, almost screeching the title in the chorus and then dropping down to confide with her chest voice: "You should be." Swift even sings about how her voice now sounds. "I wanna snarl and show you just how disturbed this has made me / You wouldn't last an hour in the asylum where they raised me / So all you kids can sneak into my house with all the cobwebs," where this crazy cat lady lives.

Those needs hit even harder in a song whose music, without the words, would mark an explosion of joy: The more crushed she feels inside, the harder she tries to project a smooth, happy exterior, at least when she faces her fans, in public, onstage. She needs us at least as much as we need her. "I Can Do It with a Broken Heart" does not address an ex or a clique of Sarahs and Hannahs exclusively. Instead it looks more broadly and generously and wrenchingly to the fans, especially those who have already paid to see the Eras Tour, where Swift can always hit her marks, "grinning like I'm winning." Sparkling electronic arrangements look back to the hi-NRG pop of the late 1980s and early 1990s: Compare the Erasure hits "Sometimes" (1987) and "A Little Respect" (1988), music designed (near the height of the HIV/AIDS crisis) for full-on queer dance-floor joy.

"I Can Do It with a Broken Heart" strives for dance-floor joy, too, in its sounds, but the words do not join that party. Instead they say how hard Swift must work to get that party started. The bop reaches out to all the people (queer or straight) defined by performance, by external validation, by applause, by straight A's. Few poems and fewer pop songs address this problem in contemporary terms. Two of the few are Laura Kasischke's poems "Miss Weariness," about a girl who gets sick of trying, and "Miss Congeniality," about a girl who dies trying instead. In the latter, "They praised my feet, the shoes / on my feet, my feet / on the floor, the floor," "the sense of despair / I evoked with my smile," Kasischke writes; they rewarded "the song / I sang," until this people-pleasing, performing girl's "bloody mattress / had washed up on the shore."[22]

That kind of exhaustion (and that kind of densely rhymed wordplay, adapted to go with music) plays off against the energy, the show-must-go-on spirit, in "I Can Do It with a Broken Heart." You can get all the way to that song—track thirteen (another important Swiftian number) on *TTPD*—before remembering that Swift must have finished writing *TTPD* during the first grueling months of the Eras Tour. That's what good girls do. "I can pass this test," she sings, being someone who's studied hard and passed all her tests, all her life. Constant eighth notes all through the three-minute tune (there's not even a bridge) insist that she can't stop moving, or working: She knows how much she depends on her fans, as well as how much her fans depend on her.

A doubter might say she embodies the American insistence that we work ourselves (like the girls in Kasischke's poems) half to death. A sympathetic listener might say instead that she knows how hard we have to work for others: Go to school, teach a class, feed a kid, drive a teen to work. Get yourself out there for the fans who believe they need you, the fans who in many cases paid four figures to be there. Each declaration overspills its measure. "I cry a lot but I am so productive, it's an art." "You know you're good when you can even do it / With a broken heart." It's a song so exhilarating, and exhausting, that after two verses it just stops. "I'm miserable," Swift exclaims, not singing, just speaking. "And nobody even knows / Try and come for my job." That line—far down in the mix, almost tossed-off, on record—turns climactic as she enunciates it onstage on the Eras Tour: "Try. And. Come. For. My. Job!"

How does Swift see that job? Writing songs, collaborating with other musicians and writers. Recording them, working with producers. Going on tour, using social media to keep fans engaged, and to help us feel seen. Feeding our own sense that she wants to feed us, that she cares about us (which, in her own careful way, she seems to do). But also, like it or not, maintaining an image, visually and reputationally, in costumes and lights, onstage and on red carpets: That's part of her art, and craft, and know-how, too.

That's the part of her job that haunts "Clara Bow." Raised—really, neglected—in New York City tenements, the real Clara Bow (1905–1965) became the biggest draw of Hollywood's silent era. Unsophisticated, kind to everyone, constantly falling in love with new men, Bow became an exploited, overworked national treasure, the face of the flapper generation. Bow at her peak, writes her biographer David Stenn, "was not just a star, but the most lucrative asset of a powerful corporation." Letters addressed only to "The 'It' Girl, Hollywood, USA" reached her, some of the more than 33,000 she received after *Red Hair* (1928). Talkies wrecked her career, not because her voice failed (in the right roles, she sounded just fine), but because she got so nervous around microphones, and because scandals finally made her less bankable.[23]

Swift seems to have identified with Bow as early as 2021, when Stephanie Zacharek of *Time* magazine noticed Swift's series of Bow-themed outfits. Swift—unlike Bow—can manage herself, and now owns rights to her own work. Unlike Bow, she controls her financial destiny. Like Bow, though, she lives in the public eye. She's been told "You're the real thing," by executives and producers and journalists whose jobs involve fakery. And like Bow, she seems at a loss when not working. "Clara's personal identity derived entirely from her professional activity," Stenn concludes. He then quotes her contemporary, the screen actor turned film historian Louise Brooks: "Off the screen, [Bow] disappeared like an overexposed negative.... The only thing she was was this *image*" (emphasis in Stenn).[24]

Could the same thing happen to Taylor Swift? Or could Swift end up more like Stevie Nicks, since (as the song suggests someone once told her) "You look like Stevie Nicks / In '75"? Nicks aged out of her alluring, carefree hippie look into the full-on sorceress of *Bella Donna* (1981), and then into an elder stateswoman of California soft rock, mentor to HAIM, and friend to Swift: She even contributed a poem, dedicated "For T—and me," to the physical CD release of *TTPD*. Nicks's presence in Taylor's second verse makes the song less crushingly fearful, more self-aware. "I have a few very close friends, most of them I've known forever, and I kind of like it," she told the *New York Times* in 2014. A Nicks-like trajectory might not be so bad.[25]

It would, at least, improve on Clara Bow's. The Dessner-assisted composition leaves plenty of space for Swift's alto register, keeping all the instrumentation low in the bass or in the wispy upper atmosphere. The bass-led, percussion-free arrangement resembles nothing Swift has done before, suggesting instead younger indie songwriters like Phoebe Bridgers or Lucy Dacus. The song then gets meta in a way that Taylor has never attempted before: "You look like Taylor Swift / In this light ... You've got edge, she never did." Could Swift imagine somebody mistaking her for a look-alike (as in the famous scene from the film *L.A.*

Confidential with the punchline, "She is Lana Turner")? Or has Swift imagined her own replacement, groomed to dazzle after she fades?[26]

At this point in *TTPD*, the last track on disc one, Matty Healy and his precursors—Jake Gyllenhaal on *Red*, Joe Jonas in "Forever and Always," even Maxim in *Rebecca*—matter less than the self-portraits that Taylor has made, the way that she seems (like the best lyric poets) to share some part of herself (whether directly or through some alter ego). Swift's loquacious extravagance fits a figure who can never get enough: not enough reassurance, not enough support, not enough applause or praise or positive feedback to hold back permanently the sense that she's worthless, or hollow, or doomed to be unlovable (as in "The Prophecy"). Each award, every number one, helps—then the void returns. After all, it was the Taylor of months ago who entertained a dying child in Sydney (look up "Scarlett Oliver"), and the Taylor of twelve years ago who got us all dancing to "Shake It Off," and helped us dump nogoodniks with "We Are Never Ever Getting Back Together." What has she done lately? What if she's done all she can ever do?

Some of us know this feeling as impostor syndrome. Others hear a fear of growing old. Politically alert fans may see in it an aspect of capitalism, with its insatiable demand for new and greater returns: what the business writer Kevin Evers, writing on Swift's own career, calls her "incontrovertible need to do more." "I Can Do It with a Broken Heart" even includes a literal crowd shouting "More!" The economist Joseph Schumpeter wrote of the "fundamental impulse that sets and keeps the capitalist engine in motion," the need to create new stuff to meet new demands. Such a way of life, he concludes, "not only never is but never can be stationary."[27]

In this sense, Swift—who famously encourages fans to buy more and more records—comes across as an engine of capitalism, and as its creation, and also as its victim. Her participation in the world economy, her ability to give us product—to produce the feelings we demand—becomes the most stable part of her identity. The social researcher Georgia Carroll even suggests, ungenerously, that Taylor's attempts at imagined connection, in songs and online, are only a "well-executed marketing strategy": Fans buy her things in the hope that she'll notice us too. And yet the songs themselves—"I Can Do It with a Broken Heart," "Florida!!!," "Cassandra"—depict a neediness less practical than emotional and existential, what the eighteenth-century critic Samuel Johnson named "that hunger of imagination which preys incessantly upon human life, and must always be appeased by some employment." His depression, too, worked the graveyard shift.[28]

Swift tends to end albums on optimistic notes ("Mastermind" on the first version of *Midnights*, "Long Live" on *Speak Now*, "New Year's Day" on *Reputation*). She could have ended this one with the fun, hope, and patience she found in "The Alchemy." Instead she closes disc one with "Clara Bow," and disc two with "The Manuscript," a slow, pensive song about closure ("The story isn't mine any more"). Before that song comes "Robin," and before that "The Bolter," the last (so far) in her handful of songs that amount to biographies: Taylor's portrait of a serial monogamist feels specific enough to reflect a historical figure. And indeed—as the fandom discovered (I learned about it from a student)—Frances Osborne's *The Bolter* (2008) describes the misadventures of Osborne's grandmother Idina Sackville (1893–1955), also the model for a character nicknamed "The Bolter" in novels by Nancy Mitford.

Marrying and then divorcing five husbands, Sackville reached her peak of gossip-page notoriety as the sponsor and host of sex parties and fluid polyamorous arrangements among the white aristocrats of 1920s Kenya, in what was then called the Happy Valley (properly the Wanjohi

Valley). Like protagonists in Swift's earlier songs, Sackville (as Osborne writes) learned the hard way that "the only way to hang on to a better life was not to stake it upon the survival of a marriage." Or even a boyfriend. But the character profiled in Swift's song does not look much like Osborne's Idina Sackville. Swift's Bolter "fell through the ice" in childhood, a detail nowhere in Osborne. She then found freedom in the marriages she repeatedly chose to leave. Each time "she just knows / She must bolt," she's proving that she can still live her own life, a proof reinforced by cascading euphony. It's a tribute to flight and to independence from men, from hot men and from needy men and charismatic tortured poet-men, and it's an almost gleeful apology for a claim that should require none: You do not have to do what your milieu expects, and you do not have to stand by your man.[29]

Sackville was no poet, no singer, and no memoirist. Nor were the men she married and left. "The Bolter" makes a superb and self-contained example for Swift's recent songcraft, but it's no place to end an album about Swift's public image, her career, her would-be art monster ex-boyfriend, and the shape of her art. That's why *TTPD*, disc two, concludes with "The Manuscript," a self-conscious piece of writing about writing if there ever was one, and a work as salty (so to speak) as Yeats could ever want. Did the song describe an actual manuscript? Could it be the manuscript for "Dear John," her first song about a doomed age-gap relationship? Or the manuscript, reproduced in the *Lover* diaries, for "All Too Well?"

We may never know, and close focus on the "real" details risks overlooking the technical achievement as well as the emotional point. Again, as in "Evermore," as in "The Smallest Man Who Ever Lived," the bridge in "The Manuscript" brings a musical time change to match the time shift in the story, from 6/8 to 4/4 as "the years passed." Lines, divorced from their tunes, flout metrical patterns, as if Swift meant to remind us that she does not write page-based poems, but songs: "He said, 'I'm not a donor but / I'd give you my heart if you needed it' / She rolled her eyes and said / 'You're a professional.'" Once again, vowel rhymes make the patterns that count. The first *o* in "donor" matches the *o* in "rolled"; the long *i* in "eyes" matches the earlier ones in "driver's license." And that's all we get. If Swift and the older seducer stay together, they'll end up with "strollers," which after four syllables matches the verse-ending "over."

Where are these sound patterns going? When will the life in the song—the life Swift has lived on this album—begin to make sense? Only in retrospect: Only after Taylor herself has some distance from this older man, and from the chaos and revelry, the sinking ships and grim prophecy, elsewhere on *TTPD*. The word "age" recurs, changing meaning (syllepsis again), first an era ("the age of him") and then "boys who were her own age." And around these key words, around the end of the album, the sounds of *or*, like boats' oars, begin to pull: doors, above board, sure; forward, score, for; shores; more. Taylor's repetitions and rhymes, along with reflection and distance and the passage of years, have salted and sealed this heartbreak, like her others, into a work of art. Romances like this one belong to the past, like the Chelsea Hotel, like the *Iliad*, like *Peter Pan*. Their story over and done, offered as models and mirrorballs for us, their storyteller can go back out there and figure out how to return to the stage.

13

ERAS

Most of us would agree, especially after the quarantines of 2020–2021, that isolation and loneliness hurt, and that art can address them, bringing people together. It's clear by now—between all the sold-out stadium shows and the string of number-one records—that bringing people together is something Taylor Swift does. And yet the most popular art, at any given time, the art that brings the greatest number of people together, may not last. It may not always reward sustained attention, or repay lasting respect.

I have been trying to show, because I feel certain it's true, that Taylor Swift does merit those things. She shows us how much, like so many of us, she wants to present a beautiful, virtuous facade, while letting us notice mistakes, wrong turns, bad feelings, and faults. She looks at why so many of us, especially girls and women, crave romance, and danger, and at the wrong turns those cravings entail. She navigates, and shows how we might navigate, between the Scylla of absolute independence (she needs us too much for that) and the Charybdis of depending totally, guilelessly, on romantic love. She lets us identify with her (she's relatable) while looking up to her, vicariously enjoying her successes, having fun (she's aspirational). And she does all those things (alongside coauthors, producers, and other musicians) in music that rewards attentive listening, in ways that let millions of us sing along. That's why Swift seems to me to be not just a force in popular culture, but also a major artist, even a genius (as it says in my title).

Such arguments ought to recognize cases against them. One such case says that she's taken advantage of privilege, of money, and of whiteness. And indeed, if you're looking for an artist devoted to overturning the entire world system of capitalism, or to wholly destroying any institution, Taylor's not your girl. She has learned to see herself as privileged, and to see privilege's obligations and problems: making known her political views; practicing, often without public notice, philanthropy; noticing, in her music as well as in her public statements, the limits of her own whiteness; standing behind (and singing about, and for) people who could use help, especially when they're fighting patriarchy. She lets those people (I'm one) see ourselves in her, from "Tied Together with a Smile" and "Dear John" through "The Man" and "The Manuscript."[1]

Another case has to do with the notion of genius. The stereotypical genius is a man who works alone and changes everything through the sheer force of his brain: someone who moves fast and breaks things; who leaves a whole art form, or a whole scientific field, or a big slice of history, totally changed. It's a stereotype that comes from modernism, from the idea, as the poet Ezra Pound put it, that the goal of great artists is always to "make it new." It's a stereotype that emerged from the ideal of tortured poets: artists who feel so out of step with normal people, and with their own time, that they may end up wrecking themselves, being too brilliant for this dull world. It's a stereotype that places the artist—as the literary scholar Bob Perelman, himself an avant-garde poet, explains—above and apart from the audience. A "modernist genius," in particular—think Pound or James Joyce in literature, Ornette Coleman in jazz, perhaps the Velvet Underground in rock music—expects society "to catch up, aesthetically or politically, to writing that it by and large didn't read and couldn't understand."[2]

Taylor Swift's music doesn't work that way. Nor does she play the role of Romantic genius, the spirit to whom great art just comes naturally, the "true genius . . . unacquainted with the rules," as Friedrich Schiller put it. Her hits, and her concerts, and her persona, never conceal the effort they involve. She's "never been a natural," or at least that's what she says: All Swift's albums carry the subtextual message "this is me trying." And that message speaks to her life as a woman, too, as someone who could never be The Man. In present-day America, the social work professor Madeline Pérez has observed, "women attribute success to effort, while men think of success in relation to ability." Women learn to disclaim, and men to claim, personal credit for accomplishments; women learn to avoid, and men to take pride in, open transgression. Boys will be boys: That's how the West was won. Girls should be dutiful daughters, people-pleasers, tendrils tucked into a golden braid. We get those messages from childhood on. Men stand out; women cooperate. Men shine, naturally; women labor, unseen.[3]

Those messages too, show why it's important to call Taylor Swift a genius, at least in the popular sense of "genius" that means "a great artist." She's neither a modernist genius, "superior . . . to everyday life" (to quote Perelman), nor a Romantic genius with semi-divine, self-destructive, break-everything gifts, an "object of awe and terror" (to quote Ralph Waldo Emerson). If Swift comes across as a "mastermind," that's not because she's smarter or more inspired than everyone else: It's because no one wanted to play with her as a little kid, and she's been working hard, looking for collaborators, willing partners, in her schemes ever since. And if she's a genius, that's not because she stands apart from everyone else or pushes us away.[4]

Instead Swift has put her powers into seeing and hearing so many of us as we already are. Readers and listeners in their own time admired Alexander Pope, and W. B. Yeats, and Willa Cather, and Carole King, and will (I think) admire Taylor Swift, not because those creators reinvented their art forms from the ground up, but because what they invented, discovered, or perfected speaks to us, profoundly and repeatedly, musically, intellectually, and emotionally. Some such artists shock the crowd; some don't. And some shocks fade. The last thing Americans, in particular, need as the 2020s roll on is another cult of creative destruction, an art devoted to tearing things down. Instead, we—not just Swifties, but Americans, readers of books, girls, women, queers, everyone really—need complex art with subtleties that do not repel newbies; art that feels familiar enough that it can comfort us while exploring our oddities; art that asks us to keep going, noticing our hopes as well as our weaknesses; art that invites us, and does not shove us away.

That's what Taylor Swift, from her debut to the present day, for a fortnight, and for nearly twenty years, has tried to give to parts of the pop music world. It's what she has noticed—what she describes, and reacts to, and sometimes reacts against—in her present-day moves as the world's most noticed songwriter. It's what makes her, in the terms of this book, a genius. And it's what we can see—what millions of us have seen, in stadiums, in movie theaters, or on the small screen—with the global success of the Eras Tour.

Taylor Swift's life as a creator and an entertainer does not just mean writing and singing, and trying to get people to hear her songs. It also means—has meant, since her MySpace days—making a public persona that speaks to her fans, one that encourages us as fans to see ourselves in her, and, if she's touring, to see her onstage. Sometimes her songs—from "The Lucky One" to "Florida!!!"—wrestle against that role. At other times—"Mastermind," say—they imply that it is what she has sought. And that's what she got with the Eras Tour.

It's what I see in Edinburgh when I go to witness the Eras Tour for myself, and it's a testament both to how she writes and to how much and how many people care. On the tram are preschoolers, and young adults, and moms, and a few dads, and women old enough to be Taylor Swift's great-aunts or grandmothers. Some girls wear cowboy hats. Others dress like faerie dryads (fit for *Folklore*). A mother and daughter wear matching denim jackets with valentine hearts and lines from Swift's mother-and-daughter song on the back: "I had the best day" (first jacket) "With you today" (second jacket). I scan the queue to get into the show, then see the queue for merchandise. One woman wears pink glitter, a bolero jacket, and a pink hijab. A T-shirt reads, "My Daughter Loves Taylor Swift More Than Me." Another shirt adapts the song "Karma": "Kermit Is My Boyfriend / Kermit Is a Frog," with the green Muppet's picture. Other shirts say "#SWIFTIEBOYFRIEND" or "In My Bestie Era." Still others duplicate the slogans from the various black-on-white T-shirts that Taylor wears when she performs "22." My own says (all caps, of course) "THIS IS NOT TAYLOR'S VERSION." More T-shirts enter my field of vision once we're in our seats: "darling I'm a nightmare dressed like a daydream," all lowercase like the *Reputation* logo; "In My Capybara Era," with photos of capybaras—chill as always—in the pattern and colors of Eras Tour merch; "KC SWIFTIES," in goldenrod and red. Someone does beard drag, hairy and proud, in a black fur throw and a white mini dress stenciled with the *Reputation* cover.

Taylor chooses, for her opening acts, her friends, or else songwriters she wants to promote. Tonight's opener, Paramore, counts as both: Lead singer Hayley Williams, one of Swift's oldest and closest Nashville pals, sprints around full of energy, almost comfortable on this enormous stage. She's literally leaning into the songs, bending forward over the microphone. She's also dressed to look unmemorable: blue work shirt, khaki pants, a ski cap with a symbol of Scotland, St. Andrew's cross. There's no stage set for Paramore, no props, nothing to see except musicians, as if to avoid competing with Taylor. Girls hold hands and sway to Paramore's "Obsession" as if cheering a football team. When Paramore plays "What Are You Gonna Do?" Williams walks all the way out to the end of the key-shaped stage. She reminds me of a stagehand, checking the planks and the pipes, making sure all the steam jets, guitar monitors, and motorized platforms will function for the star.

A giant digital clock counts down minutes and seconds. At 2:23 the digits disappear, replaced by an old-style clock face with Roman numerals, and the background music changes to "You Don't Own Me," by Lesley Gore. The point, of course, is that Taylor owns herself. Crabby lefties, if any paid to attend the show, might complain that she celebrates ownership, that her stagecraft and her public image make her a creature of capital: Certainly (the lyrics to "Change" notwithstanding) she has not worked to foment revolution. At the same time, even before she takes the stage she's sending another message: You don't own me, because no one owns anyone, and no one can own you—not a management company, not an employer, not even the most devoted public, and certainly not your boyfriend. You belong *to* you, whether or not (as the song says) you belong *with* me. And then we begin: "Miss Americana," truncated, leads into "Cruel Summer," the single from *Lover* that hit (perhaps thanks to the tour) four years after that album came out. Broad metallic bricks, thick enough to support Taylor's body, rise and fall below her as she belts out the bridge: "I don't want to keep secrets just to keep you."

This summer of Eras in Edinburgh and *TTPD* everywhere doesn't feel cruel: It feels like the transformation of life into art. The literary critic Kenneth Burke argued way back in 1931 that no matter how strong an emotion an artist wants to represent, no matter how important an artist's topic, "the artist's means are always becoming ends in themselves," ways to appreciate artistic technique. That's one reason art about sadness can bring us joy, one reason tragedy gives pleasure, one reason you might become an artist, one reason an artist might be a "work person." And it's on display in Taylor's work. Start with a cruel summer, and end up with "Cruel Summer"; start with a good cry and end up exultant onstage. Taylor's Eras, as the essayist Maggie Nelson points out in a fanzine, reflect her work: they are not "stations of life," like "maiden, wife, mother," but phases of her art: "the story of your life is literally what your art makes of it."[5]

"This crowd's different, huh?" Taylor says. "Okay! All right. So you decided in the first song you're gonna prove to me that you are the best crowd. You're amazing now. Edinburgh. This one will be good." She says that, or something like it, to all the crowds, and we know she means it each time: Part of a great Taylor Swift song, like part of a show, involves this heady mix between the obviously generic and the apparently individual, the way we feel that she sees us, really knows us, speaks to the root of our feelings, even when she's saying something banal. We might not even mind knowing how she's repeating herself. Kenneth Burke, again, explains why: Music, "fitted less than any other art for imparting information, deals minutely in frustrations and fulfillments of desire, and for that reason . . . can bear repetition without loss."[6]

Given the stagecraft, the talent, and the expense of the Eras Tour, we might expect concertgoers to treat it as a spectacle, astonishing, alien, out-of-this-world. And yet to read accounts of the Eras Tour—and to attend it—is to find, over and over, a spectacle minimized: a monumental effort treated almost like intimate, personal communication. The Eras Tour shows have the same sets every night, of course—a set change is a big deal. Swift did change the roster of songs in 2023, switching "Invisible String" out for "The 1," perhaps to mark her breakup with Alwyn; and she changed the order more drastically when she returned to the tour after *TTPD* came out, combining the *Folklore* and *Evermore* sets to make room for new material near the end, and eliminating a few more earlier songs—among them, bizarrely, "Long Live"—so the show wouldn't get overlong.

But there's something unique, if not personal, at every show: the surprise songs, solo performances, often keyed to the city where the show takes place (for example, "Paris" in Paris). During the first American legs of the tour, in 2023, surprise songs meant whole songs, usually one on acoustic guitar and one on piano. As the Eras Tour rolled on—and as Swift came close to running out of songs she had never performed on this tour—this part of the show became an occasion for medleys, which fans insisted on calling mashups: two or three songs on guitar, two or three on piano, often making a point about the occasions, or themes, or sounds, that the songs shared.

Once the show has started, informed Swifties know what's coming next, in broad outline, except for those surprise songs. And yet online Swifties—ever eager for more connections to our icon—made up a game where we guess the details: It's called Swiftball, and thousands of fans played each night, for over a year, in Discord and on the app once known as Twitter, as well as through the bespoke phone app called SwiftAlert. Swiftball players guessed which dress our girl will wear for each Era; which slogan T-shirt she'll pick for "22"; what colors her color-coordinated sets will use; whether a special guest will show; whether something "unhinged" will take place (Will she announce a new re-recorded album? or a new single? or the end of the world?); what the surprise songs will be on guitar and piano, or, an easier guess, what albums she'll draw them from; and whether she'll give a speech. Swiftballers filled out ballots before each concert, then watched the live feed to see what they got right. The game brought Swifties together: as usual, the entity with her at its center thrives by connecting so many of us on its margins.

The live concert displays Swift's mastery of marketing, public appearances, social media, and, not least, practical stagecraft: extra-musical skills in logistics, materiel, and people management, skills that the albums, necessarily, conceal. For example, "Lover" (a long slow song and a bit of a drag) remained in the Eras Tour set in 2024 even after Taylor cut the fan favorite "Long Live," and long after she broke up with its real-life subject, Joe Alwyn. Why? For one thing, its molasses-paced, molasses-sweet direct address lets Taylor onstage sing to her imagined boyfriend while really singing to the live (and mostly female) audience: We love her too. For another, the song allows the members of her band to walk out onstage, slowly, while Taylor walks offstage for a costume change. (Anytime something about a large pop concert baffles you, it's safe to guess there's a set or costume change involved.) Again, she's demonstrating skill, collaboration, competence; again, she's showing her work.

TAYLOR'S VERSION

Taylor told CBS News in 2011—though the clip never aired until 2024—"I think you kind of get set in how you feel when you're in school. I could be sitting in the front row at an awards show and I still don't feel like a cool kid." One way to address your own sense of insecurity—sometimes the best way—involves reaching out to others, to see them, to help them feel secure. Some of the stagecraft here seems designed to do that. For "Love Story," the lights around the thrust part of the stage align like an airport's landing strip, as if she's touching down to meet us. At the end of "22," as always, she gives the bowler hat she wore onstage to a small child in the audience. The big screens behind Taylor show the child who gets the hat as she cycles through little-kid emotions: astonishment, near-crying, disbelief, and then a high-five.[7]

Between songs from her *Red* era, Taylor in Edinburgh improvises a sentence fragment into the mic: "When you had the dream of doing this, the crowd looked exactly like this." Her "you" means "I." Her first "this" means her tour. Her second "this" means us: The biggest tour yet from the biggest pop star on the planet still seems to single its listeners out, or tries to. Before "All Too Well," she asks—as always—our permission to take up ten minutes of our time: She still wants our approval, so many years after turning twenty-one. Then she runs through all that song's emotions—heady limerence, deepening contentment, surprised suspicion, grief, anger, melancholic resignation, as autumn chill becomes wintertime cold. "You lost the one real thing you've ever known," she tells her ex (but I will be fine, she implies: Look, I wrote this song). As she reaches that line, the colored confetti of autumn leaves changes to white snow-dust.

Physically demonstrating, recapitulating, the changes Swift's art has gone through, while staying relatable and aspirational, owning them all and repudiating none, Swift's Eras Tour also sets examples that no album, in isolation, could. It's a way to show how she's changed and remained herself, to show how the eras and parts of her life and her challenges and surprising joys hold together, how she continues to sound like herself. And that means that the Eras Tour, above and apart from the albums it contains—and far more than another kind of concert tour that just mixed songs together—offers models for us as fans, who might make new connections and change our own lives. We can dress up as one era, our favorite, too, or show off our own changes.

Bryan West's delightful book about the Eras Tour and its superfans, *This Swift Beat*, records such multiple fashion choices: "I was going for 'Lover,'" says one Cincinnati concertgoer, "but at heart I'm an 'Evermore' girl." Sarah Chapelle's book on Taylor's outfits emphasizes what those outfits tell fans. Often they cast her as accessible, imitable, "a delight for fans to replicate," though the outfits also acknowledge her "natural thinness, blondeness, and modelesque height." The tour gives fans—who may not be thin, or blonde, or tall—occasions for feeling seen—if not by Taylor herself, then by the other Swifties who gather around her.[8]

The set for "The Man," an open-plan office, and the starker, brighter, similar set for ". . . Ready for It?" both invite us to join Taylor, to see ourselves in her, in ways that highlight rage. Taylor isn't fighting one bad man, she's fighting a system, and not in the name of absolute freedom (whatever that would mean), but in the name of a better system that might elevate us, too. On platforms for *Reputation*-era songs, not only the star, but her band members and dancers, can ride up and down. The dancers for "Look What You Made Me Do" dress up as previous Taylors: the Junior Jewels girl from "You Belong with Me," the ballerina from "Shake It Off," her VMA Awards costume. The effect is to tie all her earlier eras, her earlier looks and personas, together: She's had to be them, and to reject them, in order to become who she is now. When the real Taylor breaks away from those dancers and steps out of her phone-booth-sized cage, it's a victory lap, a way of sharing freedom. Maybe she'll help us get out of our own cages, too.

The set that Swifties call *folkmore*—a combination of *Folklore* and *Evermore*, created in 2024 to make room for *The Tortured Poets Department*—starts with the rising yellow light of fireflies, a moon reflected in ponds and rushes. When we see Taylor she's lying on a cottage roof, getting ready to sing "Cardigan." If you're seeing it for the first time, it's a wonder, a sudden trip to a magic wood. If you've seen it before, you might realize that this set also lets Taylor's body get physical rest: She's not keeping us waiting (we see her onstage), but for a few minutes she doesn't have to stand or move or dance. Again—and in contrast to other great pop performers—Taylor's providing a spectacle while reminding us that she's never been superhuman. She needs this pause more than we do.

At this point, she plays "Betty" alone onstage, on acoustic guitar, until James, the persona who voices the song, "[shows] up at [the] party." Then the band and the dancers appear. After Taylor plays "Champagne Problems," showcasing her solo piano skills, she stands and pauses for applause, always one to three minutes' worth (Swiftballers guess the time). We're cheering her resilience, her ability (as she puts it in "Willow") to come back strong like a 1990s trend.

Nobody thought of *1989* as an angry album when it came out. Swifties loved (or disliked) it for its bangers, its celebrations, its back turned on Nashville, its welcome to New York. The *1989* set here, though, emphasizes power, pride, and (again) gleeful rage. Taylor takes up a golf club to "smash" a convertible on risers, just as she did in the video for "Blank Space." For "Bad Blood," cannons shoot fire above the roof of the stadium: We can feel the heat flare. When the fires recede, we see the moonscape that signals *The Tortured Poets Department*, with a fresh series of glowing traps from which Taylor must escape. Again, "growing up precocious sometimes means not growing up at all": You become an adult, but you're still in a cage. (Some *TTPD* songs, including "But Daddy I Love Him," have lost their second verses for the sake of the run time: I realize, crestfallen, that I may never hear Taylor sing that favorite line.)

Eras Tour stagecraft reaches its purposefully cheesy peak in "I Can Do It with a Broken Heart." Dancers in old-school formalwear set Taylor on a fainting couch, as if she has collapsed from exhaustion. Then—once again—she emerges, empowered, in the new album's unambiguous banger, a song about being on tour forever, going out in front of every stadium, and selling big songs like this one. It's as meta as Taylor has ever been. The crowd literally screams "More!" She knows she's won our hearts by baring her heart, telling us that she really did get her heart broken, and then she performs for us, singing about the stress of performing with your heart crushed anyway. *Should* we be shouting "more," now that we know? Should we have given her space and left her alone?

Coming onstage with this song, she gives us her answer: There's no place that she'd rather be. Disaster in love, complete romantic collapse, doesn't have to mean your life is over, because—it's what Taylor has been saying off and on since *Taylor Swift*—you may well fall hard for the wrong guy, but you don't have to build your entire life around him: He can't own you. You may need help—you can't do everything on your own; no one can—but you own yourself. It is, if you like, a disability rights message: total self-reliance isn't a worthy goal so much as it is an ableist mirage. The live version of "I Can Do It with a Broken Heart" builds up the confidence that the recorded version struggles to project. Taylor visits the edge of the stage and enunciates that final line in the bridgeless song, one word per downbeat, with gestures to match. We saw that line in the previous chapter: "Try. And. Come. For. My. Job."

Now that she's doing mashups for surprise songs—two or three spliced into one another on guitar, then two or three more on piano—she can give her audiences hints about how the songs interact. Tonight in Edinburgh, "It's Nice to Have a Friend," about kids who grow up together and stay together, leads into "Dorothea," a plea from a kid who stayed home to a former beau who moved away. We can see Taylor both as the would-be star in LA and as the boy, or the girl, she left back in Tupelo. The relatable Taylor pines for the aspirational Taylor, and we know that they're two sides of one golden coin.

The Eras Tour does not only show how much Swift's art remains both aspirational and relatable, how much we can hear her songs as about us, and for us. It also underlines her need to show her work, to show us how hard she works. After *Reputation* and its unusual, almost stuntlike publicity, Taylor told *Vogue*, "I wanted to say to people, 'You realize writing songs is an art and a craft and not, like, an easy thing to do?'" In his poem "Adam's Curse," W. B. Yeats makes the same complaint: Non-poets usually overlook the work it takes "to articulate sweet sounds together." To which Yeats's friend replies, "To be born woman is to know— / Although they do not talk of it at school— / That we must labour to be beautiful."[9]

So many of us labor too, whether beside our mirrors at 6 a.m., working to get our blush just right over foundation, or over a standardized test score we hope to raise, or over our own writings, or else at a take-home test, a workbench, a spreadsheet. So many of us feel that we have no choice: That's one more reason—besides our romantic ups and downs, besides our life under patriarchal limits—that so many fans still see our lives in Swift's. She's the good girl, growing up precocious (no wonder she falls for the bad guys), always striving to earn the next accolade, being the best Taylor that she can be, following the instructional template that so many of us have long received, especially (but not only) if we are American girls, raised on promises. She really did get the gold stars, and yet she keeps working to garner even more: Even if she imagines an escape, or really escapes—for example, to Florida (or "Florida!!!")—we know she'll return.

It's as if she can't help it—no more than we can help coming from the achievement-oriented, high-pressure beauty cultures and school systems and families to which so many Swifties belong. We hear that growing up that way gives us privilege, and we may accept it, and yet we may feel that we're not lucky so much as obliged. The essayist, cultural critic, and fat activist Anne Helen Petersen has written beautifully about how Taylor negotiates that dilemma. "Trying to fit into society's understanding of 'good girl' is a trap," Petersen explains, "the same way the 'model minority' and the 'good gay' and the 'good fatty' are all traps. . . . Even when you succeed at it you lose, because these roles are ultimately means of containment: of circumscribing power by putting exacting, contradictory standards" on what you can do with it. And, Petersen continues, people who "identify with Swift—particularly with the Eldest-Daughter, Type-A, highly regimented, no-choice-but-to-be-a-good-girl part of her"—tend to defend her, even against the cultural critics (such as Petersen) who are not really attacking her, but pointing out her contradictions instead.[10]

TAYLOR'S VERSION

Being Taylor Swift—the Eras Tour wants us to know—means a lot of work: It means trying to get everything just right. Sometimes our lives feel like a lot of work too. We want to please everyone, to look acceptable, if not beautiful, to shine, never to let anyone down. And that's one reason fans collect, and cherish, the moments when something goes harmlessly wrong. It's not only the surprise songs, and the micro-decisions about vocal performance, and the various guest stars, that set each show apart. It's also, sometimes, the comedic mistakes: getting stuck on the roof of the *Folklore* house; tangling herself up in a billowing sleeve; rushing past a dancer to make a missed cue; dancing around a metallic cube that won't move with the choreography as it should; improvising after the "piano" (really an electronic keyboard) coughs up a string of unaccountable, unpredictable, metallic sounds, having apparently short-circuited in the torrential rain on the night before. You can watch these mistakes in the fan-made blooper reels known as "Errors Tour" videos, and they're a hoot. Like all blooper reels, they bring the star closer to us.

Other unrepeatable moments show Swift going out of her way to help fans. In Philadelphia, night two, she told a security guard to keep his hands to himself, without breaking the pace of the song: "Now we got bad blood—Stop! She wasn't doing anything! Used to be mad love—Hey, stop!" "She wasn't doing anything" became a meme, and a remix, and a T-shirt. Bryan West writes that in Europe, Swift "paused at least 18 of her 48 shows to ask staff to help concertgoers." When her elbow catches on her gown, or when she stops the show to call off a cop, we remember that nothing about this tour, and none of these songs, comes effortlessly or automatically. All these songs and minutes and sets and dances come out of collaboration and conscious choices. And—because it's Taylor—they come with humorous, back-on-her-feet, can't-miss-a-beat recoveries.[11]

After the last surprise song, in this Edinburgh concert as on every tour, Swift dives (so it seems) under the stage and into a pool of moving water, swimming like an Olympian or a mermaid. The move allows the singer to change costumes again before the *Midnights* set. It also looks back to the other transformations she has chosen to undergo: "You can either stand there and let the wave crash into you," she said in 2019, "or you can dive under the water, hold your breath, wait for it to pass and while you're down there, try to learn something." As she has, showing her work, and setting another example.[12]

The *Midnights* set, and the whole show, ends with "Karma." But if that set has a center, it's "Mastermind." It's a song about her relationship with her fans just as much as it's a song about how she caught and enticed her best guy. Nothing we've seen, for the last three and a half hours, maybe the last fifteen years, was accidental. It was all by design. An album about her sleepless days, her insecurities, all the nights when her depression works the graveyard shift and she feels like a monster, becomes, by the end of this set, the end of the evening, a monument to coming back, to taking charge when you can, to changing when you need to change, to accepting help while knowing that you belong to you. It's a monument full of glow and glitter, too—the glitter of "Bejeweled," and the over-the-top shimmer of "Karma," with seemingly all her dancers onstage. All of us, wearing her light-up bracelets, can imagine a small slice of her power—not her economic clout, but her power over herself, her voice, her poise. It's nice to have so many friends.

On our way out of Murrayfield Stadium we notice two girls in white *Folklore* chemises, strings of lights attached to each, literally skipping. Our bracelets change color and glow—violet, red, blue, white—as the crowds disperse. Looking at my wrists, at the dim streetlights, at the queue for the tram, I think about how the driven, exhausted Taylor of "I Can Do It with a Broken Heart"; and the delighted, controlling Taylor of "Mastermind"; and the love-struck woman, who changes a line in "Karma" when her boyfriend shows up at a concert (he's the guy on the Chiefs), are all the same person, about how the costume changes and the personae are who she is, just as much (at the least) as whatever private life paparazzi try to steal. I think about how she says regularly from the stage that she's as happy on this world tour as she has ever felt: Maybe that's the real Taylor. Not Harry Styles, but "Style"; not Matty Healy so much as "But Daddy I Love Him"; not any one romance, but "New Romantics." Every show is like a battle; every show is like a dream.

Every show was also streamed online, through the good offices of perhaps a dozen figures (the best known, Tess Bohne, goes by @Tess-Dear) on Instagram, TikTok, and YouTube, or in de facto watch parties on Discord. The linguistics professor Gretchen McCulloch has described such online social spaces as "third places," neither home nor work nor school, "distinguished by an emphasis on conversation and playfulness, regular attendees who set the tone for newcomers, the freedom to come and go as you please, a lack of formal membership requirements, and a warm, unpretentious feeling of home away from home." The sociologist Ray Oldenburg coined the term "third place" in 1989, referring to physical sites such as coffee shops and pubs. Many of us now find them online instead, which is McCulloch's point, not about Swifties but about fandom spaces in general.[13]

What distinguishes Swifties from other fandoms? For one thing, size; for another, its multigenerational nature (remember those great-aunts and mothers and nieces or daughters, all together on the tram). For another, the feeling of safety, both social and physical. People just getting into, say, Brahms, or Batman, or the Boston Bruins, might feel unwelcome among the tough guys or nerdy know-it-alls. With Swifties, we're welcome. The Swiftie universe also manifests—thanks to its size—in many offline, real-world gatherings: not just an Eras Tour show, but a local dance party, or a campus Swift night, or fans "congregating by the thousands to sing songs in the street," as West put it, after the canceled shows in Vienna—an Eras Tour event without the tour. Relentlessly cheerful, hoping to leave no one out, Swift in her songs, as well as when she's not singing, seems to know how many of us find one another through her.[14]

I almost wrote, just now, not "when she's not singing," but "when she's not performing." But it's not clear when, if ever, Taylor Swift is not performing. That's not a jab at her authenticity but a claim about her personality, as she describes it in songs and in interviews. She always (like it or not) knows that we're watching, and she doesn't want to let us down. Does she write, sing, and perform in order to live her life? Or does she live to write, sing, and perform? For an artist like Swift the question has no answer. If I'm not writing, if nobody's reading what I write, if nobody likes it, if nobody hears or sees me, who am I? Such questions animate so much of the music that Taylor Swift has made, from the insecurities of "Fifteen" and "Tied Together with a Smile" to the insecurities of "I Can Do It with a Broken Heart" and "Clara Bow." It's no wonder that so many of us around the world—especially so many girls and women, so many people shaped by cultures of people-pleasing, of giving back, of gratitude—have seen our own faces and heard our own voices here too.

And it's no wonder that the last surprise songs for the last Eras show, Vancouver, night three, addressed her relationship to her fans, a relationship—as I've been saying all along—that relies on how the words fit the music, that remains both aspirational and relatable, that shows the inevitable, impossible effects of her nonstop striving to be good, do better, do more. In picking her last surprise songs, Swift tells the crowd in Vancouver, she asked "which songs really encapsulate how I feel about the end of this tour, and I decided to go back to the beginning." First, from *Taylor Swift*, "A Place in This World," relatable to a T, heart on sleeve, rhymes pointedly obvious, telling us it's okay to be wrong, not to know what comes next, reaching up with the chorus's rising vocal line. Second, her song about coming together in third places, outside expectations and incentives and classrooms: "We're the New Romantics," she sings. "The best people in life are free."

Her last-ever piano surprise songs this night start so slow that it takes a few measures before Vancouver realizes what it's hearing: "Long Live," and then "New Year's Day," her song about keeping things going after a mega-party ends, and then "The Manuscript," the last song on (so far) her last album, to match "Tim McGraw" (Glendale, night one), the first song on her first. Swift sings the end of "The Manuscript" over the piano part that goes with "New Year's Day": "Now and then I reread the manuscript / But the story isn't mine anymore."

Swifties may want to pretend to be Taylor Swift's friends; Swift may encourage, or revel in, that pretense. We may use her music both as an escape from our lives and as a way to understand those lives. Where does Swift go when she wants to escape from her own? Dani Winchester and Olivia Kotarski have now recorded over a hundred installments (and counting) of their popular, thoughtful Swiftie podcast *Taylearning*. Most episodes address one album, one song (check out the way they break down "The Archer"), or one figure from Swift's cast of characters (Taylor Lautner, Sabrina Carpenter, Kanye West). One of their most heavily researched episodes addresses Swift's private jet, much criticized in 2023 for its supposedly out-of-line carbon emissions. Dani and Olivia point out that in her choice of vehicle, as in so much else, Swift gets held to an almost uniquely high standard. And they point out that Swift has little choice: Imagine New York La Guardia once passengers saw that Taylor would be on their plane.[15]

Swift needs that jet to get from show to show while on tour. But she also needs it to get away: to see her family, and her squad, and her boyfriend, the Kansas City Chiefs tight end Travis Kelce, who happens to live in a city that loves his team, and harbors few paparazzi, a city that seems, from afar, to embody the loyalty and the enthusiasm of fandom, without the telescopes and microscopes and scrutineers of New York or LA. What's it like there? What does Taylor see, and how do fans see Taylor, when she's not recording, not touring, and not leading a wholly public life? Dani and Olivia invited me to KC to find out.

What I see is another way that Taylor's music—and her life—can bring people together. It's cold on the plane, and I'm wearing a thick denim jacket with painted logos for all Taylor's albums, a gift from my Swiftie friend Kristie. A woman with long black hair and a plaid poncho tells me she loves my jacket. I notice her earrings: Chiefs arrowheads. "Go Chiefs!" she exclaims, assuming I'm a fan too. At the Kansas City International Airport's souvenir store, I spot sweatshirts in Chiefs colors, goldenrod on deep red, with a slogan that reads, "I'm Just Here for Taylor." (And so I am.)

In Kansas City, Olivia and Dani and their friend Rebecca take me to Piropos, the Argentine steakhouse that Taylor and Travis selected in October 2023 for their first public date. With rainbow-glass sculptures, brass railings, and a view of the lit-up city center, the place hits the sweet spot for a fancy dinner. High school girls, hardly able to move in their spangly dresses, gather in groups of four to six, blocking the stairs: It's homecoming week. Near our table, a couple in or past their sixties lean back, nursing cocktails. Our server tells us that Taylor and Travis's single visit transformed the restaurant's profile, though not its menu or décor. A Nickelodeon TV host made a YouTube episode there about "the Taylor Swift experience." People order whatever she ordered (the halibut). Sometimes they want to buy her chair (not for sale).

The next day, Dani and Olivia and I go to the "MADE IN KC" store, which offers locally sourced products. I've never set foot in any city where so many people wear sports team logos (and I live in Boston). Here, Chiefs pride has subsumed Taylor pride. One sweatshirt at the store reads, "WORLD CHAMPS: Taylor's Version." A white T-shirt with overlapping outlines of a running Travis Kelce (overlapping because he moves faster than the eye can see) puns on her name and his skill: "Mr. Swift." Another T-shirt mimics the T-shirts Taylor wears for the Eras Tour version of "22": "WHO'S TRAVIS KELCE ANYWAY? EW." Across the street, at EB and Co., a store for locally created jewelry, the feast of "Tayvis" merchandise continues. I purchase earrings with enamel images of Taylor's rag-doll cat Benjamin. I see, but do not purchase, rings with Travis's number 87; a beaded purse with the *Lover* logo; enormous beaded earrings in the shape of the *Reputation* snake; and buttons that say "KAN ZEH SWIFTY," with a Y, because Swift herself has registered as a trademark the word "Swiftie" with an "ie."[16]

The following day we go to Rye, a fancy brunch place that Taylor and Travis sometimes visit. We order Travis's supposed favorite: a cinnamon roll the size of a box turtle, meant for a split among three or four people, with shiny, soft, off-white icing that looks like lava overflow. Half of the other tables have at least one patron wearing a Chiefs jersey: Most of those jerseys feature the "87." That afternoon we hit an unpretentious, joyful, video-game-themed bar called the DoubleTap. Everyone there is watching the Chiefs play the Chargers. When Travis makes his first catch, the whole room roars. It's a refreshing look at how fandoms can work. Rather than reorganize itself around Taylor or send a pack of celebrity chasers after her (as happened in New York City), KC has folded Swifties into a preexisting enthusiasm. It's as close to a refuge from her own prominence as Taylor seems likely to get without retreating entirely (as she did in 2016–2017).

But that's not very close. "The Manuscript" reminds us that Swift is a writer, just as "Long Live" and "I Can Do It with a Broken Heart" remind us that she's a performer. Is she a poet? I get that question a lot. The title, and the material, on *TTPD* prompted acres of unproductive debate as to whether her lyrics count as poetry. These debates echoed similar arguments around the Beatles, around Joni Mitchell, around Tupac, around Kendrick Lamar, around Bob Dylan and his Nobel Prize. Is Kendrick a poet? Is Dylan a genius? Will any or all of them matter as much (whatever that means) or last as long as, say, Emily Dickinson?

For what it's worth, I have made my own preferences clear: I hear Swift as one of the world's great songwriters—a genius of making (alone and with coauthors) pop songs. Song lyrics, at least in our day, words made to fit repeated vocal melodies, amount to an art form distinct from page-based poetry, just as stage plays constitute an art form distinct from novels (and rap lyrics, like screenplays, an art form distinct from both). That said, Swift's powers let her do some things that, in past societies, poets have done: She holds up a mirror (or a mirrorball), gives shape to shared experience, takes us for an emotional ride, and represents large groups, generations, or nations. It's in this sense that, as the Italian literary theorist Guido Mazzoni puts it, "rock and pop and today's hip-hop and rap have a social mandate that modern poetry has lost. . . . Songs have taken the place of poems for the educated lay public," with their "simple, direct and immediate passions . . . transfigured by music."[17]

Pop songs like Taylor's, lyrics like Taylor's, in other words, can seem easy to hear, and easy to like, as well as hard to achieve. The novelist Rachel Kushner has written about her own years in San Francisco rock clubs. One night, "PJ Harvey played two sold-out shows at the Warfield, and after her second show she played a secret impromptu set at the Hotel Utah, a dive bar. . . . I think I left at about five a.m., and she was still playing. She did not get tired, and she did not look tired." Kushner concludes, from hearing that musician, that "to be truly good at something is the very highest joy."[18]

Taylor Swift would never say as much outright, but it's been her message too, from Sydney to Vancouver, Wyomissing to Edinburgh. And Kushner might have taken, from PJ Harvey or from Taylor, another message: For some of us, that joy demands to be shared. Art wants an audience; energy wants to circulate, even if the only "message" it brings is the possibility of that joy. And songwriting—music with words about the human experience—can carry other messages on top of that one, above all the message that pain can turn into joy, especially when the audience sticks around.

Willa Cather concluded *The Song of the Lark*—her great novel about the youth of a classical singer—by claiming that an adult artist's development finally sets her apart from the facts of her life. "Here we must leave Thea Kronborg. . . . The growth of an artist is an intellectual and spiritual development which can scarcely be followed in a personal narrative. This story attempts to deal only with the simple and concrete beginnings which color and accent an artist's work." Swift's body of work speaks, constantly, to the kind of effort, the "life of disciplined endeavor," that she, too, has made for herself. And yet Swift's body of work so often asks us *not* to discard her "personal narrative," to figure it into her triumphs, as Cather's own life in fact figures into hers.[19]

Swift speaks to her audience almost from a position of equality, as Cather's proud grown-up artists never would. Swift seems to care about us, within certain boundaries. She has what the poet Gerard Manley Hopkins called the virtue of "bidding," "the art or virtue of saying everything right to or at the hearer," making the hearer feel always "addressed or at least concerned." And if "But Daddy I Love Him," "Clara Bow," and "Call It What You Want" established Swift's boundaries, pushing back against the stans, then the Eras Tour, and "New Romantics," and "The Manuscript" remind us how much Swift still speaks to us, for us, how much her music lets us feel close to her.[20]

Near the end of *The Song of the Lark*, Thea's mentors and teachers talk about how Thea got so good. The musician who understood her best, the Hungarian émigré Harsanyi, explains that "every artist's secret . . . is passion. That is all. It is an open secret, and perfectly safe. Like heroism, it is inimitable in cheap materials." "Passion" here does not mean Thea's flimsy love affairs, but her attention to what she sings and how she sings. That passion, in turn, lets Thea do something that some of us have seen Swift herself do, something inherently aspirational (we wish we could do it) even if it seems impossible; something inherently relatable (she has invited us to join in, even given one of us a bowler hat), even though we know she's not literally our friend. But let Cather (who, again, might have disdained Swift) say it:

> While she was on the stage she was conscious that every movement was the right movement, that her body was absolutely the instrument of her idea. Not for nothing had she kept it so severely, kept it filled with such energy and fire. All that deep-rooted vitality flowered in her voice, her face, in her very finger-tips. She felt like a tree bursting into bloom. And her voice was as flexible as her body; equal to any demand, capable of every *nuance*. With the sense of its perfect companionship, its entire trustworthiness, she had been able to throw herself into the dramatic exigencies of the part, everything in her at its best. [Emphasis in original.]

"Companionship." "Trustworthiness." Even this clearly non-pop version of vocal and lyrical excellence requires such things. Swift has brought them to her songs since the first time she sang about moonlight on a lake. After so many years, she can still feel like our companion, our super-ultra-mega-famous friend. After so many heartbreaks and reversals, she can still look like someone that many of us, especially the good girls and precocious "work people" and often-rewarded children, want to be. And when she has more to say, or to sing, we'll be listening.[21]

When TV and radio journalists interviewed me, after my lecture class on Swift had ended, during the last months of the Eras Tour, they often asked me what I thought Swift would do next. I wanted to tell them, quoting "Death by a Thousand Cuts," that they might as well ask the traffic lights. I said "I don't know." And I remembered Yeats's thoughts, at twice Taylor's age, as he wrote about himself:

All his happier dreams came true . . .
"What then?" sang Plato's ghost. "What then?"

"The work is done," grown old he thought,
"According to my boyish plan;
Let the fools rage, I swerved in naught,
Something to perfection brought";
But louder sang that ghost, "What then?"

Swift, at the conclusion of the Eras Tour, has exorcised her prior selves, and brought much of her catalog to perfection, as well as bringing it to over 10 million concertgoers, on 149 dates, on five continents. Only she can say whether she, too, has heard this ghost, insisting that no achievement is enough, that no realized work of art can fulfill an artist's every dream: Only another work, another show, and another manuscript will do.[22]

ACKNOWLEDGMENTS

No project this size finds anything like its right shape without plenty of help. If this one works, it does so thanks to more friends, students, writers, and additional Swifties than I have space to name. If you helped and your name's not here, please know that I'm grateful!

My editor Lara Heimert watched over me, reassured me, and set me on the right paths when I strayed from our purposes. She also offered a tall stack of good ideas, most of which I hope I've incorporated. If you find something enlightening in this book, there's a big chance it began with her. My agent, Matt McGowan, talked me through the initial stage of the project, did the hard parts and the numbers, and made the right match: I remain a major Matt fan. My kind editors on other continuing book projects—Carmen Giménez, Philip Leventhal, Sharmila Sen, and Jeff Shotts—happily gave me the space to drive this one. Other editors, I will see you soon.

This book could not remotely have come to life had I not first taught a course about Taylor, a shockingly big one. That course would have crashed and burned without the intellectual, practical, and pedagogical energies, and the kindness, of MJ (Merlin) Cunniff. Other teaching

ACKNOWLEDGMENTS

fellows for that course made it work in other ways, with music they played and lectures they gave: Avery Blankenship, Imani Davis, Elisa Fuhrken, Jaime Gordon, Sharri Hall, Jenny Henderson, Matthew Jordan, and Walter Smelt. Chloe Chapin contributed both her knowledge of pedagogy and her expertise with costume and fashion. Some students from that course affected this book as well, in ways that could not help but make it better: among them (not an exhaustive list) Elizabeth Ambrose, Dannie Bell, Betsy Bennett, Brady Billingsley, Maya Bodnick, Cole Hahn, Cameron Hosain, Siena Lerner-Gill, Angela Lin (from MIT), Olivia Ma, Elixandra Ocasio, Mary Pankowski, Aaron Rosales, Cormac Savage, and Catherine Stanton.

Harvard's a weird place but it's been good for me, thanks in part to the colleagues and department chairs who've welcomed me and listened to me there: Particular warmth, in the year-plus over which this book got made, goes out to Dan Donoghue, Deidre Lynch, and Leah Whittington; to department chairs Glenda Carpio, John Stauffer, and Nicholas Watson; and to nonfaculty staff, among them Lauren Bimmler, Rhiannon Gentile, Case Kerns, Sol Kim-Bentley, Anna McDonald, and Gwen Urdang-Brown.

Some of my favorite Swifties came through for me. Bryan West of *USA Today* did as much as he could to help me teach and to show me around Nashville. Dani, Olivia, and Rebecca from *Taylearning* came to Boston, lent me the mic for their podcast, and also showed me around Kansas City: I hope this book conveys my gratitude, along with the enthusiasms we share. The very kind Zan Romanoff and Sarah Enni let me onto their podcast as well: You should check out their novels! Second to none in Swifthood comes the poet, friend, and editor Kristie Dougherty, the mastermind behind the Swiftie anthology *Invisible Strings*, who answered all my questions, at all hours, and put her own

ACKNOWLEDGMENTS

weekend on hold to show me around Nashville. Friendship bracelets are just where it starts.

Kristin Nelson Patel, Paras Patel, Catherine Rockwood, and Rachel Trousdale welcomed me into their homes and families: Consider, please, reading Rachel's and Catherine's own poems! Brian Hanechak and Kate Fractal provided warmth, nerds, and refuge, along with countless messages from the stars. Connor Kennedy entered my life as I finished writing this book, bringing only the finest wags, scritches, and taste tests.

Rachel Gold understands me like nobody else, and like I thought nobody ever would. They see the world—or the plurality of worlds—as I do, and they've shown me more than a small part of those worlds: Consider reading their novels too (Swifties new to the Goldverse can begin with *In the Silences*). Mara Hampson tells me the stories we both need to hear: Together we boldly go. I love how we keep going (and purring). I want to thank La, and also Kam, here, too: I couldn't imagine more generous metamours.

Jessica Bennett and I have been in love since the mid-1990s. Yup, we still are. It's nice to have a you. Together we live with two very astonishing young people. Cooper, your strength of character matches your wisdom, your artistic talent, and your dexterity in creating characters; Millie, being around you feels like music (complimentary) even when you're not playing music. I'll even drop you off around the block: I've had so many best days with you.

NOTES

Chapter 1. . . . Ready for It

1. As of early 2025, the Swiftie Tube map remained online. See "Taylor Swift Tube Map Released as Star Plays London," BBC, June 24, 2024, www.bbc.com/news/articlescrgg097rg7no.

2. *Journey to Fearless*, dir. Don Mischer and Ryan Polito (The Hub, 2010). The guitar teacher and computer repairman Ronnie Cremer later tried to capitalize on his pupil's success, giving disrespectful interviews and setting up websites to flaunt his connection to her, until the Swift family shut him down. See Holly Herman, "Berks County Man Says He Taught Taylor Swift to Play Guitar," *Reading Eagle*, February 12, 2015, www.readingeagle.com/2015/02/12/berks-county-man-says-he-taught-taylor-swift-to-play-guitar.

3. Joanna Hillman, "Taylor Swift Interviews Rock 'n' Roll Icon Pattie Boyd on Songwriting, Beatlemania, and the Power of Being a Muse," *Harper's Bazaar*, July 10, 2018, www.harpersbazaar.com/culture/features/a22020940/taylor-swift-interviews-pattie-boyd; Kelefa Sanneh, *Major Labels* (New York: Penguin, 2021), 71; "73 Questions with Taylor Swift," YouTube, posted by Vogue, April 19, 2016, www.youtube.com/watch?v=XnbCSboujF4 (after 1:20).

4. Swifties, from high school students to professors like me, have often written about her "English!" references. For an articulate high school student's observations, see Whitney Knotts, "Taylor Swift Was an English Teacher in Her Past Life," in *Talon*, the student newspaper of Academic Magnet High School in North Charleston, South Carolina, May 5, 2021, https://amhsnewspaper.com/46386/ae/taylor-swift-was-an-english-teacher-in-her-past-life. For professors' views, see especially Betsy Winakur Tontiplaphol and Anastasia Klimchynskaya, eds., *The Literary Taylor Swift* (New York: Bloomsbury, 2024); Elly McCausland, *Stars Around My Scars: The Annotated Poetry of Taylor Swift* (New York: Andrews McMeel, 2024); Elly McCausland, *Swifterature: A Love Story* (New York: Pegasus, 2025); and Kirsty Fairclough, *Swiftly Iconic* (Manchester, UK: Manchester University Press, 2026).

5. Chris Willman, "Read Taylor Swift's Speech Welcoming Carole King, 'the Greatest Songwriter of All Time,' into Rock and Roll Hall of Fame," *Variety*, October 30, 2021, https://

variety.com/2021/music/news/taylor-swift-carole-king-full-speech-rock-roll-hall-fame-1235101292.

6. "Google Books Ngram Viewer" for the term "relatability," https://books.google.com/ngrams/graph?content=relatability&year_start=1800&year_end=2019&corpus=en-2019&smoothing=3; Samuel Johnson, "The Life of Gray," edited by Jack Lynch from *The Lives of the Poets*, ed. G. B. Hill, 3 vols. (Oxford: Clarendon, 1905), https://jacklynch.net/Texts/gray.html; Helen Vendler, *Part of Nature, Part of Us* (Cambridge, MA: Harvard University Press, 1980), 237; Tavi Gevinson, *Fan Fiction* (Los Angeles: Heavy Manners, 2024), 8, available at www.mirrorball.org.

7. For an annotated list, see Rob Sheffield's running tally: "All 274 of Taylor Swift Songs, Ranked," *Rolling Stone*, April 25, 2024, www.rollingstone.com/music/music-lists/taylor-swift-songs-ranked-rob-sheffield-201800.

8. Melanie Dunea, ed., *My Country* (New York: Rodale, 2010), 72.

9. Alex Suskind, "New Reputation: Taylor Swift Shares Intel on TS7, Fan Theories, and Her Next Era," *Entertainment Weekly*, May 9, 2019, https://ew.com/music/2019/05/09/taylor-swift-cover-story.

Chapter 2. Debut

1. Casey Lawrence, "Before Jennifer Lawrence and Taylor Swift Were Famous, They Modeled for Abercrombie & Fitch," *Teen Vogue*, January 31, 2014, www.teenvogue.com/gallery/abercrombie-and-fitch-celebrity-models.

2. Casey Sennett, "Taylor Swift," Pennsylvania Center for the Book, Literary and Cultural Heritage Maps of Pennsylvania, https://pabook.libraries.psu.edu/literary-cultural-heritage-map-pa/bios/swift__taylor, accessed March 13, 2025; Dan Gelston, "Taylor Swift's Connections to Sports Go Back to Her Early Days Performing the National Anthem," NBC10 Philadelphia, February 9, 2024, www.nbcphiladelphia.com/news/local/taylor-swifts-connections-to-sports-go-back-to-her-early-days-performing-the-national-anthem/3772093. For more on Swift's early life, see Chloe Govan, *Taylor Swift: The Rise of the Nashville Teen* (London: Omnibus, 2012), and Louisa Jepson, *Taylor Swift* (London: Simon and Schuster, 2013).

3. Govan, *Taylor Swift*, 67, 91–93; Melanie Dunea, ed., *My Country* (New York: Rodale, 2010), 72.

4. Alexander Pope, *The Poems*, ed. John Butt (New Haven, CT: Yale University Press, 1963), 195, 210 (capitalization modernized); W. B. Yeats, "He Tells of a Valley Full of Lovers," in *Collected Works*, vol. 1, *The Poems*, 2nd ed., ed. Richard J. Finneran (New York: Scribner, 2010), 67.

5. Govan, *Taylor Swift*, 44, 29, 32–33, 54.

6. Chris Willman, "Taylor Swift's Road to Fame," *Entertainment Weekly*, February 5, 2008, https://ew.com/article/2008/02/05/taylor-swifts-road-fame.

7. Sterling Whitaker, "Veteran Songwriter Liz Rose Shares Secret to Co-writing with Taylor Swift: 'I Didn't Get in Her Way,'" August 16, 2014, Taste of Country, https://tasteofcountry.com/liz-rose-taylor-swift-co-writing. Rose has since released a fine album on her

NOTES TO CHAPTER 2

own, *Swimming Alone*; to compare Rose's work there, and for other performers, is to see how much Taylor Swift put her own verbal energies into the Swift/Rose songs.

8. Kevin Evers, *There's Nothing Like This: The Strategic Genius of Taylor Swift* (Boston: Harvard Business Review Press, 2025), 14. Borchetta had apparently heard Swift's songs a few days before, when Swift came to his office, but the Bluebird showcase convinced him to sign her.

9. Sarah Chapelle, *Taylor Swift Style* (New York: St. Martin's, 2024), 8; Evers, *There's Nothing Like This*, 25.

10. Fans and journalists do not agree on the name of the senior: It's widely reported as Brandon Borello, but may also be Drew Dunlap, or an imaginary composite. See, for example, "Rosie," *All Too Well* (blog), July 4, 2013, https://13alltoowell-blog.tumblr.com/post/54582711529; Nate Jones, "What Happens to Boys After Taylor Swift Writes Songs About Them?," *Vulture*, October 27, 2014, www.vulture.com/2014/10/what-happens-to-boys-after-taylor-swift.html; Christina Capatides, "Match These Taylor Swift Songs to Her Ex-Boyfriends," CBS News, September 7, 2016, www.cbsnews.com/pictures/match-these-taylor-swift-songs-to-her-ex-boyfriends/16.

11. Glenn McDonald, *You Have Not Yet Heard Your Favorite Song: How Streaming Changes Music* (Kingston-upon-Thames: Canbury, 2024), 86; Taylor Swift, *Lover* diaries, entry for June 16, 2003; Chet Flippo, "Tanya Tucker: The Teenage Teaser," *Rolling Stone*, September 26, 1974, 85.

12. "Mary's Song (Oh My My My)," Swiftipedia: Taylor Swift Wiki, accessed March 13, 2025, https://taylorswift.fandom.com/wiki/Mary%27s_Song_(Oh_My_My_My).

13. "Picture to Burn," Taylor Swift Switzerland, accessed April 17, 2025, https://taylorswiftswitzerland.ch/index.php/albums/taylor-swift-album/taylor-swift-songs/picture-to-burn.

14. For Swift's full essay on Lee, see Holly Gleason, ed., *Women Walk the Line* (Austin: University of Texas Press, 2017), 41–42.

15. "Tied Together with a Smile," Swiftipedia: Taylor Swift Wiki, accessed March 13, 2025, https://taylorswift.fandom.com/wiki/Tied_Together_with_a_Smile; Erving Goffman, *The Presentation of Self in Everyday Life* (Chicago: University of Chicago Press, 1959 [1956]), 150–151.

16. Jepson, *Taylor Swift*, 35.

17. Robyn Schiff, "Lion Felling a Bull," in *A Woman of Property* (New York: Penguin, 2016), 68.

18. "The Outside," Swiftipedia: Taylor Swift Wiki, accessed March 13, 2025, https://taylorswift.fandom.com/wiki/The_Outside; Swift, *Lover* diaries, entry for February 14, 2004.

19. Swift, *Lover* diaries, entry for June 3, 2006; Chris Willman, "Getting to Know Taylor Swift," *Entertainment Weekly*, July 25, 2007, https://ew.com/article/2007/07/25/getting-know-taylor-swift; Jepson, *Taylor Swift*, 53.

20. Austin Scaggs, "Taylor Swift: Country, Metal, Hip-Hop and Jamming with Superfans," *Rolling Stone*, November 27, 2008, www.rollingstone.com/music/music-news/taylor-swift-country-metal-hip-hop-and-super-fans-236671; Jon Caramanica, "My Music, MySpace,

My Life," *New York Times*, November 7, 2008, www.nytimes.com/2008/11/09/arts/music/09cara.html?; Willman, "Taylor Swift's Road to Fame."

21. Scott Miller, *Music: What Happened?* (Alameda, CA: 125 Books, 2010), 87.

Chapter 3. Fearless

1. Ken Tucker, "The Billboard Q&A: Taylor Swift," *Billboard*, March 26, 2008, www.billboard.com/music/music-news/the-billboard-qa-taylor-swift-1046063; Associated Press, "Taylor Swift Receives Her High School Diploma," *Houston Chronicle*, July 27, 2008, www.chron.com/culture/main/article/taylor-swift-receives-her-high-school-diploma-1545672.php.

2. Allen Grossman, with Mark Halliday, *The Sighted Singer* (Baltimore: Johns Hopkins University Press, 1992), 369.

3. John Liberty, "An Unassuming Ride to Teen Queendom," *Kalamazoo Gazette*, January 31, 2008, www.mlive.com/kalamazoo_gazette_extra/2008/01/an_unassuming_ride_to_teen_que.html; William Wordsworth, "Lines Composed a Few Miles Above Tintern Abbey," in William Wordsworth and Samuel Taylor Coleridge, *Lyrical Ballads*, ed. Fiona Stafford (Oxford: Oxford University Press, 2000 [1798]), 197.

4. "Fifteen," Taylor Swift Switzerland, accessed March 14, 2025, taylorswiftswitzerland.ch/index.php/albums/fearless-album/fearless-songs/fifteen.

5. Greil Marcus, *The History of Rock 'n' Roll in Ten Songs* (New Haven, CT: Yale University Press, 2015), 103, 106.

6. Tracey Thorn, *Naked at the Albert Hall* (London: Virago, 2016), 103, 106.

7. Dave Itzkoff, "In Defense of Taylor Swift," *New York Times*, February 4, 2010, https://archive.nytimes.com/artsbeat.blogs.nytimes.com/2010/02/04/taylor-swift-defended-by-record-label-executive/index.html; Thorn, *Naked at the Albert Hall*, 26.

8. Ilana Nash, *American Sweethearts: Teenage Girls in Twentieth Century Popular Culture* (Bloomington: Indiana University Press, 2010), 24.

9. Chloe Govan, *Taylor Swift: The Rise of the Nashville Teen* (London: Omnibus, 2012), 148; "Truck Driver's Gear Change," TV Tropes, accessed March 14, 2025, https://tvtropes.org/pmwiki/pmwiki.php/Main/TruckDriversGearChange.

10. Kristen Hé, "Taylor Swift's 'Love Story' Re-Recording Gently Reinvents a Modern Classic," *Billboard*, February 12, 2021, www.billboard.com/music/pop/taylor-swift-love-story-rerecording-versions-compared-9525463; Melanie Dunea, ed., *My Country* (New York: Rodale, 2010), 72.

11. Jocelyn Vena, "Taylor Swift Talks About Joe Jonas Breakup Online, on the Radio, on TV and in Her New Album," MTV, November 6, 2008, archived at WayBack Machine, https://web.archive.org/web/20140904221949/http://www.mtv.com/news/1598752/taylor-swift-talks-about-joe-jonas-breakup-online-on-the-radio-on-tv-and-in-her-new-album; "Taylor Swift's Message to Joe Jonas," YouTube, posted by okGrace, November 5, 2008, www.youtube.com/watch?v=9NyEWGAlFr8.

12. Richard Rys, "Exit Interview: Taylor Swift," *Philadelphia Magazine*, October 21, 2008, www.phillymag.com/news/2008/10/21/exit-interview-taylor-swift; Govan, *Taylor Swift*, 158.

NOTES TO CHAPTER 4

13. James Merrill, "Matinees," in *Collected Poems*, ed. J. D. McClatchy and Stephen Yenser (New York: Knopf, 2001), 269.

14. Dave Pell, "For Sale on the Web: You!," NPR, January 27, 2011, www.kunc.org/2011-01-27/for-sale-on-the-web-you.

15. Olivia Ordoñez, "'I'm Still Trying Everything to Keep You Looking at Me': Taylor Swift and the Autotheoretical Construction of Public Selves," *Feminist Studies* 49, nos. 2–3 (2023): 394–420.

16. Stephen Betts, "Taylor Swift's 'Hey Stephen' Inspiration Returns the Favor," The Boot, May 5, 2011, https://theboot.com/stephen-barker-liles-taylor-swift-song.

17. Govan, *Taylor Swift*, 152.

18. Kelefa Sanneh, *Major Labels* (New York: Penguin, 2021), 162.

19. Robert Frost, *The Notebooks of Robert Frost*, ed. Mark Richardson (Cambridge, MA: Harvard University Press, 2007), 283.

Chapter 4. Speak Now

1. Taylor Swift, webcast, quoted in Louisa Jepson, *Taylor Swift* (London: Simon and Schuster, 2013), 184, 158; Brian Hiatt and Erik Madigan Heck, "Taylor Swift: The Rolling Stone Interview," *Rolling Stone*, September 18, 2019, www.rollingstone.com/music/music-features/taylor-swift-rolling-stone-interview-880794, quoted in Caroline Sullivan, *Taylor Swift: Era by Era. The Unauthorized Biography* (New York: Andrews McMeel, 2024), 125.

2. "Songs on *Speak Now*," Taylor Swift Switzerland, accessed March 14, 2025, https://taylorswiftswitzerland.ch/index.php/albums/speak-now-album/speak-now-songs.

3. Nicki Cox, "Take a Peek Inside Taylor Swift's $2M Eclectic, 'Alice in Wonderland'–Inspired Penthouse Apartment in Nashville," Page Six, March 1, 2024, https://pagesix.com/lifestyle/take-a-peek-inside-taylor-swifts-2m-eclectic-alice-in-wonderland-inspired-penthouse-apartment-in-nashville.

4. Sarah Chapelle, *Taylor Swift Style* (New York: St. Martin's, 2024), 66, 144; Julia Serano, "Femmephobia," Julia's Trans, Gender, Sexuality, & Activism Glossary!, accessed March 14, 2025, www.juliaserano.com/terminology.html#femmephobia. The A-line skirt and matching top come from the *1989* era, but Chapelle's larger point—first advanced for the flowy *Speak Now* look—remains.

5. Barry Egan, "Don't Go Breaking My Heart," *Irish Independent*, January 27, 2025, www.independent.ie/entertainment/music/dont-go-breaking-my-heart-taylor-swift-opens-up/30683975.html.

6. Ewen McAskill, "Obama Calls Kanye West a 'Jackass,'" *Guardian*, September 15, 2009, www.theguardian.com/world/2009/sep/15/obama-kanye-west-mtv; Joel Meares, "A Profile Written Through Tweets," *Columbia Journalism Review*, August 27, 2010, www.cjr.org/the_kicker/a_profile_written_through_twee.php.

7. "Taylor Lautner Calls 2009 VMAs Moment with Ex Taylor Swift His BIGGEST Regret," YouTube, posted by Entertainment Tonight, February 2, 2023, www.youtube.com/watch?v=vOhQbaDEk-A.

NOTES TO CHAPTER 4

8. Chuck Klosterman, "Taylor Swift on 'Bad Blood,' Kanye West, and How People Interpret Her Lyrics," *GQ*, October 15, 2015, www.gq.com/story/taylor-swift-gq-cover-story.

9. Megan Vick, "Taylor Swift Reveals 'Speak Now' Track List," *Billboard*, September 22, 2010, www.billboard.com/music/music-news/taylor-swift-reveals-speak-now-track-list-956160.

10. Shaun Cullen, "The Innocent and the Runaway," *Journal of Popular Music Studies* 28, no. 1 (2016): 33–50, 40.

11. "Adam Young: What Really Happened with Taylor Swift," *US*, June 15, 2011, www.usmagazine.com/entertainment/news/owl-citys-adam-young-2011156.

12. Tom Roland, "Taylor Swift Ready to 'Speak Now,'" Reuters, October 15, 2010, www.reuters.com/article/lifestyle/taylor-swift-ready-to-speak-now-with-third-album-idUSTRE69E5RK.

13. Emily Nagoski, *Come Together: The Science (and Art!) of Creating Lasting Sexual Connections* (New York: Ballantine, 2024), 26; Annie Zaleski, *Taylor Swift: The Stories Behind the Songs* (San Diego: Thunder Bay, 2024), 65.

14. Chapelle, *Taylor Swift Style*, 66.

15. Arielle Zibrak, *Guilty Pleasures* (New York: New York University Press, 2021), 122–123.

16. Lizzie Widdicombe, "You Belong with Me," *New Yorker*, October 3, 2011, https://newyorker.com/magazine/2011/10/10/taylor-swift-profile-you-belong-with-me.

17. Richard Lawson, "Taylor Swift and John Mayer Probably Aren't Getting Back Together," *Vanity Fair*, August 21, 2014, www.vanityfair.com/hollywood/2014/08/taylor-swift-john-mayer-chateau-marmont.

18. Chloe Govan, *Taylor Swift: The Rise of the Nashville Teen* (London: Omnibus, 2012), 210.

19. Jepson, *Taylor Swift*, 178–179.

20. Kelsie Gibson, "Who Are Taylor Swift's Speak Now Songs About?," *People*, July 10, 2023, http://people.com/who-are-taylor-swift-speak-now-songs-about-7557272; Devon Price, *Unlearning Shame* (New York: Harmony, 2024), 129.

21. Price, *Unlearning Shame*, 129, 144.

22. Margaret Rossman, "Taylor Swift, Remediating the Self, and Nostalgic Girlhood in Tween Music Fandom," *Transformative Works and Cultures* 38 (2022), journal.transformativeworks.org/index.php/article/view/2287.

23. Dan Grote, "Editorial: Why the From the Ashes X-Men Comics Have More New Mutants Than New Mutants," ComicsXF, September 8, 2024, https://comicsxf.com/2024/09/08/xmen-fromtheashes-new-mutants. Solfège (the do-re-mi system) properly represents minor keys with *do* as the root and *me*, *le*, and *te*, rather than *mi*, *la*, *ti* for the third, sixth, and seventh notes of the scale; for simplicity's sake, in this book I represent them instead by taking *la* as the root.

24. Hannah Dailey, "Emma Stone Reacts to Rumors," *Billboard*, December 7, 2023, http://billboard.com/music/music-news/emma-stone-reacts-taylor-swift-when-emma-falls-in-love-rumors-1235544422; Jepson, *Taylor Swift*, 244.

NOTES TO CHAPTER 5

25. The queer sex therapist Casey Tanner, for example, remembers (with a hint of sarcasm) "those moments growing up in high school where I was like, well, do I want to be her? Or do I want to date her? Right. That sort of common friendship experience." Casey Tanner (guest), "Queer and Questioning," *Call Your Girlfriend* (podcast), June 4, 2021, www.callyourgirlfriend.com/episodes/2021/06/04/queer-questioning; Anna Marks, "Look What Taylor Swift Made Us Do," *New York Times*, January 4, 2024, www.nytimes.com/2024/01/04/opinion/taylor-swift-queer.html. On Gaylorism, see also James Factora, "USA Today Is Hiring a Taylor Swift Reporter," Them, September 12, 2023, www.them.us/story/usa-today-taylor-swift-reporter.

26. Marisa Meltzer, "When Two Thumbs Down Are a Sign of Approval," *New York Times*, August 9, 2011, www.nytimes.com/2011/08/11/fashion/hand-heart-gesture-grows-in-popularity-noticed.html; Rossman, "Taylor Swift, Remediating the Self."

27. Kathleen Hanna, *Rebel Girl* (New York: HarperCollins, 2024), 136.

28. Jepson, *Taylor Swift*, 78; Hanna, *Rebel Girl*, 169.

Chapter 5. Red

1. Alyssa Bailey, "Taylor Swift Says *Red* Is Her Only 'True Breakup Album,'" *Elle*, October 28, 2020, www.elle.com/culture/celebrities/a34506168/taylor-swift-red-breakup-album; Kevin Evers, *There's Nothing Like This: The Strategic Genius of Taylor Swift* (Boston: Harvard Business Review Press, 2025), 98–99 ("Swift has copped to crying while listening to Blue . . . and it's hard to imagine that it wasn't influencing her"); Grady Smith, "Taylor Swift's New Single 'We Are Never Ever Getting Back Together,'" *Entertainment Weekly*, August 14, 2012, https://ew.com/article/2012/08/14/taylor-swift-we-are-never-ever-getting-back-together-red/; Caroline Sullivan, *Taylor Swift: Era by Era. The Unauthorized Biography* (New York: Andrews McMeel, 2024), 147; CD insert to *Red*, 2012.

2. R. O. Kwon, ed., *Kink* (New York: Simon and Schuster, 2021), 3.

3. Ursula K. Le Guin, *The Birthday of the World* (New York: Harper Perennial, 2003), 146; William Empson, *The Structure of Complex Words*, ed. Helen Thaventhiran and Stefan Collini (Oxford: Oxford University Press, 2021 [1951]).

4. Niall Stokes, *U2: Into the Heart* (New York: Thunder's Mouth, 2005), 10, 17.

5. Courtney Conley, "Crash and Burn: Taylor Swift's Lyrics on Dating Bad Drivers," Safe2Drive, September 24, 2024, www.safe2drive.com/blog/Crash-and-Burn-Taylor-Swifts-Lyrics-on-Dating-Bad-Drivers.

6. Sullivan, *Taylor Swift*, 145.

7. Jason Lipshutz, "Taylor Swift Reveals 'Never Ever' Inspiration," *Billboard*, September 24, 2012, www.billboard.com/music/music-news/taylor-swift-reveals-never-ever-inspiration-474960; Savannah Dantona, "Eat Your Hearts Out, Pop-Hating Ex-BFs," *American Songwriter*, November 26, 2023, https://americansongwriter.com/the-meaning-behind-we-are-never-ever-getting-back-to-together-by-taylor-swift.

NOTES TO CHAPTER 5

8. "Rockism"—and its opposite, "poptimism"—have a long and involuted history, beginning with the English New Wave artist Pete Wylie, who apparently coined the term in 1981. One good introduction is Jody Rosen, "The Perils of Poptimism," Slate, May 9, 2006, https://slate.com/culture/2006/05/does-hating-rock-make-you-a-music-critic.html.

9. Chas Newkey-Burden, *Taylor Swift: The Whole Story*, 2nd ed. (New York: Harper-Collins, 2024), 182; John Seabrook, *The Song Machine* (New York: Norton, 2015), 308.

10. "Exclusive: Taylor Swift Sheds Light on 'Red' Bonus Tracks," Yahoo, October 24, 2012, https://sg.news.yahoo.com/exclusive-taylor-swift-sheds-light-red-bonus-tracks-180547365.html.

11. Rob Sheffield, "All 274 of Taylor Swift Songs, Ranked," *Rolling Stone*, April 25, 2024, www.rollingstone.com/music/music-lists/taylor-swift-songs-ranked-rob-sheffield-201800.

12. Scott Huver, "Dazed and Confused at 30," AV Club, September 19, 2023, www.avclub.com/dazed-and-confused-at-30-aimless-teens-timeless-story-1850850421; Jill Filipovic, "The Problem with Men who Date Much Younger Women," Substack, September 9, 2022, https://jill.substack.com/p/the-problem-with-men-who-date-much.

13. Melanie Dunea, ed., *My Country* (New York: Rodale, 2010), 77; Rob Sheffield, *Heartbreak Is the National Anthem* (New York: HarperCollins, 2024), 75. Number two through five are "One" by U2; "You Were Mine" by the Chicks; "Breathe" by Faith Hill; and "Can't Tell Me Nothin'" by Tim McGraw.

14. Sarah Chapelle, *Taylor Swift Style* (New York: St. Martin's, 2024), 123. Telling a story through a moving object, Swift joins a centuries-old tradition, from Joseph Addison's "The Adventures of a Shilling" (1710) through Annie Proulx's novel *Accordion Crimes*.

15. Nine syllables, not ten, in "The idea you had of me, who was she," thanks to an effect called elision, where the short vowel at the end of "the" and the long vowel *i* in "idea" run together.

16. Helen Vendler, *The Odes of John Keats* (Cambridge, MA: Harvard University Press, 1983), 283.

17. Betsy Tontiplaphol, "Baby, We're the Late Romantics," in *The Literary Taylor Swift: Songwriting and Intertextuality*, ed. Betsy Tontiplaphol (New York: Bloomsbury, 2024), chap. 5.

18. Sullivan, *Taylor Swift*, 153. In Shaw's play *Back to Methuselah* the devil says that line about things that never were to Adam and Eve.

19. Ciprian Floria, "The Story of the Oldsmobile 'Rocket' 88, America's First Muscle Car," Autoevolution, September 8, 2021, www.autoevolution.com/news/the-story-of-the-oldsmobile-rocket-88-america-s-first-muscle-car-168929.html.

20. Michael Bull, "Soundscapes of the Car," in *Car Cultures*, ed. Daniel Miller (Oxford: Berg, 2001), 185–202, 186, 193.

21. Newkey-Burden, *Taylor Swift*, 147.

22. Ed Masley, "Taylor Swift Inspired by Phoenix Mother's Grief," *Arizona Republic*, September 11, 2012, www.usatoday.com/story/life/music/2012/09/11/taylor-swift-inspired-by

NOTES TO CHAPTER 6

-phoenix-woman-blog-on-sons-death/1413411; Maya Thompson, "Where Is Ronan," Rock Star Ronan, May 9, 2011, https://rockstarronan.com/2011/05/09/where-is-ronan.

23. Jem Aswad, "Taylor Swift Named Country Songwriter of the Year," *Rolling Stone*, November 10, 2010, www.rollingstone.com/music/music-country/taylor-swift-named-country-songwriter-of-the-year-70024.

24. Sheffield, *Heartbreak*, 58.

25. Amber Tamblyn, "This Hollywood Horror Film Hit Close to Home," *New York Times*, October 20, 2024, www.nytimes.com/2024/10/20/opinion/hollywood-horror-the-substance.html.

Chapter 6. 1989

1. Helen Vendler again: "When a poet puts off an old style he or she perpetrates, so to speak, an act of violence on the self. It is not too much to say that the old body must be dematerialized if the poet is to assume a new one." *The Breaking of Style* (Cambridge, MA: Harvard University Press, 1995), 1–2.

2. Dave Tompkins, *How to Wreck a Nice Beach: The Vocoder from World War II to Hip-Hop. The Machine Speaks* (Brooklyn: Melville House, 2010), 256.

3. "Taylor Swift Talking About Why She Named Her Album '1989,'" YouTube, posted by Celebs tea, July 18, 2021, www.youtube.com/watch?v=ZRM9lF2VJNQ.

4. Kelefa Sanneh, *Major Labels* (New York: Penguin, 2021), 191.

5. Chas Newkey-Burden, *Taylor Swift: The Whole Story*, 2nd ed. (New York: HarperCollins, 2024), 218; Louisa Jepson, *Taylor Swift* (London: Simon and Schuster, 2013), 281, 192; Dan Stubbs, "Taylor Swift: Power, Fame and the Future," *NME* (*New Musical Express*), October 9, 2015, www.nme.com/features/taylor-swift-power-fame-and-the-future-the-full-nme-cover-interview-549.

6. Stubbs, "Taylor Swift: Power, Fame and the Future"; Anne Helen Petersen, "Taylor Swift and the Gray Area of Disordered Eating," BuzzFeed, February 8, 2020, www.buzzfeednews.com/article/annehelenpetersen/taylor-swift-miss-americana-disordered-eating-body-image; *Miss Americana*, dir. Lana Wilson (Tremolo, dist. Netflix, 2020).

7. Scott Raab, "The ESQ&A: Taylor Swift, Between Fans (Published 2014)," *Esquire*, July 7, 2024, www.esquire.com/entertainment/music/a30491/taylor-swift-1114. She told almost the same story, in almost the same words, to Chuck Klosterman for *GQ*.

8. Newkey-Burden, *Taylor Swift*, 211; Jem Aswad, "Taylor Swift 'Shake It Off' Copyright Lawsuit Dropped," *Variety*, December 12, 2022, https://variety.com/2022/music/news/taylor-swift-shake-it-off-lawsuit-dropped-1235458220.

9. Jocelyn Vena, "Taylor Swift 'Hyperventilating' over 'Shake It Off' Flash Mob," *Billboard*, August 23, 2014, www.billboard.com/music/music-news/taylor-swift-hyperventilating-over-shake-it-off-flash-mob-6229161; Caroline Sullivan, *Taylor Swift: Era by Era. The Unauthorized Biography* (New York: Andrews McMeel, 2024), 169.

NOTES TO CHAPTER 6

10. Riley Utley, "Why Are Australian Swifties Screaming 'Sydney'?," CinemaBlend, February 26, 2024, www.cinemablend.com/television/why-are-australian-swifties-screaming-sydney-taylor-swift-blank-space.

11. "Taylor Swift Breaks Down 'Style,'" YouTube, posted by On Air with Ryan Seacrest, October 31, 2014, www.youtube.com/watch?v=7A3VAM7vZIs.

12. Matt BaileyShea, *Lines and Lyrics: An Introduction to Poetry and Song* (New Haven, CT: Yale University Press, 2021), 47.

13. Francesca Bacardi, "Even Taylor Swift's Mom Thought She Was Singing 'Starbucks Lovers' in 'Blank Space,'" E! News, May 26, 2015, www.eonline.com/news/659883/even-taylor-swift-s-mom-thought-she-was-singing-starbucks-lovers-in-blank-space; BaileyShea, *Lines and Lyrics*, 50.

14. Amy Gahran, "Riding the Relationship Escalator," *Solo Poly* (blog), November 29, 2012, https://solopoly.net/2012/11/29/riding-the-relationship-escalator-or-not.

15. Kelsie Gibson, "Who Are Taylor Swift's '1989' Songs About?," *People*, October 27, 2023, https://people.com/who-are-taylor-swift-1989-songs-about-8383220; Annie Zaleski, *Taylor Swift: The Stories Behind the Songs* (San Diego: Thunder Bay, 2024), 110; "Taylor Swift Breaks Down 'Style,'" On Air with Ryan Seacrest, YouTube.

16. Jeff Dolven, *Senses of Style: Poetry Before Interpretation* (Chicago: University of Chicago Press, 2017), 163; Jack Elving, "Re-Examining Spider Man," *Elving's Musings* (blog), January 9, 2022, https://elvingsmusings.wordpress.com/2022/01/09/re-examining-spider-man-06-illusions-behind-the-illusion-of-change.

17. Arielle Zibrak, *Guilty Pleasures* (New York: New York University Press, 2021), 86.

18. Kristin Harris, "Here's Harry Styles's Paper Plane Necklace Taylor Swift Is Singing About," BuzzFeed, October 14, 2014, www.buzzfeed.com/kristinharris/heres-harry-styles-paper-plane-necklace-taylor-swift-is-sing.

19. "Taylor Swift: The 1989 World Tour Live (Remastered)," YouTube, posted by EAS Music Channel, May 28, 2022, www.youtube.com/watch?v=P5JLMp08GC0.

20. Willa Cather, *The Song of the Lark*, ed. Janet Sharistanian (New York: Oxford University Press, 2000 [1915]), 177.

21. Cather, *Song of the Lark*, 181, 320.

22. Raab, "The ESQ&A."

23. Tavi Gevinson, "Taylor Swift Has No Regrets," *Elle*, May 7, 2015, www.elle.com/fashion/a28210/taylor-swift-elle-june-cover-2015.

24. Glenn McDonald, *You Have Not Yet Heard Your Favorite Song: How Streaming Changes Music* (Kingston-upon-Thames: Canbury, 2024), 115.

25. Cather, *Song of the Lark*, 86–87.

26. The song apparently refers to the literal home, and to the supportive romance, that Swift's friend Lena Dunham shared with Swift's collaborator Jack Antonoff. Swift told Tavi Gevinson in 2015, "I wrote that song about things that Lena has told me about her and Jack." Gevinson, "Taylor Swift Has No Regrets."

NOTES TO CHAPTER 7

27. "Taylor Swift's 1989 Secret Session," YouTube, posted by Sara, February 11, 2022, www.youtube.com/watch?v=50ZLsEck030; Hermione Hoby, "Taylor Swift: 'Sexy? Not on My Radar,'" *Guardian*, August 23, 2014, www.theguardian.com/music/2014/aug/23/taylor-swift-shake-it-off.

28. Pat Pattison, *Writing Better Lyrics*, 2nd ed. (New York: Penguin, 2009), 48; Chuck Klosterman, "Taylor Swift on 'Bad Blood,' Kanye West and How People Interpret Her Lyrics," *GQ*, October 15, 2015, www.gq.com/story/taylor-swift-gq-cover-story.

29. W. B. Yeats, "The Friends That Have It I Do Wrong," in *Collected Works*, vol. 1, *The Poems*, 2nd ed., ed. Richard J. Finneran (New York: Scribner, 2010), 557.

30. Courtney Gibson, "I Host Huge Dance Parties Across America," *Newsweek*, March 21, 2022, www.newsweek.com/i-host-taylor-swift-dance-parties-across-america-1690080.

31. Liberty Dunworth, "Taylor Swift Shouts Out Griff's New Song," *NME* (*New Musical Express*), September 5, 2023, www.nme.com/news/music/taylor-swift-shouts-out-griffs-new-song-vertigo-3493472.

32. Rachel Aroesti, interview with Griff, *Guardian*, July 12, 2024, www.theguardian.com/music/article/2024/jul/12/griff-music-interview-vertigo-taylor-swift-wembley.

Chapter 7. Reputation

1. Asir F, "Villareal, a Texas Author, Calls Taylor Swift a 'Billionaire Racist' and 'Nazi Barbie,'" *The Independent* (Singapore), April 23, 2024, https://theindependent.sg/villarreal-a-texas-author-calls-taylor-swift-a-billionaire-racist-and-nazi-barbie; Leah Donnella, "Taylor Swift, Aryan Goddess?," NPR, *Code Switch* (podcast), May 27, 2016, www.npr.org/sections/codeswitch/2016/05/27/479462825/taylor-swift-aryan-goddess; Mitchell Sunderland, "Can't Shake It Off: How Taylor Swift Became a Nazi Idol," *Vice*, May 23, 2016, www.vice.com/en/article/cant-shake-it-off-how-taylor-swift-became-a-nazi-idol.

2. "Taylor Swift and Calvin Harris's Relationship Timeline," *Us*, October 27, 2023, www.usmagazine.com/celebrity-news/news/taylor-swift-and-calvin-harris-romance-timeline-w200954; Alyssa Bailey, "Taylor Swift and Tom Hiddleston Relationship Timeline," *Elle*, September 9, 2016, www.elle.com/culture/celebrities/news/a39043/taylor-swift-tom-hiddleston-romance-timeline; "Lorde Sorry After Saying Taylor Swift Is 'Like Having a Friend with an Autoimmune Disease,'" BBC, June 20, 2017, www.bbc.com/newsbeat-40339923.

3. Kirk Mitchell, "Jury Finds That Radio Host Groped Taylor Swift Before Denver Concert," *Denver Post*, August 14, 2017, www.denverpost.com/2017/08/14/jury-finds-radio-host-david-mueller-groped-taylor-swift-denver-concert.

4. Elle Hunt, "Taylor Swift Is Excused from Jury Duty," *Guardian*, August 30, 2016, www.theguardian.com/music/2016/aug/30/taylor-swift-excused-jury-duty-nashville.

5. Caroline Framke, "Who Is Taylor Swift Voting For?," *Vox*, November 8, 2016, www.vox.com/culture/2016/11/8/13565144/who-is-taylor-swift-voting-for-clinton-trump-election.

6. Grace Gavilanes and Sophie Dodd, "A Complete Timeline of Taylor Swift and Kanye West's Feud," *People*, December 8, 2023, https://people.com/music/kanye-west-famous

-inside-his-and-taylor-swifts-relationship-history; Kirsty Thatcher, "A Complete Timeline of Taylor Swift and Kim Kardashian's Feud," *Elle*, June 24, 2024, www.elle.com.au/culture/taylor-swift-kim-kardashians-feud-timeline.

7. Raisa Bruner, "Read the Transcript of Kanye West's Phone Call with Taylor Swift," *Time*, July 18, 2016, https://time.com/4410370/taylor-swift-kim-kardashian-kanye-west/; Melody Chio, "Taylor Swift and Kanye West's 'Famous' Phone Call Leaks," *People*, March 21, 2020, https://people.com/music/taylor-swift-kanye-west-famous-phone-call-leaks.

8. Bridie Jabour, "Taylor Swift's 'Downfall': What the Online Celebrations Really Say,'" *Guardian*, July 18, 2016, www.theguardian.com/commentisfree/2016/jul/18/taylor-swift-kanye-west-kim-kardashian-west-famous-reaction; "A Timeline of Taylor Swift's Feud with Kanye West and Kim Kardashian," *Cosmopolitan*, April 24, 2024, www.cosmopolitan.com/uk/entertainment/news/a41965/taylor-swift-kanye-west-feud-timeline.

9. Jon Caramanica, "Taylor Swift Is a 2017 Pop Machine," *New York Times*, November 9, 2017.

10. Robin Bernstein, *Racial Innocence: Performing American Childhood from Slavery to Civil Rights* (New York: New York University Press, 2016), 8; Ba Parker and Leah Donnella, "Taylor Swift and the Unbearable Whiteness of Girlhood," NPR, *Code Switch* (podcast), January 31, 2024, https://open.spotify.com/episode/3yDoS0QCMiJlYlbzs48CKZ, transcript at Discover Shows, accessed March 18, 2025, https://app.podscribe.ai/episode/95522404.

11. "Taylor Swift ft. T-Pain—Thug Story (Official Video)," YouTube, posted by MASTER RJ, February 21, 2024, www.youtube.com/watch?v=ZUKdhXL3NCw; Chloe Govan, *Taylor Swift: The Rise of the Nashville Teen* (London: Omnibus, 2012), 172. T-Pain later endured his own years of depression and exile from the music industry, thanks to reactions against Auto-Tune, though he's come back, with untreated vocals. See Leila Fadel and Ziadd Burch, "Rapper T-Pain Has a Simple Message for Those Who Think He Can't Sing: Shut Up," NPR, March 31, 2023, www.npr.org/2023/03/31/1167297060/auto-tune-made-him-famous-t-pain-shows-off-his-natural-singing-voice-on-a-new-al.

12. Cydney Henderson, "Charli XCX Claims No Bad Blood," *USA Today*, August 7, 2019, www.usatoday.com/story/entertainment/music/2019/08/07/charli-xcx-clarifies-comparing-taylor-swift-fans-5-year-olds/1940233001; Kim Novak, "Fans Clap Back as Charli XCX Says Supporting Taylor Swift on Tour Was Like Performing 'to 5-Year-Olds,'" *Metro*, August 6, 2019, https://metro.co.uk/2019/08/06/fans-clap-back-as-charli-xcx-says-supporting-taylor-swift-on-tour-was-like-performing-to-5-year-olds-10529980.

13. Kitty Empire, "Taylor Swift: Reputation Review," *Observer*, November 12, 2017, www.theguardian.com/music/2017/nov/12/taylor-swift-reputation-review; TaylorSwift.com, viewed June 7, 2025. The *Observer* was until 2025 the Sunday edition of the *Guardian*.

14. Caroline Sullivan, *Taylor Swift: Era by Era. The Unauthorized Biography* (New York: Andrews McMeel, 2024), 178, 180; Sarah Chapelle, *Taylor Swift Style* (New York: St. Martin's, 2024), 181.

15. On Taylor's track-and-hook songwriting, see especially Nate Sloan, "Taylor Swift and the Work of Songwriting," *Contemporary Music Review* 40, no. 1 (2021): 11–26.

NOTES TO CHAPTER 7

16. Kelefa Sanneh, *Major Labels* (New York: Penguin, 2021), 150, 152.

17. Sullivan, *Taylor Swift*, 185.

18. Tayter-Swift, Tumblr, December 16, 2018, 10:17 p.m., www.tumblr.com/tayter-swift/181191669738/taylor-swift-honors-dancer-loie-fuller-during-her; "Taylor Swift Tribute to Loie Fuller," Filmgeschiedenis, accessed March 18, 2025, http://filmgeschiedenis.be/portfolio/taylor-swift-tribute-to-loie-fuller; Mia Generoso, "Meet Taylor Swift's Muse," *Teen World Arts*, July 12, 2019, https://teenworldarts.com/magazine/loie-fuller; Susan Jones, *Literature, Modernism and Dance* (Oxford: Oxford University Press, 2013), chap. 1; Zvi Rosen, "Fuller v. Bemis and the Failed Prehistory of Choreographic Copyright," Mostly IP History, March 20, 2013, https://mostlyiphistory.com/2023/03/30/fuller-v-bemis-and-the-failed-prehistory-of-choreographic-copyright; Nicholas Arcomano, "The Copyright Law and Dance," *New York Times*, January 11, 1981, www.nytimes.com/1981/01/11/arts/the-copyright-law-and-dance.html. Fuller lost the case, *Fuller v. Bemis*. Not until the Copyright Act of 1976 did American law clearly recognize choreography as a copyrightable art.

19. Laura Snapes, "Taylor Swift: 'I Was Literally About to Break,'" *Guardian*, August 24, 2019, www.theguardian.com/music/2019/aug/24/taylor-swift-pop-music-hunger-games-gladiators.

20. Empire, "Taylor Swift: Reputation Review"; Nadia Laswi, "'Thank u, Next' to Racial Identity: Pop Star Ariana Grande's Record of Racebending," *BerkeleyB-Side*, November 9, 2022, https://berkeleybside.com/thank-u-next-to-racial-identity-pop-star-ariana-grandes-record-of-racebending.

21. Megan Friedman, "The Internet Is Convinced Taylor Swift's New Song Is Actually About Arya Stark," *Cosmopolitan*, August 25, 2017, www.cosmopolitan.com/entertainment/music/a12096106/taylor-swift-look-what-you-made-me-do-arya-stark; Rebecca Skane, "Is Taylor Swift's 'Look What You Made Me Do' a Tribute to Arya Stark?," *Portsmouth Review*, October 10, 2017, https://portsmouthreview.com/taylor-swifts-look-made-tribute-arya-stark; Alex Suskind, "Taylor Swift Reveals How *Game of Thrones* (and Arya's Kill List) Inspired Reputation," *Entertainment Weekly*, May 9, 2019, https://ew.com/music/2019/05/09/taylor-swift-game-of-thrones-reputation. *Game of Thrones* followers will know already that the Dothraki and their drums come with their own set of unexamined racial stereotypes. See especially Tyler Dean, "Game of Thrones' Complex Relationship to Racism and Colonialism," Reactor, June 10, 2019, https://reactormag.com/game-of-thrones-complex-relationship-to-racism-and-colonialism. Rumors that Swift also wrote songs inspired by *Gilmore Girls*, alas, have no support beyond a few superfans' Tumblrs. See Kelly Conaboy, "All the Evidence I Could Find That Taylor Swift Is a *Gilmore Girls* Fan," Vulture, February 6, 2024, www.vulture.com/article/taylor-swift-songs-about-gilmore-girls-theory.html.

22. Alexander Pope, *The Poems*, ed. John Butt (New Haven, CT: Yale University Press, 1963), 598, 604, 607 (capitalization modernized).

23. Pope, *The Poems*, 607, 608.

24. danah boyd, *It's Complicated: The Social Lives of Networked Teens* (New York: New York University Press, 2013), 35.

NOTES TO CHAPTER 7

25. Chas Newkey-Burden, *Taylor Swift: The Whole Story*, 2nd ed. (New York: HarperCollins, 2024), 235.

26. Kathleen Hanna, *Rebel Girl* (New York: HarperCollins, 2024), 104–105.

Chapter 8. Lover

1. Caroline Sullivan, *Taylor Swift: Era by Era. The Unauthorized Biography* (New York: Andrews McMeel, 2024), 213, 214; "Taylor Swift on 'Lover' and Haters," YouTube, posted by CBS Sunday Morning, August 25, 2019, www.youtube.com/watch?v=nDzhoofkRJI.

2. For Swift's original Instagram endorsement, dated October 7, 2018, see www.instagram.com/taylorswift/p/BopoXpYnCes.

3. Abby Aguirre, "Taylor Swift on Sexism, Scrutiny and Standing Up for Herself," *Vogue*, August 28, 2019, www.vogue.com/article/taylor-swift-cover-september-2019.

4. Nick Romano, "A Guide to the Hidden References and Easter Eggs in Taylor Swift's 'The Man' Video," *Entertainment Weekly*, February 27, 2020, https://ew.com/music/2020/02/27/taylor-swift-the-man-music-video-easter-eggs. "Leo" is Leonardo DiCaprio, the *Titanic* star known, by then, for dating remarkably young women. On *Karma*, see (or hear) in particular *Taylearning* (podcast), episode 126, "All We Think About Is Karma," https://podcasts.apple.com/is/podcast/126-all-we-think-about-is-karma-the-missing-album/id1662665657?i=1000703716174.

5. "Taylor Swift on 'Lover' and Haters," CBS Sunday Morning, YouTube.

6. Nick Romano, "Taylor Swift Learns How to Adjust Her [REDACTED] in 'The Man' Making-of Video," *Entertainment Weekly*, March 6, 2020, https://ew.com/music/taylor-swift-the-man-making-of-video.

7. Makena Kelly, "Meet the Swifties Campaigning for Kamala Harris," *Wired*, July 31, 2024, www.wired.com/story/swifties-campaigning-for-kamala-harris; Tom Tomorrow.

8. See Lauren Berlant, *Cruel Optimism* (Durham, NC: Duke University Press, 2011), and also Barbara Ehrenreich, *Bright-Sided: How Positive Thinking Is Undermining America* (New York: Picador, 2010).

9. The post, from August 2019, is archived at Reddit, "Taylor Confirmed the Fishbowl Theory on Tumblr!," www.reddit.com/r/TaylorSwift/comments/cu6rpa/taylor_confirmed_the_fishbowl_theory_on_tumblr. Confusingly, the Reddit thread screenshots a Tumblr post that itself includes a screenshot from Twitter: a Russian doll of an Easter egg, if you like.

10. "Taylor Swift—BBC Radio 1 Live Lounge 2019 (Full Show)," September 3, 2019, YouTube, posted by Taylor Nation International, March 8, 2021, www.youtube.com/watch?v=aB_3-8ebkfs, at 15:10; Annie Zaleski, *Taylor Swift: The Stories Behind the Songs* (San Diego: Thunder Bay, 2024), 155.

11. Asa Seresin, "On Heteropessimism," *New Inquiry*, October 9, 2019, https://thenewinquiry.com/on-heteropessimism.

12. Sullivan, *Taylor Swift*, 153.

NOTES TO CHAPTER 9

13. Zaleski, *Taylor Swift*, 169; Evan Agostini, "Regents Park Music School Is Glad to Have a Friend in Taylor Swift," *Toronto Star*, August 26, 2019, www.thestar.com/entertainment/music/regent-park-school-of-music-is-glad-to-have-a-friend-in-taylor-swift/article_fedc1e88-eb66-51a7-970c-3708b9748d65.html.

14. Aguirre, "Taylor Swift on Sexism."

15. @ashleytrabue, Threads, August 20, 2024, www.threads.net/@ashleytrabue/post/C-55wxdyB9k?xmt=AQGze3lZFbPz9MgwDQIJD6AZVvYTC3ky94D_fBGdvDxTpQ. The phrase "compulsory heterosexuality" owes its origin to Adrienne Rich's 1980 essay "Compulsory Heterosexuality and Lesbian Existence," collected in Rich, *Blood, Bread and Poetry* (New York: Norton, 1986).

16. Kevin Evers, *There's Nothing Like This: The Strategic Genius of Taylor Swift* (Boston: Harvard Business Review Press, 2025), 204.

17. Chas Newkey-Burden, *Taylor Swift: The Whole Story*, 2nd ed. (New York: Harper-Collins, 2024), 260, 261.

18. Jael Goldfine, "Is Taylor Swift Re-Recording Her Old Music Under a New Name?," *Paper*, May 26, 2020, www.papermag.com/taylor-swift-killing-eve-jack-leopard-dolphin-club#rebelltitem10. Sullivan, for whatever reason, does not acknowledge the version as Taylor's. See Sullivan, *Taylor Swift*, 209–210.

19. Katie Atkinson, "Taylor Swift Officially Cancels Lover Fest Concerts," *Billboard*, February 26, 2021, www.billboard.com/pro/taylor-swift-lover-fest-tour-canceled; *Miss Americana*, dir. Lana Wilson (Tremolo, dist. Netflix, 2020).

20. Jessica Booth, "All About Taylor Swift's Cats," *People*, October 18, 2024, https://people.com/pets/all-about-taylor-swift-cats; "Taylor said it . . . ADOPT CATS!," TikTok, posted by A Better Life—Pet Rescue, October 14, 2024, www.tiktok.com/@abetterlifepetrescue/video/7289825133470977310?lang=en.

Chapter 9. Folklore

1. *Folklore: The Long Pond Studio Sessions*, dir. Taylor Swift (Disney+, 2020).

2. Dave Fawbert, quoted in Laura Snapes, "'Genuine': Why Taylor Swift Can Celebrate More Than an Album Release," *Guardian*, October 14, 2022, www.theguardian.com/music/2022/oct/14/taylor-swift-celebrate-album-release-midnights-pop-acclaim, also quoted in Caroline Sullivan, *Taylor Swift: Era by Era. The Unauthorized Biography* (New York: Andrews McMeel, 2024), 220.

3. Willa Cather, "Escapism," in *Stories, Poems, and Other Writings*, ed. Sharon O'Brien (New York: Library of America, 1992), 965–968, 965.

4. Mark Slobin, *Folk Music: A Very Short Introduction* (Oxford: Oxford University Press, 2011), 2.

5. Marcus Wratten, "Taylor Swift Personally Offered Heartstopper Her Song," Pink News, August 7, 2023, www.thepinknews.com/2023/08/07/heartstopper-season-two-music-taylor-swift-darcy-tara-seven.

NOTES TO CHAPTER 9

6. Heran Mamo, "Ryan Reynolds Still 'Can't Believe' Taylor Swift Musically Name-Checked His and Blake Lively's Daughters," *Billboard*, August 6, 2021, www.billboard.com/music/pop/ryan-reynolds-reflects-taylor-swift-betty-9611748.

7. William Wordsworth, "Preface to *Lyrical Ballads*," in *Romanticism: An Anthology*, ed. Duncan Wu, 5th ed. (Oxford: Blackwell, 2024), 277.

8. Daniel Kreps, "Taylor Swift Shares Orchestral Version of 'The Lakes' on 'Folklore' Anniversary," *Rolling Stone*, July 24, 2021, www.rollingstone.com/music/music-news/taylor-swift-orchestral-version-the-lakes-folklore-anniversary-1201754; TaylorSwift, Tumblr, July 24, 2021, https://taylorswift.tumblr.com/post/657595827641073664/its-been-one-year-since-we-escaped-the-real-world.

9. Elise Taylor, "The Outrageous Life of Rebekah Harkness, Taylor Swift's High-Society Muse," *Vogue*, July 29, 2020, www.vogue.com/article/the-outrageous-life-of-rebekah-harkness-taylor-swifts-high-society-muse; Cameron Katz and Katie Buck, "Taylor Swift's 'The Last Great American Dynasty' and the St. Louis Heiress Who Inspired It," *Teen Vogue*, October 27, 2023, www.teenvogue.com/story/taylor-swift-the-last-great-american-dynasty; Craig Unger, *Blue Blood* (New York: William Morrow, 1988).

10. James Merrill, "Mirror," in *Collected Poems*, ed. J. D. McClatchy and Stephen Yenser (New York: Knopf, 2001), 83; also at Poetry Foundation, www.poetryfoundation.org/poetrymagazine/poems/27569/mirror-56d2118331ae5.

11. Erwin Panofsky, *Philosophy and History: Essays Presented to Ernst Cassirer* (Oxford: Oxford University Press, 1936), 314.

Chapter 10. Evermore

1. Claire Shaffer, "Aaron Dessner on How His Collaborative Chemistry with Taylor Swift Led to 'Evermore,'" *Rolling Stone*, December 18, 2020, www.rollingstone.com/music/music-features/aaron-dessner-interview-taylor-swift-evermore-1105853.

2. "Taylor Swift's Songwriting Process on 'Evermore,'" YouTube, posted by Apple Music, December 15, 2020, www.youtube.com/watch?v=CQacWbsLbS4&t=6s.

3. Eve Kosofsky Sedgwick, *Tendencies* (Durham, NC: Duke University Press, 1991), 5.

4. Robert Frost, *The Poetry of Robert Frost*, ed. Edward Connery Lathem (New York: Henry Holt, 1969), 105, 377; David Orr, "The Most Misread Poem in America," *Paris Review*, September 11, 2015, www.theparisreview.org/blog/2015/09/11/the-most-misread-poem-in-america. See also David Orr, *The Road Not Taken: Finding America in the Poem Everyone Loves and Almost Everyone Gets Wrong* (New York: Penguin, 2016).

5. Zane Lowe, Apple Music Interview with Taylor Swift, YouTube, December 15, 2020, www.youtube.com/watch?v=CQacWbsLbS4; The Taylor Swift Fanbook, Icons Series, no. 38 (2024): n.p.

6. For example, "Green Light x Gold Rush (Lorde x Taylor Swift Mashup)," YouTube, posted by Honeymoon Mixes, December 16, 2020, www.youtube.com/watch?v=DIFV7haGvcM; "A Cappella Cover of Green Light / Gold Rush by Lorde / Taylor Swift: The Sil-

NOTES TO CHAPTER 11

houettes," YouTube, posted by LUC Silhouettes, March 9, 2022, www.youtube.com/watch?v=Luuh5W3Hv_I.

7. Angel Shaw, "Who Was Marjorie? The Inspiration for Taylor Swift's Evermore Song and Lyrics Meaning Explained," *Screen Rant*, March 15, 2024, https://screenrant.com/taylor-swift-the-eras-tour-marjorie-song-lyrics-inspiration; Louisa Jepson, *Taylor Swift* (London: Simon and Schuster, 2013), 5.

8. "Taylor Swift's Songwriting Process on 'Evermore,'" Apple Music, YouTube; Ashley Iasimone, "Taylor Swift in Awe of What Fans Did During 'Marjorie' in Nashville: 'So Meaningful and So Special,'" *Billboard*, May 6, 2023, www.billboard.com/music/music-news/taylor-swift-marjorie-nashville-video-1235323118.

9. "Taylor Swift's Songwriting Process on 'Evermore,'" Apple Music, YouTube; Daphne du Maurier, *Rebecca* (London: Gollancz, 1980 [1938]), 46.

10. Du Maurier, *Rebecca*, 122, 171, 274.

11. Du Maurier, *Rebecca*, 287–288.

12. Any song in 5/4 can be rescored as 10/8, and vice versa. Aaron Dessner describes the song as 10/8. See Annie Zaleski, *Taylor Swift: The Stories Behind the Songs* (San Diego: Thunder Bay, 2024), 197.

13. "So What Is Hyperpop Anyway?," WKNC 88.1 (blog), April 15, 2021, https://wknc.org/2021/04/15/so-what-is-hyperpop-anyway.

14. Nic Johnson, "How Hyperpop Gives Trans Artists a Voice," *Ringtone* (blog), August 12, 2020, www.ringtonemag.com/articles/how-hyperpop-gives-trans-artists-a-voice.

15. Jamie Lynne Burgess, "How Bad Can They Be? The Villains of Midnights Admit Their Crimes," Swifticism, November 14, 2022, available on Medium, https://medium.com/swifticism/how-bad-can-they-be-the-villains-of-midnights-admit-their-crimesf2359ee6ef72.

16. John Keats, *Complete Poems*, ed. Jack Stillinger (Cambridge, MA: Harvard University Press, 1982), 176–177.

17. "Taylor Swift's Songwriting Process on 'Evermore,'" Apple Music, YouTube.

18. Alexandra Lange, *Meet Me by the Fountain: An Inside History of the Mall* (New York: Bloomsbury, 2022), 5, 154.

19. Lange, *Meet Me by the Fountain*, 153.

20. Richard Thompson, with Scott Timberg, *Beeswing: Losing My Way and Finding My Voice 1967–75* (Chapel Hill, NC: Algonquin, 2021), 254.

Chapter 11. Midnights

1. Lauren Huff, "Everything to Know About Taylor Swift's *Midnights* Album," *Entertainment Weekly*, October 23, 2022, https://ew.com/musiceverything-to-know-taylor-swift-midnights-album.

2. *Let's Ask Taylor Swift* (podcast), "Introducing," November 21, 2024, https://pod.link/1779581115/episode/9804d35544791bb9657c235467fbc5bc.

3. Brittany Spanos, "Is 'Karma' Real? Inside the Mystery of Taylor Swift's 'Lost' Album," *Rolling Stone*, September 26, 2022, www.rollingstone.com/music/music-features/taylor

NOTES TO CHAPTER 11

swift-karma-lost-album-real-1234598609; *Taylearning* (podcast), episode 126, "All We Think About Is KARMA," April 16, 2025, https://www.taylearningpodcast.com/episodes/all-we-think-about-is-karma-the-missing-album-theory-explained; Annie Zaleski, *Taylor Swift: The Stories Behind the Songs* (San Diego: Thunder Bay, 2024), 220.

4. Amber Tamblyn, *Era of Ignition* (New York: Crown, 2019), 126–127.

5. Rania Aniftos, "Taylor Swift Deletes 'Lavender Haze' Explanation," *Billboard*, May 1, 2023, www.billboard.com/music/music-news/taylor-swift-deletes-lavender-haze-explanation-video-1235319256.

6. Lina Das, "Taylor Swift: 'Men Hand Me Inspiration on a Plate,'" *Daily Mail*, October 29, 2012, www.dailymail.co.uk/home/you/article-2218012/Taylor-Swift-Men-hand-inspiration-plate.html; Louisa Jepson, *Taylor Swift* (London: Simon and Schuster, 2013), 8.

7. Christopher Grobe, *The Art of Confession* (New York: New York University Press, 2017), 23, 25. Halsey and girl in red (always lowercase) are stage names for (respectively) Ashley Nicolette Frangipane and Marie Ulven Ringheim.

8. Taylor Swift, Instagram, October 2, 2022, www.instagram.com/reel/CjPMULyPp9V.

9. Thania Garcia, "Taylor Swift's 'Anti-Hero' Video Edited to Remove 'Fat' Reference Following Online Criticism," *Variety*, October 26, 2022, https://variety.com/2022/music/news/taylor-swift-anti-hero-video-edited-fat-scale-1235414992; Catherine Mhloyi, "Taylor Swift's 'Anti-Hero' Music Video Scale Scene Perpetuates Fatphobia," *Teen Vogue*, October 26, 2022, www.teenvogue.com/story/taylor-swift-anti-hero-music-video-scale-scene-fatphobia; Zan Romanoff, *LOOK* (New York: Dial, 2020), 219.

10. *Star Trek* (original series), episode titled "The Enemy Within," dir. Leo Penn, first aired October 6, 1966. See https://memory-alpha.fandom.com/wiki/The_Enemy_Within_(episode).

11. Quinn Moreland, "Midnights," *Pitchfork*, October 22, 2022, https://pitchfork.com/reviews/albums/taylor-swift-midnights; Vrinda Jagota, "6 Takeaways from Taylor Swift's New Album *Midnights*," *Pitchfork*, October 21, 2022, https://pitchfork.com/thepitch/takeaways-from-taylor-swifts-new-album-midnights.

12. Rebecca Schiller, "Taylor Swift Accepts Woman of the Decade Award," *Billboard*, December 13, 2019, www.billboard.com/music/awards/taylor-swift-woman-of-the-decade-speech-billboard-women-in-music-8546156.

13. Paul Morley, *Words and Music: A History of Pop in the Shape of a City* (Athens: University of Georgia Press, 2005), 204–205.

14. Romanoff, *LOOK*, 104, 177; Zaleski, *Taylor Swift*, 218.

15. @ally_sheehan, Twitter, March 6, 2023, https://twitter.com/ally_sheehan/status/1632639015643123713 ("the fact that john mayer lived in a literal converted church building with actual stained glass windows when he dated teenage taylor swift . . . every lyric hits harder"). For images of the building, see Adriane Quinlan, "A Two-Story Condo in a Former Parish House," *Curbed*, January 2023, www.curbed.com/2023/01/former-church-parish-house-condo-pictures.html.

16. Danielle Campoamor, "People Who Have Had a Miscarriage Say One Taylor Swift Song Has a Powerful Meaning for Them," *Today*, October 21, 2022, www.today.com/parents/pregnancy/taylor-swift-song-miscarriage-bigger-than-the-whole-sky-rcna53433.

NOTES TO CHAPTER 12

17. Rebecca Jennings, Gabriela Fernandez, and Shira Tarlo, "Every Song on Taylor Swift's *Midnights*, Explained," *Vox*, October 21, 2022, www.vox.com/culture/2022/10/21/23416464/taylor-swift-midnights-lyrics-explained-anti-hero-video.

18. American Heart Association, Facebook, November 30, 2023, www.facebook.com/story.php?story_fbid=7544863667121908&id=100064525011058; Zaleski, *Taylor Swift*, 229.

19. Rania Aniftos, "Taylor Swift Is 'Never Beating the Sorcery Allegations' After Perfectly Timed Eras Tour Moment," *Billboard*, November 13, 2023, www.billboard.com/music/music-news/taylor-swift-sorcery-allegations-labyrinth-eras-tour-moment-1235471193.

20. Legacy Russell, "On #GLITCHFEMINISM and the Glitch Feminism Manifesto," Res., October 2017, https://beingres.org/2017/10/17/legacy-russell. See also Legacy Russell, *Glitch Feminism: A Manifesto* (London: Verso, 2020).

21. Lennard J. Davis, *Bending Over Backwards: Disability, Dismodernism and Other Difficult Positions* (New York: New York University Press, 2002), 30–31.

Chapter 12. The Tortured Poets Department (The Anthology)

1. Alyssa Bailey, "Taylor Swift and Matty Healy's Relationship Timeline, from 2014 Rumors to 2023's Brief Fling," *Elle*, January 20, 2025, www.elle.com/culture/celebrities/a43874381/taylor-swift-matty-healy-relationship-timeline. For the most detailed, responsible explainer, see (or rather hear) *Taylearning* (podcast), episodes 94 and 96, "The Muses: Matty Healy," parts 1 and 2, June 20 and August 28, 2024, available at Spotify, https://open.spotify.com/show/3TVFyyiSkAb9aVXGCwv4JC, or Apple Podcasts, https://podcasts.apple.com/us/podcast/taylearning-a-taylor-swift-podcast/id1662665657.

2. Friedrich Schiller, "Naïve and Sentimental Poetry," trans. Julias Elias (New York: Ungar, 1967); τοῦτο τοίνυν τὸ κάλλιον ὑπάρχει σοι παρ' ἡμῖν, ὦ Ἴων, θεῖον εἶναι καὶ μὴ τεχνικὸν περὶ Ὁμήρου ἐπαινέτην: "I'll choose the prettier option, Ion, and [rather than calling you dishonest] say it's a god who inspires you, [since you have] no laudable skill about Homer." Plato, *Ion*, 530b.

3. Jenny Offill, *Dept. of Speculation* (New York: Knopf, 2014), 4.

4. For these and many other rhetorical terms explained in clear English, the best source as of 2025 remains Gideon Burton's Forest of Rhetoric, accessed April 19, 2025, https://rhetoric.byu.edu.

5. Quoted in unattributed English translation in Niv Allon and Diana Craig Patch, *Romance Along the Nile: Ancient Egyptian Love Poetry* (New York: Metropolitan Museum of Art, 2015), 7.

6. Sophie Schillaci, "Taylor Swift's Ex Matty Healy Talks His Love of Typewriters in Resurfaced Clip After 'Tortured Poets' Release," *Entertainment Tonight*, April 22, 2024, www.etonline.com/taylor-swifts-ex-matty-healy-talks-his-love-of-typewriters-in-resurfaced-clip-after-tortured-poets; Jamie Lerner, "Matty Healy Has More Than 20 Tattoos, Each with a Different Meaning and Backstory," *Distractify*, April 19, 2024, www.distractify.com/p/matty-healy-tattoos-explained.

7. Nathaniel Rich, "Where the Walls Still Talk," *Vanity Fair*, October 8, 2013, www.vanityfair.com/culture/2013/10/chelsea-hotel-oral-history.

NOTES TO CHAPTER 12

8. For a similar argument (organized around motherhood), try Mairead Small Staid, "Moving Past the Myth of the Art Monster," *Jezebel*, October 14, 2019, www.jezebel.com/moving-past-the-myth-of-the-art-monster-1838526171.

9. Molly Mulshine and Alyssa Bailey, "Taylor Swift and Joe Alwyn's Complete Relationship Timeline," *Elle*, January 5, 2025, www.elle.com/culture/celebrities/a25654362/taylor-swift-joe-alwyn-relationship-timeline. Neither Swift nor Alwyn have discussed any mental health diagnoses in public, but journalists' and fans' reactions to *TTPD* described him repeatedly as depressed or suffering from depression. See, for example, Zara Woodcock, "Joe Alwyn Fans Rally to Support British Actor as They Slam Taylor Swift's 'Manipulative' Album Jibes," *Daily Mirror*, April 20, 2024, www.mirror.co.uk/3am/celebrity-news/joe-alwyn-fans-rally-support-32633170; Constance Grady, "Taylor Swift Seems Sick of Being Everyone's Best Friend," *Vox*, April 19, 2024, www.vox.com/culture/24134809/taylor-swift-tortured-poets-department-matty-healy-joe-alwyn.

10. Bailey, "Taylor Swift and Matty Healy's Relationship Timeline."

11. On Matty Healy's history with addictions and substance abuse, see Jon Bilstein, "The 1975's Matty Healy Opens Up About Heroin Addiction and the 'Emotional Hangover' That Followed His Bandmate's Intervention," *Rolling Stone*, October 12, 2022, www.rollingstone.com/music/music-news/the-1975-matty-healy-heroin-addiction-intervention-1234609776, and Jia Tolentino, "Who Is Matty Healy?," *New Yorker*, May 29, 2023, www.newyorker.com/magazine/2023/06/05/who-is-matty-healy.

12. Darren Wershler-Henry, *The Iron Whim* (Ithaca, NY: Cornell University Press, 2007), 6. On typewriter poetry, see also Brian Sonia-Wallace, *The Poetry of Strangers: What I Learned Traveling America with a Typewriter* (New York: HarperCollins, 2020).

13. "Taylor Swift Interview: Screen Test," YouTube, posted by the New York Times, December 4, 2009, www.youtube.com/watch?v=XarVd2TSmqI.

14. Shaad D'Souza, "Demanding Taylor Swift Dump Matty Healy? Fan Culture Is Out of Control," *Guardian*, May 20, 2023, www.theguardian.com/commentisfree/2023/may/30/taylor-swift-matty-healy-fan-culture.

15. For controversy over "all the racists"—"the first time that Swift has sung about race" directly—see, especially, Jay Stahl, "Why Taylor Swift's 'All the Racists' Lyric Is Dividing Fans," *USA Today*, April 24, 2024, www.usatoday.com/story/entertainment/music/2024/04/24/taylor-swift-lyrics-song-i-hate-it-here-1830s-divides-fans/73437328007.

16. Willa Paskin, "Taylor Swift's Precociousness Problem," *Vulture*, December 13, 2011, www.vulture.com/2011/12/taylor-swifts-precociousness-problem.html.

17. Michael O'Neill, ed., *A Routledge Literary Sourcebook on the Poems of W. B. Yeats* (New York: Routledge, 2004), 31.

18. For Healy getting upset about his height ("I'm a big boy!"), see, for example, Dani Medina, "Matty Healy Is 'Sick to F— Death' of Fans Who Think He's Short," The 1975 Radio, iHeart, December 3, 2022, www.iheart.com/content/2022-12-03-matty-healy-is-sick-to-f-death-of-fans-who-think-hes-short-watch; Danielle Chelosky, "Matty Healy Only Seems Short Because the Rest of The 1975 Are Huge, the 'Sick to F*cking Death' Singer Explained," Uproxx, December 2, 2022, https://uproxx.com/indie/the-1975-matty-healy-short-height.

NOTES TO CHAPTER 13

He seems to be 5'10" or 5'11", but the other members of The 1975 all stand several inches taller, which makes him look shorter than he otherwise would—some fans allege that he's really 5'5".

19. For these references and more, see Alyssa Bailey, "Taylor Swift's 'The Black Dog' Lyrics Detail a Brutal Discovery," *Elle*, April 19, 2024, www.elle.com/culture/music/a605 48186/taylor-swift-the-black-dog-lyrics-meaning-matty-healy.

20. Francesca Street, "What It's Like Inside the Black Dog, the London Pub Made Famous by Taylor Swift," CNN, April 24, 2024, www.cnn.com/travel/black-dog-vauxhall -london-pub-taylor-swift/index.html. Horace's original Latin reads "Non horam tesse esse potes . . . teque ipsum vitas fugitives et erro / iam vino quaerens, iam somno fallere Curam; / frustra; nam comes atra permit sequiturque fugacem" (Horace, Satires II:7, 112–115). See also Paul Bernard Foley, "'Black Dog' as a Metaphor for Depression: A Brief History," Black Dog Institute (Australia), January 2005, available at StudyLib, https://studylib.net /doc/8100530/-black-dog--as-a-metaphor-for-depression--a-brief; Michael Thomas Kincella, "Why Is Depression Sometimes Called 'The Black Dog'?," Mental Floss, June 17, 2024, www.mentalfloss.com/posts/black-dog-depression-metaphor.

21. Bryan West, "Taylor Swift Sings 'thanK you aIMee,' Performs with Hayley Williams at Eras Tour in London," *USA Today*, June 22, 2024, www.usatoday.com/story/entertainment /music/2024/06/22/taylor-swift-eras-tour-london-surprise-songs/74182602007.

22. Laura Kasischke, *Lilies Without* (Keene, NY: Ausable, 2007), 6, also available at https://cat.middlebury.edu/~nereview/26-4/Kasischke.html.

23. David Stenn, *Clara Bow: Runnin' Wild* (New York: Cooper Square, 2000), 138.

24. Stephanie Zacharek, "What Taylor Swift's 'Clara Bow' Does—and Doesn't—Have to Do with the Famous Superstar," *Time*, April 19, 2024, https://time.com/6969048/clara-bow -taylor-swift-song; Stenn, *Clara Bow*, 261.

25. Joan Anderman, "Stevie Nicks: Just Following Her Muse," *New York Times*, February 4, 2024, www.nytimes.com/2014/02/04/booming/stevie-nicks-just-following-her-muse.html.

26. Roger Ebert, "L.A. Confidential," Roger Ebert, September 19, 1997, www.rogerebert .com/reviews/la-confidential-1997.

27. Kevin Evers, *There's Nothing Like This: The Strategic Genius of Taylor Swift* (Boston: Harvard Business Review Press, 2025), 237; Jürgen Backhaus, ed., *Joseph Alois Schumpeter: Entrepreneurship, Style and Vision* (New York: Kluwer, 2003), 129.

28. Georgia Carroll, "Like Some Kind of Congressman: The Tactical Creation of Taylor Swift's 'Brandom,'" in *The Psychgeist of Pop Culture: Taylor Swift* (Pittsburgh: Play Story, 2024), 67–81, 78; Samuel Johnson, "The History of Rasselas, Prince of Abyssinia" (1759), ed. Jack Lynch, https://jacklynch.net/Texts/rasselas.html.

29. Frances Osborne, *The Bolter* (New York: Vintage, 2010), 200.

Chapter 13. Eras

1. See Hannah Dailey and Raina Aniftos, "A Timeline of Taylor Swift's Generosity," *Billboard*, January 17, 2025, www.billboard.com/lists/taylor-swifts-charity-donations -gifts-timeline/october-2011-she-donates-70000-in-books-to-her-hometown-library;

NOTES TO CHAPTER 13

Amelia Hill, "Taylor Swift Donation Enables Cardiff Food Bank to Buy Lorry Full of Supplies," *Guardian*, June 25, 2024, www.theguardian.com/music/article/2024/jun/25/taylor-swift-donation-enables-cardiff-food-bank-lorry-supplies.

2. Bob Perelman, *The Trouble with Genius: Reading Pound, Joyce, Stein, and Zukofsky* (Berkeley: University of California Press, 1994), 7.

3. Friedrich Schiller, "Naïve and Sentimental Poetry," trans. Julias Elias (New York: Ungar, 1967), 96–97; Madeline Pérez, "Obtaining Academic Success: Nurturing Grit in Students," *Journal of Interpersonal Relations* 8 (2015): 56–63, 62.

4. Perelman, *Trouble with Genius*, 16; Ralph Waldo Emerson, "The Poet" (1844).

5. Kenneth Burke, *Counter-Statement*, 2nd ed. (Berkeley: University of California Press, 1951), 55; Maggie Nelson, *The Slicks* (Los Angeles: Dopamine, 2024), 29–30.

6. Burke, *Counter-Statement*, 36.

7. Aliza Chasan and Jane Greeley, "Grammy Winners and Nominees on *60 Minutes* Through the Years," CBS News, January 31, 2025, www.cbsnews.com/news/grammys-60-minutes-list.

8. Bryan West, *This Swift Beat* (Vancouver, WA: USA Today/Pediment, 2024), 27; Sarah Chapelle, *Taylor Swift Style* (New York: St. Martin's, 2024), 153.

9. Chapelle, *Taylor Swift Style*, 260; W. B. Yeats, "Adam's Curse," in *Collected Works*, vol. 1, *The Poems*, 2nd ed., ed. Richard J. Finneran (New York: Scribner, 2010), 80, available at Poetry Foundation, www.poetryfoundation.org/poems/43285/adams-curse.

10. Anne Helen Petersen, "Taylor Swift and the Good Girl Trap," Substack, February 7, 2024, https://annehelen.substack.com/p/taylor-swift-and-the-good-girl-trap.

11. Pallabi Bose, "Funniest Viral Memes and Moments from Taylor Swift's Eras Tour," *Prestige*, March 8, 2023, www.prestigeonline.com/sg/lifestyle/culture-plus-entertainment/best-and-funniest-moments-and-memes-of-taylor-swift-eras-tour; West, *This Swift Beat*, 98; Kat Pettibone, "Taylor Swift Stops Edinburgh 'Eras' Tour Show, Refuses to Continue Until Fans Get Help," *Us Weekly*, at Yahoo, June 7, 2024, www.yahoo.com/entertainment/taylor-swift-stops-edinburgh-eras-185251299.html.

12. Chapelle, *Taylor Swift Style*, 178.

13. Caroline Sullivan, *Taylor Swift: Era by Era. The Unauthorized Biography* (New York: Andrews McMeel, 2024), 196–197; @tessdear, LinkTree, https://linktr.ee/tessdear; Tess Bohne, Instagram, accessed April 25, 2025, www.instagram.com/tessbohne/reels/#; Gretchen McCulloch, *Because Internet: Understanding the New Rules of Language* (New York: Riverhead, 2019), 220–221.

14. West, *This Swift Beat*, 104.

15. *Taylearning* (podcast), "About," www.taylearningpodcast.com/about; *Taylearning*, episode 83, "Is Taylor Swift the 'Anti-Hero' of the Climate? A Deep Dive into Taylor's Carbon Emissions," April 3, 2024, www.taylearningpodcast.com/episodes/is-taylor-swift-the-anti-hero-of-the-climate-a-deep-dive-into-taylors-carbon-emissions. For more on Swift's carbon emissions, see the 2024 *Vice* interview with climate change expert Austin Whitman, who urges her to speak now about renewable energy and fossil-fuel dangers, but agrees that she could not fly commercial: Nick Thompson, "How Bad Are Taylor Swift's Private Jet Emissions? An Expert Explains," *Vice*, February 9, 2024, www.vice.com/en/article/taylor-swift-private-jet-emissions-explained.

NOTES TO CHAPTER 13

16. Rachel Mulumba, "Taylor Swift Trademarks," Michelson Institute for Intellectual Property (blog), September 28, 2023, https://michelsonip.com/taylor-swift-trademarks.

17. Guido Mazzoni, *On Modern Poetry*, trans. Zakiya Hanafi (Cambridge, MA: Harvard University Press, 2022), 229–231.

18. Rachel Kushner, *The Hard Crowd: Essays, 2000–2020* (New York: Scribner, 2021), 111.

19. Willa Cather, *The Song of the Lark*, ed. Janet Sharistanian (New York: Oxford University Press, 2000 [1915]), 405.

20. Quoted in Jill Muller, *Gerard Manley Hopkins and Victorian Catholicism* (New York: Routledge, 2003), 32, also available at Gerard Manley Hopkins, "Selections from Hopkins's Letters," Poetry Foundation, www.poetryfoundation.org/articles/69476/selections-from-hopkinss-letters.

21. Cather, *Song of the Lark*, 403–404.

22. Yeats, "What Then?," in *The Poems*, 302.

INDEX

Aaron Academy, 40
Abercrombie & Fitch, 18, 43–44
accessibility, 35, 39, 44, 187–188, 223, 281
"Adam's Curse" (Yeats), 284
Adams, Ryan, 182
Adeem the Artist, 148, 167
Adelicia apartments (Nashville), 62
adulthood, 77, 106, 116, 124, 146, 158, 217
   Black, 140–141
   representations of, 148
age-gap relationships, 42, 95, 268
"The Alchemy," 249, 267
alcohol, 141, 252. *See also* drinking
"All the Small Things" (Blink-182), 30
"All Too Well," 87, 92–98, 100, 107, 112, 280
"All You Had to Do Was Stay," 125
Alwyn, Joe (boyfriend), 141, 145, 157, 164, 175–176, 182
   "Champagne Problems" cowriter, 214
   "Exile" collaboration, 216
   on Instagram, 225
   split with, 237, 246, 253, 278
   "The Tortured Man Club" and, 251
   William Bowery alias, 188, 203, 222
ambition, 9, 21, 28, 36, 43, 103
   artistic, 29, 58, 202
   drive and, 33, 102, 125, 225
   insecurities and, 16, 225

American culture, 11, 95, 100–101, 140, 150
"American Girl" (Petty), 36
American Heart Association, 237
Amos, Tori, 6, 32, 57
Anacreontic (poetic genre), 143
Anderson, Abigail, 28, 42, 47, 54
Anderson, Laurie, 110–111
angst, 28, 53, 131, 184, 235, 243
   in "Hits Different," 242
   meta-, 10
"Anti-Hero," 30, 226, 227–229, 233, 236, 246
Antonoff, Jack, 196–197, 203, 227, 230, 255
   as coauthor, 121, 177, 207
   "Cruel Summer" cowritten with, 172
   Dessner and, 188, 242
   fun. band and, 242–243
   One Chance soundtrack and, 110
anxiety, 121, 177, 211, 221–222, 235, 256
   approval and, 237
   fame and, 232–233
   in *Folklore*, 189
   sleepless nights and, 234
apologia, 143, 155
approval, 16, 113, 114, 183, 237
   on the Eras Tour, 280
   good girl, 246
   Taylor Swift ("Debut") and, 36

INDEX

Arbuthnot, John, 128, 154
"The Archer," 176–177, 180, 181, 291
archetypes, 55–56
art monsters (Offill), 248, 250, 252–253, 257, 259–260, 268
Arya Stark (fictional character), 152–153, 241
aspiration
    accessibility combined with, 39
    independence and, 59–60
    reinvention and, 124
    relatability and, 29, 31, 37, 84, 91, 121, 161, 290
    representation mixed with, 44
"August," 195
Augustine (fictional character), 194, 197, 218
authenticity, 37, 63, 199–200, 232, 257, 289
autonomy, 90, 101, 240, 241
Auto-Tune, 87, 111, 140, 147
"The Awakening" (Chopin), 159

"Back to December," 65–66, 70, 80, 212
"Bad Blood," 111, 117, 283, 286
BaileyShea, Matt, 117, 118
Ballerini, Kelsea, 103, 212
banjo, 23, 26, 37, 45, 55, 60, 87, 195
Bates, Tracey, 137
Baudelaire, Charles, 251
the Beatles, 2, 88, 258, 293
Beauvoir, Simone de, 169
"Before He Cheats" (Underwood), 27
"Begin Again," 98, 101, 106
"Bejeweled," 226, 232, 234, 287
Berks Youth Theatre Academy, 21
Berlant, Lauren, 173
Bernstein, Robin, 140–141
"The Best Day," 11–12, 13–14, 48–49, 61–62, 98, 275
"Better Than Revenge," 64, 88
Betty (fictional character), 194, 195, 197, 206, 216, 218
"Betty," 194–195, 282

Beyoncé, 36, 66, 145
Big Machine Records, 23, 93, 161, 163, 181
"Bigger Than the Whole Sky," 235
Bikini Kill, 32, 80, 157. *See also* Hanna, Kathleen
Billboard (magazine), 34, 112, 113, 230
Black adulthood, 140–141
Black culture, 115, 135, 144, 150
"The Black Dog," 247, 259–260
Black music, 115, 135, 139–140, 148–150, 159
Blackburn, Marsha, 164, 180
Black-coded music, 142, 150
Blackness, 134, 141, 149–150
"Blank Space," 116–118, 123, 219, 282–283
Blink-182, 30
Blue Blood (Unger), 198
Bluebird Cafe, 23, 56–57, 58, 111
"The Bolter," 267–268
The Bolter (Osborne), 267–268
Bombalurina, 180
Bon Iver, 189. *See also* Vernon, Justin
Borchetta, Scott, 23, 44, 69, 87–88, 163, 181
Bow, Clara, 264–265. *See also* "Clara Bow" (song)
Bowery, William. *See* Alwyn, Joe
Bowie, David, 8–9, 14
boyd, danah (sociologist), 156
Braun, Scooter, 163, 168, 182
breakup songs, 65, 176
    on *Red*, 83, 86, 89, 90–91, 96–97
bridge (musical device), 13, 43, 54, 61–62, 64, 78, 88, 92, 136, 158, 199, 214, 216, 279
    folk music and, 191–192
    "I Can Do It with a Broken Heart" lacking, 263, 283–284
    as metaphor, 200, 258
    time signature change in, 268–269
Bridgers, Phoebe, 105
Britney Spears Camp for the Performing Arts, 19
Bronte, Charlotte, 195

INDEX

Brooklyn, NY, 96–97, 129
Brooks, Louise, 265
Bryan, Zach, 58
Bull, Michael, 101
bullying, 33, 62, 165–166, 167, 193, 261
Burgess, Jamie Lynne, 213–214
Burke, Kenneth, 277–278
Burton, B. J., 211
"But Daddy I Love Him," 253, 255, 256, 283, 288, 295

"Call It What You Want," 158, 295
cadence (musical device). *See* chord progressions; deceptive cadence; key change
cancellation (online attacks), 139, 157
Caramanica, Jon, 34, 139–140
"Cardigan," 192, 194, 195, 282
Carroll, Georgia, 267
cars, 10, 84, 87, 94
    American culture and, 100–101
    speeding, 101, 103, 106, 119, 147
"Cassandra," 247, 267
"Castles Crumbling," 77–78, 218
Cather, Willa, 122–123, 126, 190, 274, 294–295, 296
cats, 54–55, 182–183, 292
Cats (movie), 180–181
CBS News (TV show), 163, 169, 280
"Champagne Problems," 214, 215, 216, 282
Chapelle, Sarah, 23, 63, 72, 96, 142, 281
Chapman, Nathan, 4, 22–23, 83, 87–88, 125
Charli XCX, 8, 141, 211
Chelsea Hotel, 252, 269
"Chloe or Sam or Sophia or Marcus," 259
Chopin, Kate, 159
chord progressions, 6–7, 124, 194, 207
Christmas tree farm, 18, 180
"Christmas Tree Farm," 180, 205
Christmastime, 205–206, 231
Churchill, Winston, 259
"Clara Bow," 44, 167, 249, 264, 289, 295

Clark, Annie ("St. Vincent"), 172
Clarke, Vince, 232
"Clean," 123–124
Clinton, Hillary, 166
"Closure," 211–212, 215, 238
coauthors, 112, 125, 229, 272, 293
    Alwyn as, 222
    Antonoff as, 121, 177, 207
    collaborators and, 60, 90, 151
    Harris, C. as, 143–144
    Little as, 170
    Rich, J. as, 55
    Thompson, M. as, 103–104
code names, 155, 215
codependence (in romantic relationships), 30–31
Coleridge, Samuel Taylor, 196, 247
collaborators, 3, 60, 71, 90, 151, 203, 247. *See also* Alwyn, Joe; Antonoff, Jack; coauthors; Dessner, Aaron; Martin, Max; Rose, Liz
    Chapman as, 4, 22–23, 83, 87–88, 125
    Orrall as, 22, 23, 30, 32
    Post Malone, 254
    Rose as, 4, 22–23, 35, 56, 127
"Come Back . . . Be Here," 91–92
Come Together (Nagoski), 70
complex words (Empson), 85
compulsory heterosexuality (Rich), 27, 179, 193
computer repairman, 4, 21
"Coney Island," 216–217, 218–219
Conley, Courtney, 87
context collapse (boyd), 156–157
control, 114, 123, 181, 182, 231–232
    confidence and, 162
    good girl image and, 226
    perfectionism and, 221, 223
"Cornelia Street," 176, 177
Cosmopolitan (magazine), 118–119, 152, 159
cottagecore (genre), 191

INDEX

country music, 17, 39–40, 43, 66, 137
  culture of, 103
  fashion and, 23
  nostalgia and, 77
  pastoralism in, 19–20, 24, 26–27, 28, 37, 63
  Taylor Swift ("Debut") and, 18–20, 22–23, 25–26, 28–29
  tropes in, 26, 27, 28, 31
  women in, 25–26
Country Music Association (CMA), 112
Country Music Television (CMT), 74, 140
COVID-19 pandemic, 129, 182, 188, 189, 192, 239
  albums during, 2, 10, 184, 211, 217, 219, 221, 257
  uncertainties of, 14, 197, 201, 213, 218
"Cowboy Like Me," 212–213
"Crazier," 32
Crimes of Passion (short film), 52
cruel optimism (Berlant), 173–174
"Cruel Summer," 172–174, 176, 180, 181, 277
Cullen, Shaun, 68
cultural appropriation, 135, 149, 167
Cyrus, Miley, 40, 49, 149

Daily Mail (newspaper), 226
Daily Telegraph, 80
"Dark Blue Tennessee," 35
Dark Phoenix Saga (Claremont and Byrne), 151
Davis, Lennard J., 241
"Daylight," 175
Dazed and Confused (movie), 95
"Dear John," 71–74, 81, 95, 175, 234, 268, 272
"Dear Reader," 226, 241
"Debut" (album). *See* Taylor Swift ("Debut")
deceptive cadence (musical device), 172, 177
Def Leppard, 19

Del Rey, Lana, 57, 230–232, 241
"Delicate," 141, 145, 156
Denver, John, 20
Dessner, Aaron, 189, 203, 205, 236, 249
  Antonoff and, 188, 242
  "Closure" collaboration, 211
  "Invisible String" and, 195
  "loml" and, 258
  "Willow" collaboration, 204
detractors, 11–12, 62, 133, 232
diaries. *See Lover,* diaries
diegetic contexts, 87
disordered eating, 29, 113–114, 227, 228–229, 233
  Miss Americana and, 114
  "Tied Together with a Smile" and, 29
"Doe, a Deer" (Rodgers and Hammerstein), 6
Dolven, Jeff, 119, 122
domesticity, 175, 214, 222, 235, 253
Donnella, Leah, 140
"Don't Blame Me," 145
"Don't Stop Believin'" (Journey), 58
Dorothea (fictional character), 205, 206, 213, 216
"Dorothea," 206, 294
"Dress," 145–146, 149–150
drinking (alcohol), 106, 143, 144, 213. *See also* alcohol
drive, ambition and, 33, 102, 125, 225
"Drops of Jupiter" (Train), 27
D'Souza, Shaad, 256
Dylan, Bob, 93, 252, 293

Easter eggs, 34, 88, 99, 155, 258, 259, 260
eating disorders. *See* disordered eating
"Edge of Seventeen" (Nicks), 44–45
Edinburgh, Scotland, 1, 275–278, 280, 284, 287–288
Eilish, Billie, 7, 96, 226
"Elegy in a Country Churchyard" (Gray), 8
Empire, Kitty (music critic), 141–142, 149
empowerment, 10, 25, 47, 63–64, 283

INDEX

Empson, William, 85
"Enchanted," 69–70
"End Game," 141, 142, 144–145, 149
Entertainment Weekly (magazine), 13–14, 29, 34, 84, 152
    Swift, Andrea and, 22
    on "The Outside," 32
"Epistle to Dr. Arbuthnot" (Pope), 128, 154
Eras Tour, 1, 191, 238, 263–264, 271–274, 282–283. *See also specific songs*
    conclusion of, 297
    Edinburgh, Scotland, 275–278, 280, 287–288
    "Errors Tour," 286
    Griff opening for, 130–131
    Kelce at, 224, 275
    Lyon, France, 53–54
    movie, 76, 223
    in Nashville, 26, 208
    surprise songs on, 284
    and Swiftball, 278–279
    "Sydney" chant, 116
    in Tokyo, 33
    TTPD and, 11, 245
    in Vancouver, 61–62, 289–290
    Vienna cancellation, 289
    West, B., on, 281
Erasure (pop duo), 112, 232, 262
"Errors Tour," 286
escapism, 20, 120, 252, 290
    Cather on, 190
    Folklore and, 195, 197, 198, 200, 219
Esquire (magazine), 114
Evanson, Caitlin, 62–63
Evermore (2020), 10, 188, 207–213, 217–219, 282
    Alwyn collaboration son, 203, 214, 216
    Christmastime and, 205–206
    Folklore in relation to, 203–204
"Evermore," 216, 268
Evers, Kevin, 23, 180, 266
"Exile," 191, 192, 216
expansive recognition (Price), 75–76

"False God," 162, 173, 176, 181
fame, 65, 102, 227, 249, 252
    anxiety and, 232–233
    cost of, 66, 121
    fear and, 77
"Famous" (West, K.), 138–139
fandoms, 113, 187, 291, 293
    boy-band, 50
    1989 effect on, 127
    parasocial relationships with, 41, 50
    superfan within, 51, 127, 281
    Swifties and, 11, 15–16, 267, 274–276, 288–289
fashion, 124, 164, 223, 242
    Chappelle on, 23, 63, 96, 142, 281
    country music and, 23
Fawbert, Dave, 189
Fearless (2008), 10, 12, 57–58, 76, 130
    "Fifteen," 40–43, 47, 54, 56
    Grammy Awards for, 39–40
    Journey to Fearless (documentary), 4, 18–19, 23, 49–53, 240
    personae in, 44, 48–49, 59
    "White Horse" almost omitted from, 55
    "You Belong with Me," 45–46
Fearless (Taylor's Version) (2021), 65, 76
Febos, Melissa, 84
feminism, 63, 79–81, 151, 157, 209, 239
fiddle. *See* Evanson, Caitlin; violin
"Fifteen," 40–43, 47, 54, 56, 62, 289
"Fifteen (Taylor's Version)," 42
figures of speech, 250
Filipovic, Jill, 95
Finlay, Marjorie (grandmother), 19, 196, 207–208, 216, 219
first loves, 28, 53, 61, 109
"Florida!!!," 256–257, 261, 267, 275, 285
Folklore (2020), 10, 14, 187, 198–199, 201–202, 282. *See also The Long Pond Studio Sessions*
    anxiety in, 189
    COVID-19 during, 188

INDEX

Folklore (2020) *(continued)*
   Evermore in relation to, 203–204
   nostalgia in, 190–191, 194, 195, 197, 200
"Forever and Always," 47, 48, 54, 74, 266
"Forever Winter," 104
"Fortnight," 249, 254, 257
"Four Letter Words" (Wilde), 102
Framke, Caroline, 137
Friedman, Megan, 152
friendship bracelets, 15–16, 54, 75–76, 233
Frost, Robert, 58, 206
Fuller, Loie, 146
Future (musician), 144–145, 151, 153

Gahran, Amy, 118
Game of Thrones (TV show), 152–153, 241
Gay and Lesbian Alliance Against Defamation (GLAAD), 165
Gaye, Marvin, 7
Gaylors, 79, 178, 192–193
genius, notion of, 3–4, 44, 121, 247, 272–274
"Getaway Car," 47, 147, 195
Gevinson, Tavi, 8
Gibson, Courtney, 129–130
Glaspell, Susan, 214
"Glitch," 238–239
"Glitch Feminist Manifesto" (Russell), 239
Goffman, Erving, 29
"Gold Rush," 206, 207
Goldfine, Jael, 182
good girl, 3, 24, 25, 134, 182–183, 285
   approval and, 246
   paradox, 16, 145, 157
   public image of, 156, 255
   rejection of, 156
   syndrome of, 77–78, 226
   in "This Is Me Trying," 197
Gore, Lesley, 276
"Gorgeous," 145
Govan, Chloe, 21
Grammy Awards, 39–40, 44, 71, 111
Grande, Ariana, 149

Gray, Thomas, 8
"The Great War," 236, 237
"Green Light" (Lorde), 207
Grey's Anatomy (TV show), 55
Griff (née Sarah Faith Griffiths), 130–131
Grobe, Christopher, 226
Grossman, Allen, 41
growing up, 7–8, 9, 14, 21, 109–110, 187
   nostalgia of, 24, 28–29
   privilege and, 285
   stories about, 60–61
Guardian (newspaper), 127, 138–139, 148, 189, 256
Gyllenhaal, Jake (boyfriend), 83, 87, 91–92, 102, 182, 266
Gyllenhaal, Maggie, 91

HAIM (pop group), 213, 261, 265
"Half of My Heart" (Mayer), 71
Hanna, Kathleen, 79–81, 157. *See also* Riot Grrrl
Hannah Montana (movie), 32, 40, 49
"Happiness," 212
happy endings, 46, 162, 173–174, 179, 181, 195
   Kate Chopin and, 159
   in "Love Story," 47
   in "Mary's Song," 27
Harkness, Rebekah, 198, 210
Harris, Calvin, 136, 143, 172, 236
Harris, Kamala, 171
haters, 46, 117, 159, 165–166, 231, 261
Hawthorne, Nathaniel, 47
Healy, Matty, 58, 246–247, 250, 251, 253–255, 266
   in "The Black Dog," 260
   in "The Smallest Man Who Ever Lived," 258
Heap, Imogen, 110, 197
Heartstopper (TV show), 193
Hemingway, Ernest, 195
Hendersonville, Tennessee, 21–22, 49, 62
Hendersonville High, 40, 48, 49

INDEX

hermeneutic friend (Grossman), 41, 70, 81, 104–105, 129, 224
heteropessimism, 176, 178
"Hey Stephen," 54, 56
Hiddleston, Tom, 136, 147, 236
"High Infidelity," 235–236
Hill, Faith, 19
Hirschberg, Lynn, 255
"Hits Different," 5–6, 242–243
"Hoax," 191
Hoby, Hermione, 127
Holiday House (Rhode Island residence), 198
Holly, Buddy, 43
"Holy Ground," 100
Hopkins, Gerard Manley, 12–13, 295
"The Human Seasons" (Keats), 215
Hunger Games (movie), 192

"I Can Do It with a Broken Heart," 9, 262–264, 266–267, 283–284, 288, 289, 293
"I Can Fix Him," 157, 260–261
"I Did Something Bad," 151, 152, 153, 210
"I Forgot That You Existed," 162, 172, 181
"I Hate It Here," 249, 256
"I Knew You Were Trouble," 88
"I'd Lie," 35
"Illicit Affairs," 193–194
"I'm Only Me When I'm with You," 30–31
imposter syndrome, 177, 227, 266
In Memoriam (Tennyson), 99
independence, 90, 118–119, 241, 268, 272
 aspiration and, 60
 commercial, 161
Inez (fictional character), 197, 206, 216
"Innocent," 68–69
insecurities, 227, 230–231, 232, 241, 280, 289
 ambition and, 16, 225
 in *Midnights*, 222, 287
Instagram, 142, 156, 164, 197, 225, 227, 288
"Invisible," 32

"Invisible String," 195, 201, 278
Ion (Plato), 248
"Irreplaceable" (Beyoncé), 36
Isbell, Jason, 148
isolation, 75, 104, 188, 190, 192, 218, 271, 281
It's Complicated (boyd), 156
"It's Nice to Have a Friend," 177–178, 193, 284
"It's Time to Go," 214
"Ivy," 211

Jabour, Bridie, 138
Jack Leopards and the Dolphin Club (band), 182
Jagota, Vrinda, 230
James (fictional character), 194–195, 197, 206, 216, 218, 282
Jane Eyre (Brontë), 195
Johnson, Nic, 212
Johnson, Samuel, 8, 267
Jonas, Joe, 48, 64, 266
Journey to Fearless (documentary), 4, 18–19, 23, 49–53, 240
"Just South of Knowing Why," 35

Kansas City Chiefs, 54, 224, 249, 291–293
Kardashian, Kim, 134, 138, 146, 157, 172, 261
Karma, 168, 223–224
"Karma," 130, 223–224, 275, 287, 288
Karyn (inflatable cobra), 142, 162
Kasischke, Laura, 263
Keats, John, 97–98, 215
Kelce, Travis, 224, 249, 291–293
Kennedy, Conor, 99
key change (musical device), 46-47, 195. *See also* trucker gearshift
Khan, Sadiq, 2
Killing Eve (TV show), 181–182
Kimmel, Jimmy, 215
King, Carole, 7–8, 57, 248, 274
"King of My Heart," 147, 152

INDEX

Klosterman, Chuck, 127
Knowles, Jay, 56–57
Kotarski, Olivia, 290–292
Kushner, Rachel, 294

"Labyrinth," 238, 239
"The Lakes," 195–197
Lambert, Miranda, 57
Lang, Jeff, 103
Lange, Alexandra, 217–218
"The Last Great American Dynasty," 198, 210, 214
Lautner, Taylor, 64, 65–66, 67
"Lavender Haze," 225, 241–242, 243
Le Guin, Ursula K., 85
Led Zeppelin, 93
Lee, Brenda, 28, 29
Lee, Stan, 120
Liles, Stephen, 54
"Lily, Rosemary and the Jack of Hearts" (Dylan), 93
"Lines Composed a Few Miles Above Tintern Abbey" (Wordsworth), 41–42
Little, Joel, 170
The Little Mermaid (movie), 255
Lively, Blake, 195
Ljungfelt, Niklas, 119
"loml," 258–259
London, England, 1–2, 157, 164, 181
"London Boy," 175, 179
London Tube map, 2, 162
"Long Live," 74–77, 81, 278, 279, 290, 293
The Long Pond Studio Sessions (documentary), 188, 190, 195, 196, 199
"Long Story Short," 211
LOOK (Romanoff), 228–229, 233–234
"Look What You Made Me Do," 142, 146–147, 152, 181–182, 281
Lorde (musician; née Ella Marjia Lani Yelich-O'Connor), 136, 170, 207, 222, 230
"Love Story," 1, 46, 47, 58, 111, 122

Lover (2019), 10, 165–167, 173–183, 187
   CBS News interview on, 169
   diaries, 32–33, 136, 157, 268
   Midnights contrasted to, 221, 224
   "Miss Americana and the Heartbreak Prince," 171–172
   politics on, 137, 161, 163–164, 168, 170, 184–185
"Lover," 162, 175–176, 181, 279
Lowe, Zane, 204–205, 207–208, 214, 216
"The Lucky One," 102–103, 275
Lynn, Loretta, 20, 148
Lyrical Ballads (Wordsworth and Coleridge), 196

Machado, Ana Clara Benevides, 235
Mad Men (TV show), 225
Maher, Brian, 35
Major Labels (Sanneh), 4–5
"The Man," 167–169, 170, 183, 272, 281
mandolin, 23, 27, 37, 40, 45, 190, 214
"The Manuscript," 95, 257, 267–269, 290, 293, 295
Marcus, Greil, 43
"Marjorie," 19, 207, 216
"Maroon," 226, 239
Martin, Max, 83, 87–88, 89–90, 110, 114, 131, 151
"Mary's Song (Oh My My My)," 26–27, 35, 178
mashups (musical medleys), 53–54, 61, 213, 237, 261, 278, 284
   on YouTube, 207
   See also "Green Light" (Lorde)
masters (audio recordings), 161, 163.
   See also Big Machine Records
"Mastermind," 223, 226, 231–232, 236, 242, 287–288
masterpieces, 11–12, 92–93, 94, 97, 111, 255
Maurier, Daphne du, 208–210
Mayer, John, 71–72, 73–74, 234–235, 250
Mazzoni, Guido, 294
McAlister, James, 211

INDEX

McCartney, Stella, 164
McCulloch, Gretchen, 288
McDonald, Glenn, 25, 124
McGraw, Tim, 23–24, 52
"Me!," 162, 164–165, 170, 179, 181, 182
"Mean," 62–63, 70, 75, 81, 261
Meet Me by the Fountain (Lange), 217
Merrill, James, 52, 200
Mhloyi, Catherine, 228
"Midnight Rain," 225, 239
Midnights (2022), 5–6, 10–11, 184, 233, 238–241, 246, 287
   Alwyn inspiring, 222, 225, 236–237, 242, 243
      "Anti-Hero," 226–229
      Del Rey and, 230–232
      sleepless nights inspiring, 221, 229, 230, 234, 235
Migliore, Steve, 19
Miller, Scott, 36
Milton, John, 15, 151
"Mine," 61, 70
"Mirror" (Merrill), 200
"Mirrorball," 199–200
Miss Americana (documentary), 139, 162, 163, 182–185
   and disordered eating, 114, 233
   politics and, 137
"Miss Americana and the Heartbreak Prince," 170–172, 184–185
Mitchell, Joni, 6, 83, 105, 189, 293
"The Moment I Knew," 91, 97
mondegreen, 117–118, 121
Moreland, Quinn, 230
Morley, Paul, 231
Morris, Maren, 103
Moyet, Alison, 232
"Mr. Perfectly Fine," 47
Mueller, David, 136, 183
music genres, 3, 116, 127, 148, 182, 294. *See also* country music; pop music
   folk, 93, 117, 188, 190, 191, 195, 197, 234
   folktronica, 189, 203, 218, 219

hip-hop, 10, 66, 94, 115, 134, 143, 147
hyperpop, 211–212, 219, 238, 241
indie-folk, 188–189, 203
punk rock, 36, 79–80
rap, 115, 134, 139, 140, 143, 150, 159
R&B, 10, 115, 134, 142–144, 146, 147, 149–150, 159
synth-pop, 10, 111, 128, 130, 134, 175, 232, 237, 249
trap, 144–145, 249
whiteness in, 115, 134, 144, 148, 151
"My Tears Ricochet," 197
MySpace, 33, 34, 48, 156, 275

Nagoski, Emily, 70
Naked at the Albert Hall (Thorn), 44
Nash, Ilana, 45–46
Nashville, Tennessee, 4, 18, 21, 26, 57, 62, 201–202
   Bluebird Cafe, 23, 56–57, 58, 111
   Rubber Duck Race in, 22
National Public Radio, 133, 140
Nelson, Maggie, 277
"Never Grow Up," 61–62, 98, 178, 217
New Musical Express (*NME*), 113
New Romantics (British youth movement), 124
"New Romantics," 124–125, 131, 288, 290, 295
"New Year's Day," 145, 146, 158, 175, 267, 290
New York City, 110, 111–112, 120, 156–157, 177. *See also* Brooklyn
New York Times, 34, 79, 139–140, 255, 265
New Yorker (magazine), 4–5, 72–73, 90
Newman, Randy, 191
Nicks, Stevie, 44–45, 62, 206–207, 265
1989 (2014), 2, 10, 13, 29, 113, 130–134, 282–283
   adulthood and, 124
   BaileyShea on, 117, 118
   "Blank Space," 116–117
   growth in fandom from, 127

INDEX

1989 (2014) *(continued)*
   reinvention in, 109–110, 111–112, 122–123, 147
   self-portraiture in, 127–128
   "Shake It Off," 114–115
   "Style," 119–121
   Taylor Parties for listening to, 129–130
   "This Love," 125–126
1989 (*Taylor's Version*) (2023), 112
"No Body, No Crime," 213–214, 261
nostalgia, 190–191, 194, 195, 197, 200, 256
   country music and, 77
   of growing up, 24, 28–29
   romantic, 98–99
   for typewriters, 254
"Nothing New," 105–107
Nowak, Nina, 96

Obama, Barack, 66
Observer (newspaper), 141–142
Occam's razor, 178
ode (poetic genre), 97–98
The Odes of John Keats (Vendler), 98
Offill, Jenny, 248
Oldenburg, Ray, 288
Oliver, Scarlett, 266
One Chance (movie), 110
One Direction, 112
"Only the Young," 182, 184–185
Ordonez, Olivia, 53
Orr, David, 206
Orrall, Robert Ellis, 22, 23, 30, 32
Osborne, Frances, 267–268
"Our Song," 15, 24, 29, 35–36, 50, 52, 92
"Out of the Woods," 121, 131
outsiderhood, 3, 32, 36, 43–44, 49
"The Outside," 32–33, 37
Owl City, 69

Panofsky, Erwin, 202
paparazzi, 121, 136, 196, 257, 288, 291
"Paper Doll" (Mayer), 73
"Paper Rings," 173, 178, 181

Parade (magazine), 78
Paradise Regained (Milton), 15
Paramore, 77, 79, 276
parasocial relationships, 41, 50
Parton, Dolly, 26, 180
Paskin, Willa, 257
pastoral (literary genre), 211, 214, 215, 219
   in country music, 19–20, 26–27, 28, 37, 63
   of *Evermore*, 203
   of *Folklore*, 189–193, 195, 197, 198–199, 202
   of Pope, 153
   in "Tim McGraw," 24
   tropes of, 20–21, 24, 26, 28
patriarchy, 93, 94, 167, 272
"Peace," 191, 192, 207
Pell, Dave, 53
Pennsylvania. *See* West Reading, Pennsylvania; Wyomissing, Pennsylvania
People (magazine), 117
people pleasers, 29, 30–32, 134, 160, 263, 273, 289
Perelman, Bob, 273
Pérez, Madeline, 273
perfectionism, 114, 225, 235, 236, 238
   control and, 221, 223
   rejection of, 115
Perry, Katy, 66, 90, 142
personae, 3, 14, 139, 189, 288
   celebrity, 59, 141–142
   in *Fearless*, 44, 48–49, 59
   people pleasing, 134
   public, 40, 51, 262, 275
   sarcastic, 143, 147
   stage, 45
"Peter," 250
Peter Pan (fictional character), 249, 269
Petersen, Anne Helen, 285
Petrarch, 251
Petty, Tom, 36
Philadelphia (magazine), 48

INDEX

Phoenix, 103
Phoenix Saga (Claremont and Byrne), 151
"Picture to Burn," 27–28, 42, 47
Pitchfork (magazine), 230
"A Place in This World," 30, 32, 290
Plato, 248
politics, 137, 161, 163–164, 168, 170, 184–185
pop music, 6, 52, 78–79, 109, 110, 126, 274
    Black, 10, 134, 141, 143, 147–148, 156
    electronic, 90, 111, 237
    modern, 46, 176, 231
    phenomenon in, 127–128
Pope, Alexander, 20, 128, 153–156, 274
Post Malone, 254
Pound, Ezra, 272, 273
Poussin, Nicolas, 202
praise, 113, 114, 124, 130, 183, 224, 266
precociousness, 16, 256, 257, 283, 285
The Presentation of Self in Everyday Life (Goffman), 29
Presley, Elvis, 25, 149, 175
Price, Devon, 75–76
Prince, 2, 8, 135
privilege, 120, 136, 165, 184, 233, 272
    growing up and, 285
    white, 69, 139, 148, 156, 158–159
"The Prophecy," 150, 266
public image, 34, 35, 36, 49–50, 70, 175
    Chapelle on, 63
    as good girl, 156, 255
    personae and, 40, 51, 262, 275

queer community, 164, 165–167, 178–179, 193, 205, 274
Queer Eye (TV show), 166

Raab, Scott, 114, 123
racism, 68–69, 133, 137, 148, 149–150
RCA (record label), 23
"... Ready for It?," 1–16, 144, 151, 281
Rebecca (du Maurier), 208–211
Red (2012), 10, 73, 84–85, 103–107, 109, 147
    American culture and, 100–101
    breakup songs on, 83, 86, 89, 90–91, 96–97
    Chapman as producer on, 87–88
    Gyllenhaal, J, influence on, 83, 87, 89, 91–92, 102, 266
    romantic nostalgia on, 98–99
Red (Taylor's Version) (2021), 92, 103
red love, 84–86, 89, 97, 103, 105–106, 207
reinvention, 85, 109–110, 111–112, 122–123, 147, 274
    challenges of, 128–129
    self-, 117, 124, 131, 151
relatability, 3, 9–11, 13–14, 16, 43–44
    in "All Too Well," 94
    aspiration and, 29, 31, 37, 84, 121, 161, 290
    of "Dear John," 73
    on *Red*, 91
    rejection and, 95–96, 144–145
    in "Ronan," 104
relationship escalator (Gahran), 118–119, 120, 125
Reputation (2017), 10, 14, 133, 152–154, 181, 210, 281–282
    apologia in, 143, 155
    Black music in relation to, 115, 135, 139–140, 148–150, 159
    "Dress," 145–146
    feminist revenge in, 151
    Karyn brought out for, 142, 162
    West, K., and, 134, 137–139, 146, 157
residences, 197–198, 236
Resisting Reader (literary concept), 151, 209
revenge, 135, 155, 156, 229, 241
    feminism, 151
    songs about, 27, 64, 88, 134, 152, 261, 262
Reynolds, Ryan, 195
"Rhiannon" (Nicks), 44
Rich, Adrienne, 8. *See also* compulsory heterosexuality

INDEX

Rich, John, 55
Rich White People Fiction (RWPF) (Zibrak), 120, 127
"Right Where You Left Me," 214
Rihanna, 136, 138, 143, 236
Rimbaud, Arthur, 251
Rimes, LeAnn, 19, 25
Rio de Janeiro, 1, 235
Riot Grrrl (feminist punk rock movement), 79–81, 157
"The Road Not Taken" (Frost), 58, 206
Roan, Chappell, 130
"Robin," 267
Rock Star Ronan (blog), 103–104
rock-and-roll traditions, 84, 100
rockism, vs. poptimism (Wilson), 90
role model, 17, 156, 184, 207
Rolling Stone (magazine), 19, 25, 60
Romanoff, Zan, 228–229, 233–234
Romeo and Juliet (Shakespeare), 46–47
"Ronan," 103–104
Rose, Liz, 4, 22–23, 35, 56, 127
Rossman, Margaret, 76, 79
"Run," 106
Russell, Legacy, 239

Sackville, Idina, 267–268
"The Saddest Man Who Ever Lived," 250
"Safe and Sound," 192, 193
Sanneh, Kelefa, 4–5, 56, 144
Sansa Stark (fictional character), 152, 153
Sapphic fans, 178–179, 180, 193. *See also* Gaylors; queer community
Saturday Night Live (TV show), 65, 67–68, 142
"Say Don't Go," 126
The Scarlet Letter (Hawthorne), 47
Schiff, Robyn, 31
Schiller, Friedrich, 247–248, 273
Schumpeter, Joseph, 266
Seabrook, John, 90
secret sessions, 127

Sedgwick, Eve, 205–206
self-harm, 104
self-portraiture, 61, 127–128
Serano, Julia, 63
"Seven," 192–193
sexism, 63
sexuality, 30, 47, 50, 70, 79
  in "Dress," 145–146
  in "You Belong with Me," 45–46
"Shake It Off," 2, 112, 113, 114–115, 123, 266
Shakespeare, William, 46, 78
Sheehan, Ally, 234–235
Sheeran, Ed, 106, 144–145
Sheffield, Rob, 92
Shellback, 83, 88, 89, 110, 114
shopping malls, 217–218
Sidoti, Paul, 86
Simon, Carly, 96
Sinatra, Frank, 2
Skane, Rebecca, 152
sleepless nights, 221, 229, 230, 234, 235
Sloan, Nate, 7, 45
Slobin, Marc, 190
slut-shaming, 46, 64
"The Smallest Man Who Ever Lived," 258, 268
Smith, Patti, 247, 252, 254
Snapes, Laura, 148
"Snow on the Beach," 231
"So High School," 249
"So Long, London," 176, 246, 249, 253, 255
social media, 11, 165, 196, 233–234, 264, 279
  blackout on, 142, 159
  good girl image on, 156
  Instagram, 142, 156, 164, 197, 225, 227, 288
  MySpace, 33, 34, 48, 156, 275
  work ethic and, 16
solfège (musical notation), 6–7
"Someone Loves You Honey" (Lee), 28
"Something Like That" (McGraw), 24

INDEX

The Song of the Lark (Cather), 122–123, 294–295
songwriting, 2–3, 64, 103, 219, 250, 294. *See also* coauthors
   codependent romances in, 30–31
   growing up and, 7–8, 9
   meta-, 24, 54
   process of, 56, 188
   with Rose, 22
   success and, 4–5, 7
"Soon You'll Get Better," 174, 181
"Sparks Fly," 61
Speak Now (2010), 10, 61–68, 75–77, 80–81
   aspiration in, 59–60
   "Dear John," 71–74
   "Enchanted," 69–70
   "When Emma Falls in Love," 78–79
Speak Now (Taylor's Version), 71, 76
"Speak Now," 61
#SpeakUpNow, 256
Spears, Britney, 19, 32, 88, 218
Spotify, 25, 35, 124
"Spring and Fall" (Hopkins), 12–13
Springsteen, Bruce, 57, 148
stagecraft, 276, 278, 279, 280, 283
"Stairway to Heaven" (Led Zeppelin), 93
"The Star-Spangled Banner," 18–19
"Starlight," 98, 99
"State of Grace," 86, 98, 100, 107
Stenn, David, 264, 265
Stokes, Niall, 86
Stone, Emma, 78
"The Story of Us," 74
"Style," 119–121
Styles, Harry, 112–113, 114, 119, 196, 288
success, 9, 16, 187, 227, 261, 273
   commercial, 79, 81, 219
   of Eras Tour, 274
   songwriting and, 4–5, 7
Sullivan, Caroline, 115, 144
The Sun Also Rises (Hemingway), 195
superfan, 51, 127, 281
"SuperStar," 50

surprise songs, 278–279, 284, 286, 289–290
Suskind, Alex, 14–15
"Sweet Nothing," 242
"Sweet Tea and God's Graces," 35
"Sweeter Than Fiction," 110
Swift, Andrea (mother), 4, 18, 21–22, 33, 34, 51
   "The Best Day" about, 13–14, 48–49
   cancer and, 164, 174
   Mueller and, 136
Swift, Austin (brother), 13, 18, 62, 182
Swift, Scott (father), 4, 18, 21, 61, 163
Swift Group, 18, 21
SwiftAlert, 279
Swiftball, 278–279, 282
Swifties, 1, 8, 74, 76, 278–279, 281, 285
   COVID-19 and, 129
   fandoms and, 11, 15–16, 267, 274–276, 288–290
   for Harris, K., 171
syllepsis, 249, 250, 269
synthesizers, 118, 124, 126, 130

"Take Me Home, Country Roads" (Denver), 20
Tamblyn, Amber, 105, 224–225
Taylearning (podcast), 75, 290–291
Taylor, James, 102, 189
Taylor Swift ("Debut") (2006), 9–10, 32–37, 39, 100, 148
   codependent romance in, 30–31
   country music influence on, 18–20, 22–23, 25–26, 28–29
   "Picture to Burn," 27–28
   role model during, 17
   "Teardrops on My Guitar," 26
   "Tim McGraw," 23–24
Taylor Swift Inspired Dance Parties, 129, 130
Taylor Swift: The Eras Tour (movie), 76, 223
   parties for, 129–130
"Taylor Swift's Lyrics on Dating Bad Drivers" (Conley), 87

INDEX

#TaylorSwiftIsOverParty, 138, 139
T-drop (musical device) (Sloan), 7, 45, 47, 231
"Teardrops on My Guitar," 9, 26
Tedder, Ryan, 110, 112
Teen Vogue (magazine), 228
Tennessean (newspaper), 44, 113, 201
Tennyson, Alfred (Lord), 99
"Thank You Aimee," 261
third places (social environments), 288, 290
"This Is Me Trying," 197
"This Is What You Came For" (Harris and Swift), 143–144
"This Is Why We Can't Have Nice Things," 146, 151, 158, 210
"This Love," 125–126
This Swift Beat (West, B.), 281
Thomas, Dylan, 247, 252, 254
Thompson, Maya, 103–104
Thompson, Richard, 219
Thompson, Ronan, 103–104
Thorn, Tracey, 44, 45, 199
3/4 time. *See* time signature; waltz time
"Tied Together with a Smile," 29–30, 114, 272, 289
time signature (in music), 210, 258–259. *See also* waltz time
"Tim McGraw," 9, 23–24, 33, 52, 213, 290
Time (magazine), 264
"Timeless," 77
"'Tis the Damn Season," 205, 206
"To Autumn" (Keats), 97–98
"Today Was a Fairytale," 55, 65
Tokyo, Japan, 33
"Tolerate It," 208–209, 210–211
Tontiplaphol, Betsy, 99
"The Tortured Man Club," 251
tortured poet (stereotype), 250, 251, 252, 261, 268, 272–273
"The Tortured Poets Department," 254–255
The Tortured Poets Department (TTPD) (2024), 11, 95, 261–269, 277, 278, 293
  Alwyn influence on, 246, 251, 253
  "The Black Dog," 247, 259–260

toxic relationships, 72, 73, 84
T-Pain, 140
T-parties, 51
Train (musical group), 27
trans people, 165, 166, 167, 169, 211
tropes, 172, 229
  in country music, 26, 27, 28, 31
  literary, 48, 251
  pastoral, 20–21, 24, 26, 28
  tortured poet, 250, 251, 252, 261, 268, 272–273
trucker gearshift (musical device), 46–47, 147, 195
Trump, Donald, 137–138, 161–162, 168, 170–171, 179, 180
"T-Swizzle" (musical alias), 140–141
Tucker, Tanya, 25
"22," 73, 88, 106
"22 (Taylor's Version)," 88

ukulele, 60, 179, 190
Underwood, Carrie, 27
Unger, Craig, 198
Universal Music, 23, 161
Urie, Brendon, 164–165
USA Today, 104, 201
U2, 86, 99

Valentine's Day (movie), 64–65
Vancouver, Canada, 61–62, 289–290
vault tracks
  1989, 125, 126, 242
  Evermore, 203
  Fearless, 47, 65, 76
  Red, 103, 105, 106
  Speak Now, 76–77, 78, 80
Vendler, Helen, 8, 98
Vernon, Justin, 189, 191, 192, 216
Video Music Award (VMA), MTV, 66–68, 133, 137, 281
"Vigilante Shit," 229–230
Villarreal, Vanessa Angelica, 133
violin, 27, 151. *See also* Evanson, Caitlin

340

INDEX

vocal melodies, 6, 46, 66, 69, 90–92, 124
   repeated, 119, 293
   T-drop in (Sloan), 7, 45, 47, 231
vocal range, 7, 47, 228, 250, 262
Vogue (magazine), 5, 157, 284
Vox (magazine), 236

Walder Frey (fictional character), 152, 153
waltz time (3/4 time), 71–73, 91, 175
Warhol, Andy, 252
Warren, Diane, 126, 127
"The Way I Loved You," 55–56
"We Are Never Ever Getting Back Together" (WANEGBT), 88, 89–90, 91, 122, 266
"Welcome to New York," 111–112, 120, 136, 165
Wershler-Henry, Darren, 254
West, Bryan, 201–202, 261, 281, 286
West, Kanye, 66–69, 77, 134, 137–139, 146, 157, 163, 172
West Reading, Pennsylvania, 18–19, 21
"What Are You Gonna Do?" (Paramore), 276
"When Emma Falls in Love," 78–79, 81
"White Horse," 55, 213
white privilege, 69, 139, 148, 156, 158–159
whiteness, 4, 23–24, 115, 133–135, 148–151, 156
   Caramanica on, 140
   limitations of, 272
"Who's Afraid of Little Old Me?," 249–250, 252–253, 256, 262
"Who's Taylor Swift anyway? Ew," 88, 102
"Why She Disappeared" (poem) (Swift), 159–160
Widdicombe, Lizzie, 72–73

Wilde, Kim, 102
"Wildest Dreams," 117
Williams, Hayley, 77, 276. *See also* Paramore
"Willow," 204, 206–207, 282
Wilson, Lana, 162, 183
Winchester, Dani, 290–292
"Windsor-Forest" (Pope), 20
"Wonderland," 128
Wordsworth, William, 41–42, 128, 195, 196
work ethic, 3, 51, 52–53, 225, 263–264
Wyomissing, Pennsylvania, 18, 19, 21, 48–49, 180, 225, 294

Yaz (musical group; also Yazoo), 232
Yeats, William Butler, 20, 128, 257, 268, 274, 284, 296–297
"You Are in Love," 126, 131
"You Belong with Me," 1, 2, 45–46, 54, 66, 266, 281
"You Don't Own Me" (Gore), 276
"You Need to Calm Down," 162, 165–167, 170, 178, 182
Young, Adam, 69
"You're Losing Me," 176, 236–237, 243, 246
"You're on Your Own, Kid," 7, 54, 86, 233, 236
"You're So Vain" (Simon), 96
YouTube, 127, 131, 207, 218, 288, 292
   MySpace and, 48
   Spotify and, 35
   VMA incident on, 67

Zacharek, Stephanie, 264
Zaleski, Annie, 70
Zibrak, Arielle, 72, 120
Zoltan, Vanessa, 223

Credit: Jessica Bennett

STEPHANIE BURT is Donald P. and Katherine B. Loker Professor of English at Harvard University. Her work appears in *The New York Times Book Review*, *The New Yorker*, and *London Review of Books*, among others. Her other books of poetry and literary criticism—fourteen in all—include *We Are Mermaids*, *Advice from the Lights*, and *Don't Read Poetry: A Book About How to Read Poems*. She lives in Massachusetts.

RAISING READERS
Books Build Bright Futures

Thank you for reading this book and for being a reader of books in general. As an author, I am so grateful to share being part of a community of readers with you, and I hope you will join me in passing our love of books on to the next generation of readers.

Did you know that reading for enjoyment is the single biggest predictor of a child's future happiness and success?

More than family circumstances, parents' educational background, or income, reading impacts a child's future academic performance, emotional well-being, communication skills, economic security, ambition, and happiness.

Studies show that kids reading for enjoyment in the US is in rapid decline:

- In 2012, 53% of 9-year-olds read almost every day. Just 10 years later, in 2022, the number had fallen to 39%.
- In 2012, 27% of 13-year-olds read for fun daily. By 2023, that number was just 14%.

Together, we can commit to **Raising Readers** and change this trend. How?

- Read to children in your life daily.
- Model reading as a fun activity.
- Reduce screen time.
- Start a family, school, or community book club.
- Visit bookstores and libraries regularly.
- Listen to audiobooks.
- Read the book before you see the movie.
- Encourage your child to read aloud to a pet or stuffed animal.
- Give books as gifts.
- Donate books to families and communities in need.

Books build bright futures, and **Raising Readers** is our shared responsibility.

For more information, visit **JoinRaisingReaders.com**

Sources: National Endowment for the Arts, National Assessment of Educational Progress, WorldBookDay.org, Nielsen BookData's 2023 "Understanding the Children's Book Consumer"